UNSUNG HEROES *of* ROCK 'n' ROLL

NICK TOSCHES

CHARLES SCRIBNER'S SONS—*New York*

Copyright © 1984 Nick Tosches

Library of Congress Cataloging in Publication Data

Tosches, Nick.
  Unsung heroes of rock 'n' roll.

  Discography: p.
  Includes index.
  1. Rock musicians—United States—Biography.
2. Rock music—United States—History and criticism.
I. Title.
ML394.T67   1984   784.5'4'00922 [B]   84–1369
ISBN 0-684-18148-7 (cloth)
ISBN 0-684-18149-5 (paper)

This book published simultaneously in the United States of America and in Canada—Copyright under the Berne Convention.

1 3 5 7 9 11 13 15 17 19   F/C   20 18 16 14 12 10 8 6 4 2

1 3 5 7 9 11 13 15 17 19   F/P   20 18 16 14 12 10 8 6 4 2

Printed in the United States of America.

Several of the chapters in this book were published, in somewhat different form, in Creem *magazine.*

The photographs in this book appear courtesy of the following: pages 23, 35, 39, 55, 59, 63, 99, 103, 115, 123, and 135—Michael Ochs Archives; pages 81, 85, 95, 119, and 131—Country Music Foundation Library; page 67—Skippy Trenier; page 109—Delta Blues Museum, Clarksdale, Mississippi.

FOR SAM

Where He Breathes

Contents

Foreword

This book will not increase the size of your penis. It will not reduce the size of your thighs. It will not teach you how to profit from the recession, or how to make love to a woman. Thirty days after reading it, your stomach will still be unflattened, and you still will not know how to pick up Jane Fonda during the coming lean years.

Such matters are paltry and laughable, however, compared to the hermetic wisdom contained in these pages. Check it out, chump:

The true meaning of Spo-Dee-O-Dee! The relation of breast size to talent! What happens to guys who spend all their money on wine! Why a black man named Doc Sausage will never be elected president of the United States!

Mafia à Go-Go! Who got Annie pregnant! How Louis Prima got that way! How to pick up Keely Smith! Why Elvis was a day late and a dollar short!

How people avoided sex before there were herpes and designer jeans! Pills that can change the color of your skin! The price of the first TV Dinner, and of fame! Why Johnny Ace blew his brains out! How Hank Williams stood off Josef Stalin!

How to determine your aptitude for a career in rock 'n' roll and/or professional wrestling! Why Joe Turner doesn't give a fuck about flattening his stomach! How heroin can harm your complexion! How much the junkman paid for that heart! How to increase the size of your Cadillac! How to go from stardom to a park bench! And sometimes back!

And much, much more! In this, the only book about rock 'n' roll that knows what it's talking about!

STAN STASIAK

Introduction

The history of rock 'n' roll has been obscured by a great deal of misknowing and ignorance, and by a great many lies. There are those who believe that rock 'n' roll was a sudden, magical effusion; that a young man named Elvis Presley one day rose, dipped his comb in water, swept his hair into a duck's-ass, bopped out into the world, and created—thank God, Alan Freed was there to give it a name—rock 'n' roll. This is perhaps the most popular and abiding myth. It is merely another lesson learnt from that cherished American history book that taught us that Peary went to the North Pole alone.

At the other extreme, there are those who believe that rock 'n' roll was created by black people, then seized and commercialized by whites. This is merely a lesson from a revised edition of that same cherished history book. One could make just as strong a case for Jews being the central ethnic group in rock 'n' roll's early history; for it was they who produced many of the most important records, wrote some of the best songs, cultivated much of the greatest talent, and operated the majority of the pioneering record companies.

Rock 'n' roll was not created solely by blacks or by whites; and it certainly did not come into being all of a sudden. It evolved slowly, wrought by blacks and by whites, some of them old and some of them young, in the South and in the West, in the North and in the East. Its makers were driven not so much by any pure creative spirit, but rather by the desire to make money. Nothing can better bring together a black man and a white, a young man and an old, a country man and a city man, than a dollar placed between them. Rock 'n' roll flourished because it sold. The more it sold, the more it flourished. The heroes, unsung and sung alike, of rock 'n' roll all had one thing in common: they liked Cadillacs. If rock 'n' roll had not been salable, they would not have been making it, or trying to make it.

A senator whom I met when I was living in Tennessee told me that he had once asked Colonel Sanders what he honestly thought of black people. "They eat chicken, don't they?" had been the Colonel's smiling reply. One can fully appreciate rock 'n' roll without knowing anything of its history. But to appreciate its history, to know anything about it, one must begin to see just how much rock 'n' roll and fried chicken have in common. It is seductively easy—and not unfitting—to rhapsodize about the classic 1947 recording of "Good Rockin' Tonight" by Wynonie Harris; but it is perhaps more enlightening to acknowledge that it was eventually followed by "Good Mambo Tonight," just as Elvis Presley's earth-shaking early records were eventually followed by "Bossa Nova Baby" and "Do the Clam." But this is what makes rock 'n' roll so intriguing. Whether one regards it as art or as business, its history—one of greed and innocence, tastelessness and brilliance, the ridiculous and the sublime (not to mention sex, violence, and pink silk suits)—is a funhouse-mirror reflection of the American dream gone gaga.

Rock 'n' roll emerged in the middle of a war, when the world was mad. As the summer of 1942 began, the outlook of the recording industry was bleak. Records were made of shellac, and the countries that were America's major sources of shellac were blockaded. The shipping and distribution of records were becoming more and more problematic, since the Office of Defense Transportation had commandeered every means of transport. When the president of the American Federation of Musicians, James Caesar Petrillo, a crusader against "the menace of mechanical music," announced on June 25 that all recording licenses would become null and void on August 1 and would not be renewed until certain excessive demands were met, the industry felt as if it had received the kiss of death. Since this warning meant that no union musicians would be making records after July 31, companies rushed to lay in enough recordings to last them through the strike.

The recording ban went on for more than a year, but it did not affect the industry the way most thought it would. Nineteen forty-three turned out to be the recording industry's most prosperous year in more than a decade. The problems caused by the shellac shortage, erratic distribution, and the A.F.M. ban were more than offset by a record-buying public who wanted dearly to be distracted from the reality of war, and who had the money to pay for that distraction. The style and spirit of popular music were changing, too; and change creates excitement. Big-band swing was still the rage. Benny Goodman, Glenn Miller, Tommy and Jimmy Dorsey, Harry James—these were the men music belonged to in the early 1940s. Goodman and James recorded for Columbia. Miller and Tommy Dorsey recorded for Victor. Jimmy Dorsey recorded for Decca.

Columbia, Victor, and Decca were the three companies that dominated the industry at the time of the A.F.M. ban. Johnny Mercer's new Capitol label, which had begun as Liberty Records on April 9, 1942, had barely gotten started when Petrillo's warning came. Yet Capitol not only survived, it thrived. Something new was going on beneath big-band swing, and Capitol was a part of it. The first record that Capitol released was "Cow-Cow Boogie" by the new-wave boogie-woogie team of pianist Freddie Slack and singer Ella Mae Morse, both of whom had worked in Jimmy Dorsey's band. "Cow-Cow Boogie" was released on July 1, and it hit the pop charts the next month. Another of Capitol's first artists—he was the third act to sign with the company—was Nat King Cole. At the age of twenty-four, Cole was already one of the most important and innovative musicians on the West Coast. By the time he drifted into mainstream popular music later in the decade, he had greatly influenced Charles Brown, Cecil Gant, Amos Milburn, and other singing pianists whose names have been more closely associated than Cole's with the early history of rock 'n' roll.

Brown and Milburn came to Los Angeles from Texas, Gant from Tennessee. From the Midwest came blues shouters Big Joe Turner and Wynonie Harris. In New York jazz bands were being rent apart. Those musicians who were not bowing their sharkskin knees in fealty to that strange new stuff called be-bop were becoming involved with that other strange new music, which as yet had no name. Decca, the least conservative of the three major companies, had signed the first of these fugitives from jazz, Louis Jordan. A former alto saxophonist in Chick Webb's band, Jordan had since the end of 1938 been leading his own group, the Tympany Five. Jordan's music had grown more audacious, louder and wilder, with the passing of time. He had all but been disowned by the jazz establishment. "It's a shame that crap like this is played by a jump band of this caliber," complained a 1941 issue of *Down Beat* in its review of one of his records. But at the same time, Jordan's records were rising high on *Billboard*'s "Harlem Hit Parade" charts; and in 1944 they began crossing over to the pop charts.

As the new music spread, and as it became obvious that the prospering major companies were for the most part uninterested in it, numerous little labels were founded by men and women who smelled money in what was going on. In 1942, during the A.F.M. ban, Herman Lubinsky started Savoy Records in downtown Newark; in Los Angeles the songwriter Otis René established Excelsior ("The All Colored Recording Company"); and Joe Davis formed Beacon Records in New York. By the end of the year Beacon already had a hit of sorts, Savannah Churchill's "Fat Meat Is Good Meat."

In 1943 Ike and Bess Berman founded Apollo Records in Harlem (they moved downtown before long); in Los Angeles Robert Scherman started Premier (which became Atlas the next year). In 1944 Jules Braun began DeLuxe Records in Linden, New Jersey; Otis René, Excelsior's founder, formed Exclusive in Los Angeles; Richard A. Nelson started Gilt-Edge, also in Los Angeles; Al Greene founded National Records in New York; Bill Quinn started Gulf Records in Houston; and Sydney Nathan opened King Records in Cincinnati. In 1945 came several more Los Angeles companies: Modern, started by Jules, Joe, and Saul Bihari; Philo, formed by Ed and Leo Mesner (Philo's name was soon changed to Aladdin due to legal difficulties); Bronze, begun by Leroy Hurte; and Four-Star, formed by Richard A. Nelson to supersede his Gilt-Edge label. In New York that year, Irving Feld and Viola Marsham started Super Disc; in Newark Irving Berman founded Manor. In 1946 Bill Quinn began Gold Star in Houston, to take the place of Gulf; Jim Bulleit started Bullet Records in Nashville; Art Rupe established Specialty in Los Angeles; men in well-cut expensive suits formed Mercury in Chicago. In 1947 Herb Abramson and Ahmet Ertegun started Atlantic Records in New York; Leonard and Phil Chess began Aristocrat in Chicago (the name of the company was changed to Chess a couple of years later). In 1949 Randy Wood started Dot Records in Gallatin, Tennessee; Saul M. Kaul founded Freedom, Macy Lela Wood formed Macy's, and Don Robey started Peacock, all in Houston; and in Los Angeles Lew Chudd began Imperial. In 1950 Lillian McMurry started Trumpet Records in Jackson, Mississippi. In 1951 Ernie Young founded the Nashboro label in Nashville. In 1952 came three Memphis companies: James Mattis's Duke Records, Lester Bihari's Meteor Records, and Sam Phillips's Sun records.

These small independent companies—mongrel labels, they were called within the industry—were the breeding grounds of rock 'n' roll. None of them had any real ethnic or esthetic identity. They all released whatever they thought might sell. Aladdin, Specialty, Mercury, Atlantic, Chess, and other labels known for their black rhythm-and-blues product all released hillbilly records on the side. King Records had both Wynonie Harris and Grandpa Jones. Thrown in among Apollo's various R&B releases were records by Dean Martin and by Smilin' Eddie Hill and the Tennessee Mountain Boys. These companies' catalogues were merely an exaggerated reflection of what was going on generally.

As black music began rocking in the 1940s, there was a parallel development in country music. It was called hillbilly boogie, when it was called anything at all. It was heard in some of the Delmore Brothers' King records—most notably in their 1946 recordings "Hillbilly Boogie" and "Freight Train Boogie"—and in the Four-Star recordings of the Maddox Brothers and Rose. "Rootie Tootie," Hank Williams's third MGM release, recorded in 1947, was rock 'n' roll as much as anything else. It became common for country singers and rhythm-and-blues singers to cover each other's material. Wynonie Harris recorded Hank Penny's "Bloodshot Eyes" and Louie Innis's "Good Mornin' Judge." Melvin Moore covered Hank Williams's "Moanin' the Blues"; Eddie Crosby covered his "Lovesick Blues." Country singer Jimmy Ballard did Bull Moose Jackson's "I Want a Bowlegged Woman." The York Brothers covered the Dominoes' "Sixty-Minute Man." By the early 1950s it was not uncommon to encounter simultaneous country and rhythm-and-blues hit recordings of the same song—"Hearts of Stone" by the Charms and by Red Foley, for instance, or "Crying in the Chapel" by Rex Allen and by the Orioles. Everybody liked chicken.

It is difficult to say precisely when the words "rock 'n' roll" came to describe what was going on. The phrase itself is immemorial. It had been popular for its sexual connotations in music of the 1920s. In the fall of 1922 blues singer Trixie Smith recorded a song called "My Daddy Rocks Me (With One Steady Roll)" for Black Swan Records. Her record inspired various lyrical elaborations: "Rock That Thing" by Lil Johnson, "Rock Me Mama" by Ikey Robinson, and so on.

By the early thirties rock 'n' roll was more than a fuck-phrase. It connoted a new sensuality of rhythm, the first inklings of that new style and spirit that were to overtake music a decade later. In 1931 Duke Ellington cut "Rockin' in Rhythm" for Victor. In *Transatlantic Merry-Go-Round,* an awful United Artists movie released in the fall of 1934, the Boswell Sisters sang a song called "Rock and Roll." Gladys Presley of Tupelo was pregnant that autumn. (And, believe me, the Boswell Sisters' "Rock and Roll" was almost as bad as "Bossa Nova Baby.")

In the 1940s the phrase gathered momentum as the music gathered momentum. By 1944 the music of the Nat King Cole Trio was being advertised as "Royal Rockin' Rhythm." In January 1947 a National Records advertisement for Big Joe Turner's "Miss Brown Blues" described its product as "GROOVY RHYTHM THAT REALLY ROCKS!" In a May 1948 ad for Brownie McGhee's R&B tribute to the first black major-league baseball players, "Robbie-Dobey Boogie," Savoy Records exclaimed, "IT JUMPS, IT'S MADE, IT ROCKS, IT ROLLS."

Roy Brown's "Good Rockin' Tonight" was released by DeLuxe in September 1947. It was not a hit. Wynonie Harris recorded the song for King in December 1947. It was issued in February 1948. Slowly but surely it ascended the "race" charts (no more "Harlem Hit Parade" for progressive *Billboard*); by June it was Number 1.

After that, if it rocked, it sold. So, in 1948: "We're Gonna Rock" by Wild Bill Moore (Savoy), "Rockin' Boogie" by Joe Lutcher (Specialty), "Rockin' the House" by Memphis Slim (Miracle), and "Rockin' Jenny Jones" by Hattie Noel (MGM); in 1949: "Rockin' at Midnight" by Roy Brown (DeLuxe), "Rock the Joint" by Jimmy Preston (Gotham), "All She Wants to Do Is Rock" by Wynonie Harris (King), and "Rock the House" by Tiny Grimes (Atlantic).

At first the industry establishment did not quite know what to make of the new music. Reviewing Johnny Otis's record "Barrel House Stomp" in January 1949, *Billboard*, nonplussed, simply declared it to be "One of the loudest records ever made." A few months later, when it reviewed Wild Bill Moore's "Rock and Roll" and Louis Jordan's "Cole Slaw," *Billboard* was valiantly but awkwardly trying to adjust. Moore's record was "Another frenetic installment in the pounding 'good rocking' serial. A potent new platter of its kind." In its finest remedial hep-talk, *Billboard* said of Jordan's record: "Band really rocks." A month later the term "race" was forsaken for the cooler "rhythm and blues."

In 1950 the real flood began: "I'm Gonna Rock" by Connie Jordan (Coral), "Sausage Rock" by Doc Sausage (Regal), "Rockin' the Blues" by Pee Wee Crayton (Modern), "Rock with It" by Johnny Moore's Three Blazers (RCA Victor), "Rockin' Rhythm" by Pee Wee Barnum (Imperial), "We're Gonna Rock" by Cecil Gant doing business as Gunter Lee Carr (Decca), "Rockin' with Red" by Piano Red (RCA Victor), "Rockin' Blues" by Johnny Otis with Mel Walker (Savoy), and "How about Rocking with Me?" by Piney Brown (Apollo).

By now it was obvious that what was going on was more than a "serial," as *Billboard* had called it in the spring of 1949. Reviewing Connie Jordan's Coral recording of "I'm Gonna Rock" in February 1950, *Billboard* whined that it was "The umpteenth variation on 'Good Rocking Tonight'." But the trade publication was at the same time becoming astute enough to notice that the record in point did not "have the real gone spirit."

In 1951 came "Rock Little Baby" by Cecil Gant (Decca), "Let's Rock a While" by Amos Milburn (Aladdin), "Rockin' and Rollin'" by Little Son Jackson (Imperial), and "Rock, H-Bomb, Rock" by H-Bomb Ferguson (Atlas). Nineteen fifty-one was also the year that Little Richard's first record, "Taxi Blues," was released by Victor, and that Bill Haley began covering R&B hits—Jackie Brenston's remarkable "Rocket '88,'" the Griffin Brothers' "Pretty Baby"—for Dave Miller's little Holiday Records company in Philadelphia.

In 1952 came Haley's version of "Rock the Joint" (Essex), "Rock, Rock, Rock" by Willis "Gator Tail" Jackson (Atlantic), "Rocking on Sunday Night" by the Treniers (Okeh), "Rock Me All Night Long" by the Ravens (Mercury), "We're Gonna Rock This Joint" by the Jackson Brothers (RCA Victor), and "Rock, Rock, Rock" by Amos Milburn. By year's-end there was even a Rockin' Records Company in Los Angeles. (There had been a Rock-It Records in Baltimore in 1948–49, but it did not last.) In 1953 came "Rockin' Is Our Business" by the Treniers (Okeh), "Rock Me" by Lucky Joe Almond (Trumpet), "Easy Rocking" by Sam Butera (RCA Victor), and "Rock Me Baby" by Johnny Otis (Peacock).

By 1954 rock 'n' roll dominated the music industry. Many of rock 'n' roll's first generation—several of whom are the subjects of this book's chapters: Roy Brown, Cecil Gant, Wynonie Harris, Louis Jordan, Amos Milburn, and others—were already over the hill, dead, or forgotten. A new breed dominated the early fifties. Their sound was less raw, more commercial. As it overwhelmed the marketplace, the industry could do nothing but bow to it.

The Dominoes' "Sixty-Minute Man" had crossed over from the R&B to the pop charts in the summer of 1951. Bill Haley's "Crazy, Man, Crazy" had been a Top Twenty pop hit in the spring of 1953. In 1954 "Gee" by the Crows, "Sh-Boom" by the Chords, and "Hearts of Stone" by the Charms were all Top Twenty pop hits. Alan Freed's first East Coast dance concert, held at the Newark Armory on May 1, 1954, drew more than ten thousand people. His late-night WINS radio show was the rage of New York. In calling the music "rock 'n' roll"—though he was certainly not the first who had done so; he was only the most influential of those who had— Freed had rinsed the Dixie Peach from its image, rendering it more agreeable to the palate of the greater public. Big Joe Turner's masterpiece, "Shake, Rattle and Roll," shook the ground that spring, summer, and fall.

The major companies were paying now for their sins. Looking askance for too long at rock 'n' roll, thinking that it was a passing trend, nothing more than the "serial" that *Billboard* had called it, they began to see exactly how much money they had been missing out on since the late forties. All the best-selling rock 'n' roll hits, all the biggest artists, had belonged to those mongrel labels.

As 1955 began, the major labels tried desperately to cash in on rock 'n' roll. Since they really did not understand what rock 'n' roll was, the maladroit rushing of their greed was ridiculous to behold. Columbia decided that Tony Bennett would be its rock 'n' roll star. "DIG THE CRAZIEST!! HE SWINGS!! HE ROCKS!! HE GOES!!" Bennett's "Close Your Eyes" was pushed as an "ASTOUNDING RHYTHM AND BLUES RENDITION." Needless to say, Tony didn't make it as a rock 'n' roll star. RCA Victor's proposal was more absurd. "DIG PERRY IN ACTION ON A GREAT 'ROCK-AND-ROLL' RECORD," implored the January 1955 ads for Perry Como's cover version of Gene & Eunice's "Ko Ko Mo." But no one was laughing at RCA Victor a year later.

Nineteen fifty-four, the year of rock 'n' roll's ascension, was a quintessentially American year all-round. It was the year of the first atomic-powered submarine, the *Nautilus,* and of Senator Joseph McCarthy's televised hearings into the Communist infiltration of the United States Army. It was the year in which RCA introduced its Compatible Color TV, and in which the United States Supreme Court ruled that racial segregation in public schools was unconstitutional. It was the year that TV Dinners were nationally marketed for the first time, and that Carter-Wallace Laboratories gave the country its first tranquilizer, the Miltown. It was the year that the Muzak Corporation came into being. And it was the year that nineteen-year-old Elvis Presley made his first records, reworking country, rhythm-and-blues, and pop songs for Sam Phillips's little Sun label in Memphis. His final Sun record, "Mystery Train," released on September 1, 1955, hit Number 1 on the country charts. On November 26 Presley, who by then was under the general management of Tom Parker (one of those colonels who understood fried chicken), signed a three-year-plus-options contract with RCA Victor. At his first RCA Victor session, held in Nashville on January 5, 1956, Elvis recorded "Heartbreak Hotel." Released in February, "Heartbreak Hotel" quickly rose to the top of both the pop and the country charts; and at the end of the following month it crossed over to the R&B charts, where fifteen years before, in the days of the "Harlem Hit Parade," it had all begun.

Elvis may very well have been the most important figure in rock 'n' roll. But had it not been for those who came before him, there would have been no rock 'n' roll. It is primarily to those, the ones who came before, that I wanted to give homage in this book. Some of them were famous, some of them were not. Some of them were brilliant, some of them were fools. Many of them ended like Long-fellow's Belisarius, begging for bread beneath the very arch of their triumphal march; others of them prevailed. Most of them made music as fine as any that has ever been heard. Furthermore, they made it first. In the context of their time—when tradition was still a force, and the mass media had not yet taken to propagating changing styles as a means of propagating themselves—a great many of these characters were far more shocking than the most diligently outrageous new rock groups of today. The grand illusion of newness is popular culture's great sucker's-racket. To begin to see that there really is nothing new under the lucky old sun is to begin to understand the nature of popular culture and the business of fame. This is important. As the fellow in the *TV Guide* commercial says, watching television is becoming more complicated every day.

The chapters in this book, each of them devoted to a single artist or group, have been arranged to loosely follow the drift of time. I have begun with Jesse Stone, also known as Charles Calhoun, because his career has spanned much of the century, from minstrelsy to swing to rhythm and blues to present-day rock 'n' roll; and his story lends perspective. A chronology at the end of these chapters attempts to place the evolution of rock 'n' roll in its larger historical setting. Finally, a comprehensive discographical section serves to chronicle the recording careers of the various characters involved. These discographies can also be used as a guide to obtaining the actual music itself. They can even be read for the song titles alone, as a documentary of slang's (and sometimes subliteracy's) progress in modern America.

I spoke before of giving homage. This homage is not always of the most pious sort. Nor is my sense of history of the most orthodox variety. If I can live with these things, so can you, gentle reader. I have tried to have a little fun on the side here, and I hope that what I have written will be read by those more inclined to laugh than to flinch at a bit of license-taking, which, after all is said and done, really is what rock 'n' roll has always been about.

Thanks are due to Dave DiMartino and Connie Kramer at *Creem* magazine; to Michael Pietsch at Scribners; to Russ Galen at the Scott Meredith Literary Agency; to Judith Wilmot, who led me to Virgil's words on the dollar bill and other, greater things; to my alma mater, the New York Public Library; of course, to the Unsung Heroes themselves; and, most of all, to me, without whom this book might never have been written.

JESSE STONE

He Who Controls Rhythm

There is not much at the heart of Laurelton, New York: a grocery store, a beautician's shop, two storefront churches, and a tavern called Little T's Inn. The small black community that lies round it is one of tree-lined streets, modest one-family houses, and neatly trimmed patches of lawn. The trees are great and ancient; their roots have long ago unsettled the slate and concrete of the pavement. Their looming shadows and the lazy summer stillness of the streets are of another place, another time. Were it not for the intermittent sudden roarings of jet planes thundering to and from J.F.K. International Airport nearby, it would be easy to forget that Laurelton is only a half-hour's train ride from Manhattan.

"I've gotten used to it here," Jesse Stone said. It was August of 1983. We were sitting in the combined studio and office which he had set up years ago on the second floor of his home on Mentone Avenue. "It's going to be a hell of a job getting all this stuff packed. It took me all night just to gather up my books in those boxes." He pointed to the corrugated cardboard cartons on the floor. They had not yet been sealed. A paperback copy of Frederick Law Olmsted's *The Slave States* lay atop one of them. "My wife, Evvi, she's the one who's really set on moving to Florida. Those are her drums there." To the right of the drums there was an upright piano. A synthesizer, guitars, recording equipment, a small desk with a typewriter, filing cabinets, a 3-M copy machine, stacks of sheet music, and the couch on which we sat crowded the remaining space. "I've got another studio downstairs, in the basement. That's where I keep all my video equipment." An airplane passed low overhead, muffling his words; but he did not acknowledge it.

Jesse Stone was born in Atchison, Kansas, on November 16, 1901. His grandfather John had been owned by a white family named Stone in Tennessee. John had come to Kansas late in the last century, and he had done well. "He was something, man. He had the first Cadillac in Kansas. Bought it at the 1904 St. Louis World's Fair. He had me polishing the brass on it every Saturday morning."

Jesse's parents, Fred and Julia, were musicians, as were many of their relatives. "All my people were in show business—cousins, grandmothers, grandfathers. I was taught at home by my parents. I had an uncle who was interested in the classics. I got the ability to write songs from my mother, because she wrote songs. My father was a producer. He arranged the numbers for the minstrel shows that we had.

"I started singing when I was four. I had a dog act. The dogs were so well-trained they could do the act without me. They just made me look good. The first instrument I played was the violin."

In the 1920s Jesse traveled frequently to Kansas City, which lay but fifty miles southeast, on the other side of the Missouri River. "It was Prohibition, and Pendergast was running the whole town like an after-hours joint. It was not to be believed. Piney Brown was in with the Pendergast mob, he was what you might call their social director. There was a lot going on musically. I first ran into Joe Turner then, when he was just a kid." He paused, as if taken aback by the realization of how long ago those days were. "Joe's gone just about senile now, I think."

He also traveled upriver to St. Joseph, which was almost as wide-open a place as Kansas City. "There was a colored Chinese fellow named Ching," Jesse recalled. "He was sort of the Piney Brown of St. Joe. Had a place called the Jazzland Café. He had concocted a non-alcoholic drink that got you drunk. It fermented in your stomach after you drank it. He made it in secret, down in the basement of the club. One of the ingredients was prunes, I know that. The drink was called a Peacock. That was the big thing in St. Joe then for show-business people. Soon as they got to town, they'd go for a Peacock. It tasted something like strawberry soda, but not so sweet. The Goetz Brewery offered Ching a million dollars for his secret, but he wouldn't sell out."

By 1926 Jesse had a band called Jesse Stone and His Blue Serenaders. Under the management of Frank J. Rock, the group recorded Jesse's "Starvation Blues" for Okeh in April 1927, in St. Louis. Jesse worked as a pianist and arranger in Kansas City

Jesse Stone, with the Cookies (the future Raylettes), c. 1955.

throughout the late twenties, taking part in Meritt and Brunswick recording sessions there with Julia and George E. Lee, in 1927 and 1929.

In the thirties he organized a bigger band and began to travel farther afield. Good fortune came in 1936, when Duke Ellington visited the Detroit club where Jesse Stone and his band were performing with an all-girl vocal group called the Rhythm Debs.

"Duke was the one who turned me loose. He brought us to New York, got us booked into the Cotton Club. He gave me to Sidney Mills at Mills Music. Sidney signed me to Mills and booked me into theatres. Duke was having problems with his wife at the time, and he gave us his apartment at 2040 Seventh Avenue, paid and all, for about four months. It was quite a thing. We'd come from practically nothing out in the Midwest, and all of a sudden things were happening.

"I started working for the Apollo Theatre. This was right after it had been turned over from being a white burlesque house. I worked for Leonard Harper, staging shows, composing songs, writing jokes and routines and such for the comedians—Pigmeat Markham, Dusty Fletcher, Sam Theard. Acts came in, did a week, then they'd be gone. I filled in missing parts for musicians' arrangements. I'd add a trumpet part that was missing, a couple of saxes or something. When I started out at the Apollo, I was making $15 a week. By the time I left, I was making $300.

"I also played with my band at the Club Renaissance in Harlem on weekends. That's where Louis Jordan picked up on my style of singing. I was doin' arrangements for Chick Webb at the time, and Louis was playin' third alto in Chick's band. He asked Chick could he sing, and Chick said yeah. Louis said, 'Well, Jesse's gonna make a couple arrangements for me.' So I made the arrangements. He tried 'em out one night and he went over great. Chick didn't like that. He wouldn't call the tunes again after that. So Louis quit. I encouraged him, told him that if he wanted to sing, he should get away from Chick. He took my band, and they became the Elks Rendezvous Band, the group on his first recordings."

Jesse did some recording work himself in the late thirties and early forties. He cut "Snaky Feeling" for Variety in 1937; he arranged at sessions for Jimmie Lunceford in 1939, for Harlan Leonard and His Rockets in 1940. But he was more concerned with songwriting.

"Cole Porter taught me a lot. He said to me, 'What tools do you use?' I didn't know what he was talking about. I had never even heard of a rhyming dictionary. I didn't know what a homonym was. I didn't know the difference between assonance and alliteration. 'Tools?' I said. 'Hell,' he said, 'if you're gonna dig a ditch, you use a shovel, don't you?' I began to approach songwriting more professionally."

The first big hit that Jesse wrote was "Idaho." It was recorded by several bands in 1942, but Benny Goodman's version on Columbia was the one that ascended the pop charts that summer.

In early 1945 Jesse and his friend Herb Abramson got involved with National Records, the company that had recently been started in New York by Al Greene. "We thought Greene wasn't handling it right. He had a lot of great black talent under contract—Billy Eckstine, the Ravens, and so forth—but he wasn't doing much with them. Herb and I came up with the idea of starting a record company of our own. We figured we could do what a guy like Greene wasn't doing. The only trouble was, Herb Abramson didn't have any money, neither did I. Then, finally, Herb ran into Ahmet Ertegun. Ahmet had money. That was the beginning of Atlantic Records.

"When Atlantic first started, at the end of 1947, we were trying to do jazz. The jazz didn't sell. We tried to analyze what was wrong. We eventually made a trip down South, Ahmet, Herb, and myself. We found out that our music wasn't right because it wasn't danceable. The kids were lookin' for something to dance to. I listened to the stuff that was being done by those thrown-together bands in the joints down there, and I concluded that the only thing that was missin' from the stuff we were recording was the rhythm. All we needed was a bass-line. So I designed a bass-pattern, and it sort of became identified with rock 'n' roll—doo, da-*doo, dum;* doo, da-*doo, dum*—that thing. I'm the guilty person that started that.

"When we started puttin' that sound out on Atlantic, we started sellin' like hotcakes. The first record we used it on was 'Cole Slaw' by Frank Culley, the sax player. He came to Atlantic one day with a song he claimed to have written. It turned out to be a song called 'Sorghum Switch' that I had written when I was a staff writer at Mills. Jimmy Dorsey had recorded it in 1942. From wherever Culley had picked it up, he had gotten the title wrong. He called it 'Sergeant.' Anyway, we let him record it for Atlantic. I changed the name of the song to 'Cole Slaw' and gave it a new arrangement."

Frank Culley's record did not become a hit. But Jesse's old friend Louis Jordan covered the song and his version did, rising to Number 7 on the R&B charts in the summer of 1949. Jesse himself recorded the song for Victor.

"The first big seller we had with the new sound was Ruth Brown, who we'd found in Philadelphia. After 1949 the hits just kept coming."

Jesse's contributions to the immense success of Atlantic Records were inestimable. Charlie Gillett, the British author of *Making Tracks*, a history of Atlantic published in 1974, was told by Ahmet Ertegun that "Jesse Stone did more to develop the basic rock 'n' roll sound than anybody else." Throughout the early fifties, Jesse wrote and arranged many of Atlantic's biggest and best hits: "Money Honey" by the Drifters (1953), "It Should Have Been Me" by Ray

Charles (1954); "Your Cash Ain't Nothin' but Trash" by the Clovers (1954). Greatest of all was the song he wrote for his old friend from Kansas City, Big Joe Turner.

"In January or February 1954, Herb Abramson said to me, 'We got Joe Turner comin' in to record and we need an uptempo blues for a change.' I threw a bunch of phonetic phrases together—'shake, rattle, and roll,' 'flip, flop, and fly'—and I came up with thirty or forty verses. Then I picked over them. I got the line about 'a one-eyed cat peepin' in a seafood store' from my drummer, Baby Lovett. He was always comin' out with lines like that."

"Shake, Rattle and Roll" was a perfect record. Its lyrics were lascivious, but not quite dirty enough to stop it from getting airplay. Joe Turner had rarely sung better. Sam Taylor's tenor sax solo was glorious. Released in early April, it stayed high on the R&B charts for close to seven months.

Like many of the other songs Jesse wrote that year, "Shake, Rattle and Roll" was copyrighted under the name of Charles E. Calhoun. "I was trying to belong to both of the performing societies, ASCAP and BMI," he explained. "I had just bought a home in Hempstead. The guy who had built the house, his name was Charles Calhoun. I had the contract for the house in my hands when Ahmet was sayin', 'You gotta pick up another name to put on these tunes.' I looked down and there it was: Charles Calhoun." (Jesse not only wrote songs under this assumed name; he eventually recorded under it as well—for MGM in 1955, for Groove and Atlantic in 1956.)

When Ed Mesner opened the New York office of his Los Angeles-based Aladdin Records in the summer of 1954, he recruited Jesse to run the company's new Lamp subsidiary. Jesse continued to work with Atlantic at the same time, but his relationship with the company was slowly beginning to dissolve.

"Ahmet was good to me. He'd say, 'You're not charging enough,' and he'd write out a figure and say, 'This is what you should get. If you don't get it, the government will.' But I was after a piece of the company, and I could never pin them down to giving it to me. They kept offering me a lifetime job, but I didn't want that. I wanted a piece."

Mesner's New York Aladdin office did not last long. Aladdin itself was starting to fall in 1956, despite the success of the label's last hit act, Shirley and Lee. "Ed Mesner owed me a bunch of money when he closed the office. He gave me all the furniture and office supplies in lieu of my back pay. That was the furniture we used—

Hal Fein, Charles Singleton, and I—when we started Roosevelt Music.

"Fein had been at Mills with me. Roosevelt Music was his idea. We knew a bunch of black writers who were having trouble with white publishers. They were writing rock 'n' roll songs, and the old, established publishers weren't taking care of them. We gathered those writers together. We gave each of them his own satellite company. It worked like this. The mother company, Roosevelt, got the first pick of each batch of songs the writer came up with. The second choice went to the writer's company. The next, back to the mother company, and so on, with each batch of songs. The writers' satellite companies were named after presidents, too. Our first big hit was probably one of Otis Blackwell's songs, one of his that Elvis Presley recorded."

The twenty years since his arrival in New York had been busy ones. The twenty before that had been something, too. As he approached sixty, Jesse Stone began to look back. He had gone from minstrel shows to swing bands to rock 'n' roll; from holding up a cooper's hoop for a trained mongrel to jump through to producing shows for the Apollo to selling songs to Elvis Presley; from drinking Piney Brown's bootleg scotch and Ching's Peacocks to smoking Cab Calloway's reefer to drinking Ahmet Ertegun's champagne. At least he had a few bucks to show for it all.

"I decided to retire. I moved out to California to take it easy. I laid out on the beach listening to ball games for about a year. Some guy came looking for me one day, told me that he was snowed under with the Twist craze, asked me if I would help him out with a few arrangements.

"I didn't know it then, but that was the end of my retirement. Before I knew it, I was doing stuff for all sorts of Hollywood people, Ann-Margret and them. I ended up at Frank Sinatra's new company, Reprise, in 1961.

"A bunch of gangsters from Chicago offered me a job running a record company there. I turned them down. They made another offer. I turned them down again. They kept raising the price. Eventually it was too good to refuse. So I moved to Chicago.

"These guys weren't interested in recording. They just wanted a front. They had the top floor of the Playboy Building. They fixed me up in the most lavish, elaborate office that I had ever seen. I said, 'I don't need all this room.'—'*Don't worry about it.*' They would come in and hang around in the morning, overseeing all the booking action that was being done on the telephones. Then, after lunch, at one o'clock, the place turned into a recording company. It was Roy Love, Huddie and those guys. Huddie at that time was the big boss of the whole North Side. The record company, Randy Records, was named after his grandkid.

"It was a mess. These guys were bringin' in whatever chicks they were involved with, Playboy bunnies, whatever, to make records. They would just feed these chicks some line and send 'em to me. None of them could sing.

"One day I said, 'The reason the records ain't selling is we're not getting any publicity. I need to send out some press releases.' They said, 'OK, we'll get you a printin' press.' I figured they'd get me one of those little things you set on a table and turn the handle. No. They got me a $30,000 A. B. Dick multicolor lithograph press. It came to the building on a big truck. 'I don't know how to work this thing!'—'*Don't worry about it.*' It was crazy.

"They were giving me plenty of money. *Plenty* of money. But I became frightened. They blew a guy away on the East Side, some guy they'd put in as alderman or something, and he'd double-crossed them. And they'd have business meetings in my office, and I'd hear them talking: 'Did you see the expression on that guy's face when I told him that this was his last day?'—this is what I would hear; they'd be talking about it like they were discussin' a poker game—'He's lookin' in the muzzle and his eyes are gettin' bigger and bigger, and I blow him away.' That sort of thing was getting to me. I figured, uh-oh, I gotta get out of here.

"I slowly turned the operation over to Huddie's son, Lenny Loveman. He'd been thrown out of a bunch of colleges, and they didn't know what to do with him. I put him in charge of the record company. They were really appreciative. They gave me $24,000, and I cut out of there. I told them I was going back to New York, but I really went to Englewood, New Jersey. I thought they might come looking for me. One day I got a call at Roosevelt Music; guy on the line said, 'Anything you ever need, you just let us know. We'll be right there.'"

While Jesse was working in Chicago, he recorded several piano concertos for RCA. He regrets that they have never been released. "I still compose some classical pieces occasionally. I've listened to Bach all my life. Bartók, Stravinsky, they're my main modern men. I've had a lot more luck with my rock 'n' roll than with my concertos, that's for sure," he laughed. "You can't do it all, I guess."

Jesse figured that he would be settled in down in Florida by December. He would be eighty-two then.

I asked him if this move was another attempt to retire.

"Oh, I don't know. They have a lot of clubs down there in Orlando, where we're moving. My wife's twenty years younger than I am, and she still enjoys performing. We'll probably play a few clubs together.

"What I really want to get more involved in is this video stuff." His eyes glimmered, and he did not look at all like a man who could have had a trained-dog act in 1905. "I've been watching a lot of that rock-'n'-roll video, taking a good look at it. The way I see it, those kids are too bogged down in that montage stuff. The way it is now, it's nothing but montage. It's getting old already. I've got a few ideas I want to work on. We'll see what happens."

He slowly rose and smiled, then bent to tuck in *The Slave States*. We left the room and walked to the floor below.

"One thing I won't miss about this house is the damned stairs," he said.

BIG JOE TURNER

Steak for Breakfast,
Gal Meat on a Rainy Day

The blues, country music, and their bastard prodigal child, rock 'n' roll, have a very basic and pervasive thing in common: stupidity. They are, in the main, more the music of folly than of wisdom.

It is hard to decide who are the more ridiculous, the sensitive wimps or the make-believe tough guys. Here is Willie Nelson, starry-eyed and wearing Judy Garland pigtails at the age of fifty; Joe Jackson, a Singing Nun trapped in the body of Porky Pig. On the other hand, there is Waylon Jennings, duded-up like an overgrown Halloween cowboy; Billy Idol, who couldn't scare his beautician's poodle, trying to seem menacing; and behind them a dozen broken-down niggers, too drunk to stand up and piss, boasting in torpid baritones of their hyperbolical virility and wily worldly ways. They are, all of them, in earnest, which only renders them all the funnier.

Those few—such as Robert Johnson, Hank Williams, and Jim Morrison—who did make from their dark attrition a music of no mean power, a poetry, really; those few, in a way, were even more stupid than the rest, because they killed themselves when they could have been walking their schnauzers instead. They figured out the racket, then bet the action rather than booked it. Their words were beautiful, but their voices were scared.

All in the way of bringing us—you and me, pal, in our mutual quest for worthless knowledge—to the not unworthy matter of a noble and mighty man named Big Joe Turner, the rock 'n' roll patriarch who has out-lived and out-rocked them all. Never has he sung scared, never has he appeared in public wearing pigtails or a chartreuse codpiece. His voice, oceanic and commanding, resonant with that rumbling deep down in the ground which is the sound of the Devil chaining his third wife down, is a voice of power. Not in all of rock 'n' roll has there been another singer quite like him.

He wasn't always the big fat fuck that he became in later years. His mother, who gave birth to him on May 18, 1911, in Kansas City, Missouri, simply called him Joe. His hometown was, in the Prohibition years of his youth, one of the most wide-open cities in the Midwest, second in notoriety only to Chicago. Booze, broads, and dice were plentiful, and so were the legendary musicians who lived in Kansas City, or passed through it, in the late 1920s and early 1930s: Count Basie, Mary Lou Williams, Lester Young, and the rest. Most important of all to young Joe Turner was the boogie-woogie piano-player Pete Johnson.

Turner's father was killed in an automobile crash when Joe was fifteen. To help support his mother, his sister, Katie, and himself, Turner shined shoes, hawked newspapers, and worked as a breakfast cook in a hotel. It was a year or so after his father's death that he began hanging around the Backbiters' Club on Independence Avenue, where Pete Johnson performed nightly. Turner, whose only previous singing had been done in the streets, asked the pianist if he could join in. Johnson liked what he heard, and in 1929 Pete Johnson and eighteen-year-old Joe Turner became a team.

They moved from the Backbiters' Club to the Black and Tan. Turner's job consisted not only of singing with Johnson, but also of tending bar and making runs for the bootleg whiskey the club sold. In 1933, when Prohibition ended, Johnson and Turner moved to the Cherry Blossom, which was located at the celebrated corner of Twelfth Street and Vine (an intersection which no longer exists, by the way). They worked there for nearly three years. In 1936 they left Kansas City, traveling to Chicago, St. Louis, and Omaha. Back home, they began working at Piney Brown's joint, the Sunset Club. It was at the Sunset Club that John Hammond, searching the town for new talent, heard Johnson and Turner perform. Hammond brought them to New York, hiring them for his big "Spirituals to Swing" concert at Carnegie Hall on Christmas Eve in 1938.

Turner and Johnson stayed awhile in New York. A few days after the Carnegie Hall show, on December 30, they cut their first record, for Vocalion: "Goin' Away Blues" and the Johnson composition that had become their signature song in the Kansas City clubs, "Roll 'Em, Pete." They went back to Kansas City in August, playing at the Lone Star Club; but their hometown, fine as it was, could no longer contain them. They were back in New York by June 1939, when they made some more records for Vocalion. This time they recorded with a full band—Hot Lips Page on the trumpet, Henry Smith on the alto sax, Eddie Dougherty on the drums, Laurence Lucie on the guitar, Abe Bolar on the bass—under the name of Pete Johnson and His Boogie Woogie Boys. Their classic version of "Cherry Red" came out of this session.

Turner and Johnson continued to perform together for several years—most notably at Café Society, a fashionable, well-fronted mob joint in Greenwich Village—but their recording careers began to diverge as Turner, throughout the 1940s, veered more and more towards that style that eventually would be known as rock 'n' roll.

On January 15, 1940, he recorded "How Long, How Long Blues" and "Shake It and Break It" with the Varsity Seven—the Varsity Records band led by Benny Carter and Coleman Hawkins. A few weeks later, on February 9, he cut two sides for Vocalion with pianist Joe Sullivan and His Café Society Orchestra. On October 15, for Okeh, he recorded "Joe Turner Blues" and "Beale Street Blues" with Benny Carter and His All-Star Orchestra. On November 11, with Pete Johnson, Hot Lips Page, and others, he cut his amazing "Piney Brown Blues," released the following year as by Joe Turner and His Fly Cats in the Decca album *Kansas City Jazz*.

He remained with Decca for four years. On November 26, he cut four sides accompanied by pianist Willie "The Lion" Smith. On January 21, 1941, he recorded with Art Tatum and His Band. The first song cut that day became one of Joe Turner's most well-known pieces, "Wee Baby Blues." After a second session with Tatum, on June 13—and all four sides which were done that day were remarkable: "Lucille," "Rock Me, Mama," "Corrine, Corrina," and "Lonesome Graveyard"—Turner left New York for Los Angeles, where he joined up with Duke Ellington in the production of the revue *Jump for Joy* at the Mayan Theatre. Back in New York the following summer, he resumed making records for Decca. By this time, the thirty-year-old singer was being billed as Big Joe Turner; and big he was.

On September 8, 1941, he recorded for the first time in Los Angeles, accompanied by Freddie Slack, the leader of the new wave of boogie-woogie piano-players. "Rocks in My Bed" and "Blues on Central Avenue" both came out of that session. He recorded with the Freddie Slack Trio again, on January 28, 1942. The national recording ban imposed that year by James Caesar Petrillo, president

Big Joe Turner smiles for the guy with the day-job; a scene from
Shake, Rattle and Rock *(1956).*

of the American Federation of Musicians—Petrillo wanted to
thwart what he called "the menace of mechanical music"—
prevented Turner (and most other singers) from recording until
November 11, 1944, when the ban was ended. Two days after that
date, in Chicago, Turner made his last records for Decca, backed up
by a trio led by Pete Johnson. He cut "Rebecca" that day, with its
memorable lyric, "You know I'll cut your head, girl, just like I'd
chop a block of wood."

He began recording for National on February 2, 1945, and was
again accompanied by Johnson. For his second National session, on
January 23, 1946, in Los Angeles (where he and Johnson had now
opened their own joint, the Blue Room Club), Turner assembled an
outstanding group of musicians which included Bill Moore on the
tenor sax, Teddy Bunn on the guitar, and John "Shifty" Henry, the
author of Amos Milburn's immortal hit "Let Me Go Home, Whiskey," on the bass. "My Gal's a Jockey" c/w "I Got Love for Sale,"

one of the singles to come out of this session, was one of the sensational records of the fall of 1946.

Turner recorded for National through 1947. In July of that year he cut a two-sided "Battle of the Blues" with Wynonie Harris, for Aladdin. At the end of the year he and Pete Johnson made a single for the little Stag label of San Francisco, where they had taken a job at the Memo Cocktail Lounge. In the summer of 1948 they cut four singles for Down Beat, including "Wine-O-Baby" and "Old Piney Brown Is Gone."

When MGM inaugurated its Ebony Series that summer, Turner did five singles for the label. There followed two singles for Aladdin, two with Dootsie Williams for his DooTone label (these singles were not released, however, for several years), two for RPM, and one—a very hot one, "Please Don't Talk Me to Death"—for Modern. In January 1949 he sang on two Excelsior sides by the Lorenzo Flennoy Trio. Later that year, in Houston, he cut five singles for the Freedom label. In 1950 he made two records in New Orleans for the recently formed Imperial label, accompanied by Dave Bartholomew's Orchestra. Before heading north, he cut one single for the little Bayou company.

By 1951, Joe Turner had had more than fifty singles on the market. Through all of them there were discernible a steady maturation of his powers and an ever-increasing distinction of the style he had begun to cultivate in 1939–40. With every singing of "Rebecca," the lines about the head and the block of wood seemed more credible; and nobody made fun of his gut. From here on in, Big Joe's style would not really change. It was only a matter of the world catching up with him.

In April 1951, a few weeks before his fortieth birthday, Turner sang with Count Basie's band at the Apollo Theatre in Harlem. After this engagement, he was offered a three-year contract by Atlantic Records, and he signed it. Atlantic wasted no time. Turner went into Apex Studios on April 19, and a single was released less than two weeks later.

Turner's last hit record, the Freedom single "Still in the Dark," had been a modest one, spending but a week near the bottom of the R&B charts in March 1950. "Chains of Love," his first Atlantic single, hit the R&B charts in June and remained on the charts for six months, rising to Number 2. More hits followed: "Sweet Sixteen" in 1952, "Honey Hush" and "TV Mama" in 1953. Then, on February 15, 1954, Big Joe Turner cut the record that was to be his laurel crown: "Shake, Rattle and Roll," written for Turner by Jesse Stone (under his pseudonym Charles E. Calhoun).

Released in April, "Shake, Rattle and Roll" spent almost seven months on the R&B charts. Though it never hit Number 1 (the Midnighters' "Work With Me, Annie" could not be overcome), it stood, and yet stands, as one of the true glories of that glorious year, 1954, which was the summit of the golden age of rock 'n' roll.

There were other, lesser hits during the next couple of years: "Flip, Flop and Fly" (the follow-up to "Shake, Rattle and Roll") and "Hide and Seek" in 1955; "Morning, Noon and Night," "Corrine, Corinna" (which crossed over to become a modest pop hit), "Rock a While," and "Lipstick, Powder and Paint" in 1956. There was a feature film appearance, in American International's 1956 *Shake, Rattle and Rock.* Now that white people had gotten wise to the term "rock 'n' roll," Big Joe Turner, at the age of forty-five, was a rock 'n' roll star.

"It wasn't but a different name for the same music I been singing all my life," Turner later explained in Whitney Balliett's superb *New Yorker* portrait of him. Turner went on singing that same music. He continued to record for Atlantic until September 1959. In 1963–64 he made a couple of singles for Coral. By then, of course, hardly anyone wanted to hear the real stuff, and hardly anyone recognized Big Joe Turner's name. This didn't much bother Turner, except financially. He had rarely even cared to look into his audiences' eyes.

Big Joe Turner has continued to make records into the 1980s, for small jazz labels such as Pablo; and he has continued to perform, at clubs such as Tramps in New York. Pete Johnson is dead now, and so is Turner's main wife, Lou Willie. (There have been two others— "Whatever money I've made, the wives about got it all"—but Lou Willie, whom he was married to from 1945 till her death in 1972, was the dark lady of the flip sides.) Big Joe Turner, however, belongs to the living. In his seventies, he can still be beheld, banging the butt of his cane on the hard barroom floor, telling Rebecca about that block of wood, and exhorting that devil in nylon hose to get out of that bed, wash her face and hands, get into that kitchen, make some noise with the pots and pans.

Survival is not the point. Any bum can survive. The trick is to survive as a big fat fuck. Joe Turner—may he hit a hundred—has done that, and more.

NAT KING COLE

Beyond Pink Cadillacs

The name of Nat King Cole has been written large in the annals of popular music. Most of us who recognize that name, however, associate it only with the sort of sophisticated romantic ballads by means of which Cole's fame and fortune were derived and maintained. Unjustly ignored and forgotten is the music that Nat Cole made before his establishment. In those years before he was swallowed up by the mainstream, Cole succeeded in creating a sound that popular music has built upon ever since. He did not merely electrify the blues (that would be done later, by displaced deep-South bluesmen such as Muddy Waters); he transformed them. Drawing from jazz, he remade the blues into a thing of his own time and place. Though possessing all the ineffable forlorn wisdom of the old blues, Cole's music also embodied the sophistication and street-smart savoir faire that was burgeoning close to both sides of the tracks in New York and Los Angeles in the early forties. Understated and subtle, but never simple or coy, Cole's small-group sound became the standard of cool. It was, plainly, the main influence on those younger and wilder singing piano-players—Amos Milburn, Charles Brown, Cecil Gant, Ray Charles, and others—who led the first great wave of West Coast rock 'n' roll in the mid-forties. Lending urbanity, class, and, most important of all, accessibility to the blues, Cole was the link between the old and the new, the dungarees and the sharkskin britches.

He was born Nathaniel Adams Coles, on St. Patrick's Day, 1919, in Montgomery, Alabama. When he was four, his family—three brothers; a sister; his mother, Perlina; his father, the Reverend Edward Coles—moved to the South Side of Chicago. The Reverend was a strict, industrious man (he eventually became the pastor of the First Baptist Church of North Chicago, a position which he held until his death in 1965). Discerning Nat's musical leanings, he steered him towards playing church organ at a young age. The boy's true love, though, was not the Holy Ghost's greatest hits, but rather the smoothly vulgar music of Earl Hines.

While attending Wendell Phillips High School, he and his brother Eddie, who sang and played bass, started a band called the Rogues of Rhythm. They made $18 a week playing at the Panama Club on 58th Street, where nobody seemed to notice that the Coles boys were lifting their arrangements almost chord for chord from Earl Hines's records.

Changing the name of the six-man band to Eddie Cole's Solid Swingers, the group recorded four sides for Decca on July 28, 1936, only a few weeks after Nat had graduated from Wendell Phillips High. He didn't sing in those days, he just played the piano.

After the two Decca releases sank unnoticed, Nat joined the Chicago troupe of a musical revue called *Shuffle Along*. Becoming enamored with a pair of legs that danced in the show's line, he went west with the show in 1937. *Shuffle Along* folded abruptly in Long Beach when an enterprising member of the cast made off with $800 in receipts; but it didn't much matter to eighteen-year-old Nathaniel Coles. He married that pair of legs, which belonged to one Nadine Robinson, and moved to Los Angeles. He dropped the "s" from his surname, adopted the sobriquet "King" (it's amazing what a pair of legs can do for a young man's ego), and, recruiting guitarist Oscar Moore and bass-player Wesley Prince, formed the King Cole Trio, which found steady work at the Swanee Inn.

Adding singer Bonnie Lake (who later replaced Lena Horne in Artie Shaw's orchestra), the group, under the name of King Cole's Swingsters, made a series of records in 1939 for the small Hollywood label of Davis & Schwegler. On a few of these obscure recordings, such as "Anesthetic for Lovers" and "Riffin' at the Bar-B-Q," Cole's style at the piano could be heard coming into its own. By December 6, 1940, when the King Cole Trio first recorded for Decca (in the interim, in May and July of 1940, Cole and Oscar Moore worked at a couple of Lionel Hampton's Victor sessions), that style, wry and cocky and cool, had become a recognizable watermark. By then, too, Cole's performances had taken a momentous turn. Prompted by the drunken insistence of a group of Swanee Inn customers one night, Nat King Cole had started to sing.

It was his gravelly, sagacious vocal on the King Cole Trio's first Decca release, a version of the 1928 hit "Sweet Lorraine," that led to its becoming one of the underground sensations of 1940. Though most of them did not sell, the King Cole Trio's subsequent Decca records—"Honeysuckle Rose," "Scotchin' with the Soda," "Call the Police," "Hit That Jive, Jack," and others—were consummate in their art and seminal in their effluence.

Cole traveled east to New York, where on October 22, 1941, the King Cole Trio's last Decca session was held. (Out of this session came Cole's first hit, "That Ain't Right," which became one of the best-selling race records of 1943.) The following month, the group made two records for the small Ammor label as the King Cole Quartet, having for the moment brought in the drummer Lee Young. Remaining in New York through 1942, Cole and Moore, joined by tenor saxophonist Illinois Jacquet, trumpeter Lester Collins, and bass-player Gene Englund, recorded a pair of records for Disc under the name of the King Cole Quintet.

Back in Los Angeles at the start of 1943, the King Cole Trio, with Johnny Miller replacing Wesley Prince on the bass, began playing regularly at the 331 Club. The group made a couple of records for Excelsior early in the year. One of these, "All for You," followed "That Ain't Right" onto the race charts. In the summer Cole did his first movie work, performing in the Republic features *Here Comes Elmer* and *Pistol Packin' Mama*.

(These movies, like most of the others mentioned in this book, have been relegated to the dimmest archival sub-basement of film history. During the forties, hastily made musical films, ranging in length from one to eight reels, were churned out in great numbers. These shorts and second features were made and distributed to coincide with current hit records. Films were used as an adjunct to the recording industry, much the same as videocassettes are today. In fact, in the early forties, a phenomenon equivalent to MTV was all the rage—"movie jukeboxes" that played three-minute Soundies of current hits in "live" performance.)

On November 2, between the releases of those films, the King Cole Trio cut two records for Premier. The second of these Premier releases, "Got a Penny," was uncanny in its foreshadowing of rock 'n' roll things to come. (On the same day when these recordings were made, Oscar Moore cut a record for Premier with his brother and fellow guitarist, Johnny, and singer Charles Brown. This record, "Tell Me You'll Wait for Me," was the beginning of Johnny Moore's

Spring, 1946.

Three Blazers, one of the most important of the West Coast's early rock 'n' roll bands. In a little while, Charles Brown, who paid close attention that day as "Got a Penny" was being cut, would take up on the piano where Nat King Cole would leave off. [And, moving here into full-blown tangential bracketdom, the flip side of that Blazers record, "Melancholy Madeline" by Oscar Moore and the Three Blazers (after all, what are brothers for?), featured as its vocalist not Charles Brown but Frankie Laine in his recording debut. How he got there, I do not know; and these brackets and parentheses are beginning to frighten me; so let's move on, into a more well-lighted paragraph.])

Eight days after the Premier session, occurred the most momentous turn in Nat King Cole's career since that night in 1940 when the Swanee Inn drunks had instigated him to sing. Glenn E. Wallichs, vice-president of the new Capitol label, caught the King Cole Trio's show at the 331 Club; and, on November 10, 1943, Cole became the third artist to be signed to Capitol. Two weeks later, on November 30, the King Cole Trio went into the studio. The very first song they cut for Capitol, a Cole original titled "Straighten Up and Fly Right," became a national pop hit, rising to Number 9 on the pop charts in June 1944. (In the meantime, Capitol had purchased and reissued the Excelsior sides "All for You" and "Vom Vim Veedle.") By then Cole had made his third and fourth movie appearances, in 20th Century-Fox's *Pin-Up Girl* and Columbia's *Stars On Parade*, both of which were in the theatres as "Straighten Up and Fly Right" was in the air.

Ironically, but not surprisingly, Cole's first crossover hit marked the end of his contributions to the birthing of rock 'n' roll. To be sure, there were after "Straighten Up and Fly Right" a great many fine Nat King Cole records—"I'm a Shy Guy" (1945), "(Get Your Kicks On) Route 66" (1946), "She's My Buddy's Chick" (1946), "The Geek" (an instrumental inspired by the movie *Nightmare Alley;* 1948), and so forth, clear through to the astounding version of "Wee Baby Blues" that he made with Count Basie's orchestra in June 1958—and Cole remained until the end a stylist in a class by himself. But in 1944 he passed the torch along and settled back to enjoy the deserts of his decade-long upwards toiling. There were baseball games to watch, Philip Morrises to chain-smoke. Life was good.

He appeared in more movies: Columbia's *Swing in the Saddle* (1944), Universal's *See My Lawyer* (1944), United Artists' *Breakfast in Hollywood* (1946), All American News' *Killer Diller* (1947). He had more and bigger hits: "(I Love You) For Sentimental Reasons" reached Number 1 on the pop charts during the 1947 Christmas season; "Nature Boy" was the all-round best-selling record of 1948.

That was Nat King Cole's year, 1948. Having been divorced the year before by the pair of legs that he had followed west and wed in 1937, Cole had taken up with a lovely lady named Maria Ellington, who had sung with, but was not related to, Duke. On Easter Sunday, 1948, a few days after "Nature Boy" was released, Nat and Maria were married at the Abyssinian Baptist Church in Harlem, in a ceremony performed by Pastor Adam Clayton Powell. This $20,000 wedding was, in the words of *Ebony* magazine (in an issue whose cover was shared by "The Nat 'King' Cole Nobody Knows" and the news that "Pills Can Change the Color of Skin"), "the second largest in Harlem history." (The biggest was that of the hair-straightener queen Mme. C. J. Walker's granddaughter, in 1923.) Honeymooning in Mexico, Cole received a call from Capitol telling him that "Nature Boy" was breaking all sales records. By the time he and Maria returned home, to a Tudor mansion that Cole had bought in the exclusive Hancock Park suburb of Los Angeles, "Nature Boy" was climbing high on both the pop and race charts. Furthermore, he found that he was being honored as Man of the Year by the Elegant Negro Men's Club of Huspo. He inserted another Philip Morris in his three-inch cigarette-holder, lit it, and leaned back with great satisfaction.

The hits continued to come, though his albums began to do better than his singles. His first album, *The King Cole Trio*, released in early 1945, had been the very first 78-rpm set to hit Number 1 on *Billboard*'s new album charts. In ensuing years, thirty-three more of Cole's albums made the charts. One of these, *Ramblin' Rose* (1962), remained on the LP charts for an astounding 162 weeks. (And people ten years later thought that Carole King's *Tapestry* was a big deal.) There were more movies: *Make Believe Ballroom* (Columbia, 1949); the Universal musical featurettes *Nat "King" Cole* (1951), *Nat "King" Cole and Joe Adams' Orchestra* (1952), and *Nat "King" Cole and Russ Morgan's Orchestra* (1953); *Small Town Girl* (MGM, 1953); *The Blue Gardenia* (Warner Bros., 1953); *The Nat "King" Cole Musical Story* (narrated by, of all people, Jeff Chandler; Universal, 1955); *Istanbul* (Universal, 1956); Sam Fuller's Vietnamese war story, *China Gate*, in which Cole played his first dramatic role (20th Century-Fox, 1957); *St. Louis Blues*, in which Cole played W. C. Handy, who died two weeks before the movie's premiere (Paramount, 1958); *Night of the Quarter Moon* (MGM, 1959); and *Cat Ballou* (Columbia, 1965).

But it wasn't always easy. Nat King Cole came to know what Lou Costello already knew, that life was a bitch, and the quest for peace a three-card monte game.

The Feds swooped down on him for back taxes, seizing his mansion in March 1951, just as his last Number 1 hit, "Too Young," was being released. On April 10, 1956, he tried to give a performance in his home state, at the Birmingham Municipal Auditorium (where, eight years later, on July 1, 1964, Jerry Lee Lewis recorded the best live rock 'n' roll album ever made). "NAT KING COLE BEATEN ON ALA. STAGE; JAIL 3" was the *Daily News* headline on the following day. A group of men, followers of Asa Carter's anti-black, anti-rock 'n' roll North Alabama White Citizens Council, had, in the wrath of their impotence, charged the stage and ganged up on the singer that their less politically correct fellow Alabamians had paid to see and hear. (It is to be regretted that Yoko Ono had not yet come on the scene to inform them and us that woman is the nigger of the world.) A few months later, on November 5, 1956, NBC began broadcasting "The Nat 'King' Cole Show." But, in spite of enthusiastic critical response, no national sponsor was willing to underwrite the show, for fear of boycotting; and, in December 1957, it was shut down. "O.K. for T.V." he had sung in 1951; and so it was.

He kept playing, here and abroad. Behind him were guitarist John Collins (Oscar Moore had left long ago, in 1947, to join his brother's Blazers), bass-player Charles Harris (Johnny Miller had left in 1949), and drummer Lee Young, who had recorded with Cole back in the lean days of 1941. In June 1961 he re-signed for another ten years with Capitol. He came through the following year with the *Ramblin' Rose* album, and in 1963 with his last Top Ten hit, "Those Lazy-Hazy-Crazy Days of Summer."

It was late the next year when he got that call from Philip Morris. Canceling an engagement at the Sands in Las Vegas, he entered St. John's Hospital in Santa Monica on December 8. On January 25, a week before his father's death in Chicago, his left lung was removed. At 5:30 on the morning of February 15, 1965, a month shy of his forty-sixth birthday, Nat King Cole died. A few days later, he was put to rest in Forest Lawn Memorial Park, Glendale. Sinatra showed up in a long black limousine.

LOUIS JORDAN

Hep and the Art of Alto Sax Repair

In the 1940s there were two black singers who crossed over from the race charts (as *Billboard* called its bluegum charts until 1949, when the phrase rhythm & blues was adopted) to the pop charts. Nat King Cole, the more successful of the two singers, was eventually swallowed by the tamer, white music. One of the most inventive West Coast R&B singers of the early forties, by the year of his death, 1965, Cole had been reduced to singing "The Ballad of Cat Ballou" with Stubby Kaye. The other singer was a man named Louis Jordan. Although he is largely forgotten today, Jordan did more to define hep and to prepare white folks for the coming of rock 'n' roll than any other man of that era.

Louis Jordan was born on July 8, 1908, in Brinkley, Arkansas, a small town halfway between Little Rock and Memphis. At the age of twelve, he ran away from home and joined Ma and Pa Rainey's Rabbit Foot Minstrels. He toured with the legendary troupe for two seasons, then returned to Arkansas. Jordan's family moved to Philadelphia in 1930, and it was there that he joined the band of trumpet-player Charlie Gaines. He made the move to New York playing with Leroy Smith, then Kaiser Marshall. In 1936 he began playing alto saxophone in Chick Webb's band, and on October 29 of that year he cut his first record, blowing almost indiscernibly behind Webb's vocalist Ella Fitzgerald. On January 15, 1937, Webb allowed Jordan to sing on record for the first time, on a song called "Gee, but You're Swell."

In 1938 Jordan left Webb's band and formed his own six-piece group. They played at the Elk's Rendezvous Lounge, a small joint in

Harlem, and soon became known as Louis Jordan's Elk's Rendezvous Band. This group cut their first records, for Decca, on December 20, 1938. By the time Jordan next recorded, in early 1939, he had changed the name of his band to Louis Jordan and his Tympany Five, a name he would continue to use, regardless of the number of men in his bands, until 1955.

Louis Jordan's first hit was "I'm Gonna Move to the Outskirts of Town" (1942), a song written and first recorded five years before by bluesman Casey Bill Weldon. In 1944 Jordan crossed over to the pop charts with "G.I. Jive," and his records continued to cross over until 1949.

Louis Jordan rarely sang sad songs. He made party music, pure and simple, in which every aspect of the expanding universe was seen in terms of fried fish, sloppy kisses, gin, and the saxophone whose message transcends knowing. In songs like "Caldonia (What Makes Your Head So Hard?)," "Choo Choo Ch'Boogie," "Beware," "Boogie Woogie Blue Plate," and "Blue Light Boogie," Jordan proved himself to be the crowning glory of postwar hep. At the height of his fame, in November 1946, he had concurrently held down the top three positions on the race charts: "Choo Choo Ch'Boogie" was Number 1, "Ain't that Just Like a Woman" was Number 2, and "Stone Cold Dead in the Market" was Number 3; his "That Chick's Too Young to Fry" was tied for Number 4 with Big Boy Crudup's "Ethel Mae." He emerged at the year's end having had four of the five most successful race records of 1946. (The fifth was Nat King Cole's "Christmas Song.")

Throughout the forties, Jordan made movies, too: *Follow the Boys* (Universal, 1944); *Meet Miss Bobby Socks* (Columbia, 1944); *Caldonia* (Soundies, 1945); *Swing Parade of 1946* (Monogram, 1946); *Toot That Trumpet* (1946); *Beware*, advertised as "The first truly great ALL COLORED Musical Feature" (Astor, 1946); *Reet, Petite and Gone* (1947); and *Look Out, Sister* (1948).

In his most impressive performance, "Let the Good Times Roll" (written by the mysterious Sam Theard, also known as Lovin' Sam and Spo-Dee-O-Dee), Jordan advised:

> *Don't sit there mumblin' and talkin' trash:*
> *If you wanna have a ball ya gotta go out and spend some*
>   *cash,*
> *And let the good times roll.*

Louis Jordan, Mystic Knight of the Sea.

As early as 1949 Jordan's own lyrics were imbued not only with
the spirit of what would come to be known as rock 'n' roll, but also
with direct references to rock, as in "Saturday Night Fish Fry":

> *It was rockin', it was rockin';*
> *You never seen such scufflin' and shufflin' till the break of*
> *dawn.*

"Saturday Night Fish Fry" was Louis Jordan's last pop hit. He had six more R&B hits; then, in 1951, he fell from fame. In 1954 Jordan left Decca and signed with Aladdin, a smaller, West Coast label. After Aladdin, he cut a handful of singles for two RCA subsidiaries, Vik and X. In 1956 he came to Mercury, for whom he made his last worthwhile recordings (mostly reworkings of his old Decca hits). After leaving Mercury in 1958, Jordan became less and less active. He recorded periodically, and with no success, throughout the sixties: for Lou-Wa and Warwick in 1960, for the British label Melodisc in 1962, for Ray Charles's Tangerine label in 1962–64, for Paul Gayten's short-lived Pzazz label in 1968, and for the French label Black & Blue in 1973. In 1974 he cut an album for Johnny Otis's Blues Spectrum label. It was his last record.

In September 1974 Louis Jordan had a heart attack in Nevada. He recovered and announced his plans to tour Europe. A few months later, however, a further attack proved fatal, and he died at his home in Los Angeles on February 4, 1975. He was sixty-six years old. *Billboard* barely mentioned it.

Louis Jordan was criticized by some for catering to his white audiences. In an interview published in the English magazine *Blues Unlimited* a few years ago, Jordan admitted that he had at times made a conscious effort to render his performances acceptable to "the white crackers." Yet his spirit of whorish compromise was ahead of his time, too, in a way. Looking back now, it's easy to see that real rock 'n' roll has always been *anti*-purity, and that Louis Jordan was no more an Uncle Tom than Jimi Hendrix or Michael Jackson. He was a snazzier dresser than either of them, to boot.

In 1946 Astor Pictures released a musical called *Beware*. It centered on the Louis Jordan hit of the same name and year. The purported star of the film was Milton Woods (described as "the colored Basil Rathbone"), but the picture belongs to Louis Jordan and his band, who, in one wild and eerie scene, emerge galloping on horseback over the range—with glistening saxophones slung over their sharkskin shoulders. What finer way to be remembered?

WYNONIE HARRIS

The Man Who
Shook Down the Devil

We know that rock 'n' roll was not a human invention, that it was the work of the Holy Ghost. When, in an article called "Women Won't Leave Me Alone," published in the October 1954 issue of *Tan*, Wynonie Harris bragged that he "started the present vogue of 'rocking' blues tunes," he failed to mention the Holy Ghost, who had chosen Harris to serve him in his work. But Wynonie Harris was like that. Not even the Holy Ghost Hisself was safe from the unmoving sword of Harris's arrogance.

At about the time that Wynonie Harris was finishing his story for *Tan*, in the summer of 1954, Sun was distributing Elvis Presley's first single. Presley's second single, which was released in September 1954, was a song learned from one of Wynonie Harris's recordings: "Good Rockin' Tonight." (Harris had cut the song for King in December 1947, and it became one of the biggest R&B hits of 1948.) On the KWKH "Louisiana Hayride" that same autumn, Presley sang another song learned from Harris: "That's the Stuff You Gotta Watch," a Buddy Johnson song which Wynonie had recorded for Apollo in 1945.

Elvis learned more than songs from Wynonie Harris. The pelvic jab-and-parry, the petulant curlings of his lip, the evangelical wavings of his arms and hands—these were not the spontaneities of Elvis, but a style deftly learned from watching Wynonie Harris perform in Memphis in the early 1950s. Henry Glover, who produced most of Wynonie's records, told me when I spoke with him in the summer of 1977, "When you saw Elvis, you were seeing a mild version of Wynonie."

Wynonie Harris was born on August 24, 1915, in Omaha, Nebraska. His parents, Luther and Nallie Harris, were church-going Baptists who wanted Wynonie to become a doctor. After graduating from Central High, he attended Creighton University as a pre-med student. He stuck it out for two years. Then, in 1934, came the calling of the Ghost. Harris began dancing for money in Jim Bell's Harlem, McGill's Blue Room, and other joints around Omaha. By the end of that year, when he was nineteen, he had married a woman named Olive Goodlow of Council Bluffs, Iowa, and he had turned from dancing to singing. Frequently making the two-hundred-mile trip from Omaha to Kansas City in the late 1930s, he learned well the lessons of the master, Big Joe Turner. In 1940 he traveled to Los Angeles, where he found a job singing for $17.50 a week in Baron Moorehead's orchestra at the Club Alabam, on Central Avenue near Forty-second. It was not long before he became a local celebrity, referred to as "Mr. Blues" by those who fancied themselves in the know. While in Los Angeles, he also took a job dancing in the Republic picture *Hit Parade of 1944*.

Returning east in early 1944, Harris headlined at the Chez Paree, then at other clubs in Kansas City. While in Kansas City, he was approached by the bandleader Lucky Millinder, who offered Harris $125 a week to be a secondary singer in his band. (Trevor Bacon was Millinder's regular vocalist.) Harris accepted and went with Millinder that spring to New York, where they opened at the Apollo Theatre. On May 26 Harris recorded two songs with Lucky Millinder and His Orchestra for Decca. The first, "Hurry, Hurry," released in July 1944, was a hit. The second, "Who Threw the Whiskey in the Well?," released in April 1945, was a bigger hit. By then Harris had left Millinder and returned to Los Angeles. The only money that he had seen from the two hits he had sung was $37.50, which Decca had paid him as a recording fee. This had taught him something. In the summer of 1945 Wynonie Harris began making records of his own.

His first solo recordings were released in September by Philo, the new Los Angeles label that Ed and Leo Mesner were running out of their Philharmonic Music Shop on West Fifth Street. (Less than a year later, due to legal problems, Philo became Aladdin.) Eight records followed on the Apollo label. Several of these songs were written by Harris. One of the best, "Time to Change Your Town," lamented the end of the flush wartime days.

Wynonie Harris, with necktie.

When your money gets low,
It's time for you to change your town,
Because the war is over,
All the shipyards are closin' down.

Them boys used to wear diamonds;
You don't see those rings no more;
They used to ride Buicks and Cadillacs,
Now they're lucky to have a Ford.

The music-business establishment was hesitant in its acceptance of Wynonie Harris and his vigorously vulgar style of shouting the blues. In its review of his "Young and Wild," *Billboard* remarked rather aloofly that the record might perhaps be "Good for the back rooms at the Harlem spots." But it sold, and that's what mattered.

Wynonie and his wife, Olive, broke up at the end of 1946. By then he had begun to cultivate the lady-killer image that he maintained for the rest of his life (though for most of those years after 1946 he remained close to his second wife, Gertrude Sloan of Chicago, whom he nicknamed Ice Cream). "I play to create impressions," he said in the *Tan* article. "The women who really know me also know part of my secret. We can laugh about it together for they know how women can get stirred up by a man who seems cruel, ornery, vulgar and arrogant."

"I've had them to take enough pills to kill a horse, follow me from town to town in Cadillacs, give me money, threaten me and fight one another like crazy. It's all because I deal in sex. . . ."

"As a statement of fact, clean of any attempt to brag about it, I'm the highest-paid blues singer in the business. I'm a $1,500 a week man. Most of the other fellows sing for $50 to $75 a night. I don't. That is why I'm no Broadway star. The crooners star on the Great White Way and get swamped with Coca-Cola-drinking bobby-soxers and other 'jail bait.' I star in Georgia, Texas, Alabama, Tennessee and Missouri and get those who have money to buy stronger stuff and my records to play while they drink it.

"I like to sing to women with meat on their bones and that long green stuff in their pocketbooks. You find them mostly down South. As a matter of fact, I like all kinds of women, regardless of what color they are or what size and shape they may have. Just so long as they're breathing, that's me.

"In Dallas, Texas, recently, where I was singing with the Big Rhythm and Blues Show that featured Joe Louis, Ruth Brown, Lester Young, Buddy Johnson and the Edwards Sisters, a white chick came out to our concert at the ball park. She sat right down front in the 'white' section and I saw her eyes following my every movement while I sang my old standby, 'Wynonie's Blues.' In it there's the line: 'Let's drink some mash and talk some trash this morning.' It's what we call in the trade, a 'rocker' or a punch line, and it seldom misses making the women squeal.

"Well, this white girl jumped up and hollered out loud as if she was in church and shouting after the preacher said something to make her 'happy.' I didn't think anything about it and took my bows and went off. When I got back to the dressing room, however, there she was. I got rather warm and sweaty when she said, 'Mister, you really thrilled me with your singing. I'm a stenographer, I'm 22 and single. Could you come to my house later on tonight and sing for me?'

"You know what I told her! I stayed in the men's room for over 45 minutes until I thought she had gone and then made a break for it in my car. . . ."

He spent money like it was going out of style. When he received a $10,000 royalty check from his Apollo records, the world became for him a new place. "I bought me two Cadillacs and hired me two chauffeurs and people used to line up around 4 a.m. when I finished for the night at the Baby Grand in Harlem and watch me come out and pick out which of my cars would take me home."

While in Nashville to perform at the Club Zanzibar in early 1946, Harris cut two records there for Jim Bulleit's new Bullet label. After that he recorded two singles in Los Angeles for Lionel Hampton's Hamp-Tone label. In 1947 he recorded again for the Mesner brothers. Then, in December of that year, he signed with King Records in Cincinnati.

He stayed with King until 1954. During his seven years with the label, he became one of the biggest R&B singers of the era, and made some of the greatest rock 'n' roll records in history.

His big hits dealt either with getting drunk ("Drinkin' Wine, Spo-Dee-O-Dee," "Bloodshot Eyes") or getting laid ("I Like My Baby's Pudding," "Lovin' Machine"). His monumental version of "Good Rockin' Tonight" (Roy Brown had done the original less than a year before) was recorded three days after Christmas 1947. Released in February, it hit Number 1 on the *Billboard* race charts, as they were still called, in early June. Although his 1949 "All She Wants to Do Is Rock" sold more copies, it was "Good Rockin' Tonight" that heralded the new era of American music.

He has been remembered by those who knew him as a wildman, a creature of lurid excesses. Roy Brown, who wrote "Good Rockin' Tonight," recalled that "He'd walk into a bar and shout 'Here comes the blues!' He was wild. He'd jump off the bar and say, 'Man, I'll eat you up!' He was like that. He got shot through the head, he got shot through the ears, he'd get beat up, but he didn't mean no harm." (For the record, the only shooting injury sustained by Harris was one in his hand, inflicted by an irate cuckold.)

Ralph Bass, who worked for King (he is the one who later brought James Brown to the label) before joining Chess in 1958, told me, "He always had a broad. Shit, man, he didn't have any respect. He'd walk up and insult a woman right in front of her man. He'd say, 'Hey, bitch, what you doin' here, whore?' And call 'em all kindsa names. And there were very few cats he respected, he stayed away from.

"One night in Cincinnati, he picked me up and he was gonna fight Ezzard Charles, when Ez was champ, 'cause Ez was hittin' on his old lady. Christ," he laughed, "what a night. That was at the old Cotton Club there.

"I remember there was five beautiful showgirls stayin' at the Manse Hotel. He was there at the same time and he had this whore from Chicago with him, and he told the whore, 'Look, don't talk to these girls. These girls are respectable girls.'

"That's the way he was. He was very arrogant. Knew what he was doing. And, what the hell, he lived." Bass paused, then burst into laughter. "At least he wasn't on drugs!"

Producer Henry Glover, grasping for kind adjectives, told me that "He was, uh, very likable. At times. He carried sort of a, I don't know, negative attitude. Really, I think it was just he was frightened at people. Didn't wanna be around 'em. Drank a lot of whiskey." At this point, Mrs. Glover, who was listening to her husband's words, interjected a few of her own—"He was very loud and very vulgar"—and Henry laughed softly and said, "This man was a concept. Hell, he was too much."

In the late 1950s, Wynonie Harris fell into obscurity. There were several comeback attempts. He cut a single for Atco in 1956, one for Roulette in 1960. Late in 1956 he told an interviewer from *Rock and Roll Roundup* that "The criticism has made Elvis Presley. I think that he is okay. Elvis has made one song that I like, 'Don't Be Cruel.' Many people have been giving him a lot of trouble about swinging his hips. I swing mine and have no trouble. He's got publicity he could not buy."

As the sixties began, Wynonie Harris was all but forgotten. He lived in St. Albans, New York. He bought a bar there. He lost the bar in 1963. He moved to Los Angeles. In 1967 Preston Love, the leader of the Motown Orchestra, asked Harris to perform with the band at Santa Monica.

"Wynonie attempted to sing. He couldn't. He sang one or two numbers. It was hopeless," Love recalled. "And I had young studio-types in the band that couldn't play anything but the spurious, synthetic, modern, mathematical blues. So I said to Wynonie, 'Man, go on. Forget it,' because the people wouldn't accept him. That's the last time he ever tried to sing. Never again. Not one more note."

Wynonie Harris was sick, but he kept on drinking and carrying on. Ralph Bass said that "Several days before he died, there was a cab driver that used to buddy with him, and he called the cab driver and said, 'Come on, pick me up.' And the cab driver said, 'No broads?' 'No, just me.' And he made all the joints in L.A. and the cab driver seemed to think Wynonie had a feeling it wouldn't be too long, he wanted to see everything. He got dressed real sharp. Every joint in L.A."

The story that Preston Love told in the liner notes of *Oh Babe!*, a 1983 Dutch anthology of Harris's recordings, is a more somber one. "We ex-Omahans who had known him all his life and were living in Los Angeles gave a benefit for Wynonie in June 1969 at the Caribbean Club. When I walked in the club, he was sitting there at the bar with Patty, his daughter by his first wife, Ollie. He was a broken, bent-over man. He looked much older than me, but he still was brave and tried to carry it through. . . . It pained me so much to see him like this and I circulated around and shook hands with some of the hometown friends. When I came back to the bar he was gone. There was a little anteroom, a little foyer in the club, where two people could step in out of the wind and come on in the second door. I looked out through a window and saw him standing out there. He was just standing there, bent-over, in terrible pain. I backed up so he wouldn't notice me. He finally got himself together and straightened up. He came on back in blustering like he was OK, but he was in terrible pain."

He died in Los Angeles little more than a week later, on June 14, 1969.

Eight years later, when I was trying to ascertain how old Wynonie Harris had been when he died, Ralph Bass advised, "Whatever age he was when he died, just double it. That's the way that motherfucker lived. Every minute, every blessed minute." Those are good closing words; but better still are those words with which Wynonie Harris closed that story he wrote on the eve of his descent into oblivion: "I don't mix the Lord with the Devil. They are the two I'm most afraid of. As long as I'm with the Devil, I'm going to shake him down for everything, every dime I can get."

ELLA MAE MORSE

The Cow-Cow Girl

Ella Mae Morse—Miss Morse to you—was born on September 12, 1924, in Mansfield, Texas, a small place not too far south of Dallas. Her mother was a pianist. Her father was a drummer. Her breasts developed at an early age. Aside from these meager facts, little is known of Ella Mae's younger years.

Full-breasted, yet un-high-schooled, Miss Morse began singing in her father's local jazz band in the late 1930s. Towards the end of 1938 Jimmy Dorsey, passing through Texas, happened to hear her. So very impressed was he with the well-gartered, fiery-voiced fourteen-year-old girl that he immediately offered her a job as lead singer in his band.

Ella Mae began traveling with the Jimmy Dorsey Orchestra in January 1939. She made it as far as the Hotel New Yorker. It was there that she posed for some fine leg art (published on page 19 of the February 1939 issue of *Down Beat*); and it was there, on February 20, that, perhaps because leg art was all Dorsey got from the fourteen-year-old girl, she was replaced by nineteen-year-old Helen O'Connell.

At the close of 1939 Freddie Slack, the legendary, twenty-nine-year-old boogie-woogie man who had been with Dorsey since 1937, quit the band to become the arranger and pianist for Will Bradley's Orchestra. Less than two years later, Slack forsook the big-band sound and formed his own group, the Freddie Slack Trio. In September 1941 and January 1942 the trio found work recording with Joe Turner in Los Angeles. Not long after these sessions (from which came the Joe Turner beauties "Goin' to Chicago" and "Blues in the Night"), Slack decided to expand his band and add a vocalist.

It was then that he remembered the teenage Texas girl with sinful bosom and voice aflame. She was all of seventeen now.

Slack was the first artist to be signed by Johnny Mercer's new Capitol label. When he went into a Los Angeles studio to record on May 21, 1942, he brought with him Ella Mae Morse. That session, Ella Mae's recording debut, resulted in the first hit in the history of Capitol Records, "Cow-Cow Boogie," a song which had been written the year before by Gene DePaul, Benny Carter, and Don Raye. (Raye had previously written the boogie classics "Down the Road a Piece," "Rhumboogie," and "Beat Me, Daddy, Eight to the Bar.")

"Cow-Cow Boogie" was released on July 1, 1942, hit the charts in August, and eventually rose to Number 9. With Freddie Slack playing piano behind her, Ella Mae performed the song in the 1943 Columbia picture *Reveille With Beverly*, a musical which also featured Count Basie, Duke Ellington, the Mills Brothers, and Frank Sinatra. Later that year, she appeared in another movie, *The Sky's the Limit*, released by RKO in August.

Before "Cow-Cow Boogie" appeared on the charts, Slack and Morse had returned to the studio, on July 20. A surprising addition to the band at this session was guitarist T-Bone Walker. Once again, Slack and Morse came up with what was to be a hit, "Mister Five by Five," which entered the pop charts in December 1942 and rose to Number 10.

Ella Mae and Slack parted company in 1943. For the next two years, she, like Slack, recorded as a solo artist for Capitol. (She also appeared in two Universal movies during 1944, *South of Dixie* and *Ghost Catchers*.) Several of Ella Mae's records during those years were hot—"Invitation to the Blues," "Patty Cake Man," "Buzz Me"—but there were no hits. On February 12, 1946, Morse and Slack reunited in the studio, joined this time by the elusive Don Raye himself. The result was one of the most apocalyptic recordings in the history of what in a few years' time would be called rock 'n' roll.

Written by Raye and Slack, "The House of Blue Lights" opened with a fast-spoken dialogue between Raye and Morse as Slack pounded piano behind them. It is perhaps the classic hep colloquy.

Well, whatcha say, baby? You look as ready as Mr. Freddy this black. How 'bout you and me goin' spinnin' at the track?
What's that, homie? If you think I'm goin' dancin' on a dime, your clock is tickin' on the wrong time.

Well, what's your pleasure, treasure? You call the plays, I'll dig the ways.

Ay, daddy-o, I'm not so crude as to drop my mood on a square from way back. I'm there and have to dig life with father—and I mean Father Slack.

Well, baby, your plate gives my weight a solid flip. You snap the whip, I'll make the trip.

Then Ella Mae—free, white, and twenty-one now—began to sing one of the roughest, sexiest hymns to the night that had ever been heard. The record was released by Capitol on April 1, 1946. Like most of Morse's records, it hit the R&B charts; but it never made the pop charts. The uncrude did, however, get to see her sing the song in *How Do You Do?,* released in September of that year by Young American Films.

Ella Mae Morse continued to record for Capitol through 1947—the raunchy "Pig Foot Pete" and the funny, nasty "Pine Top Schwartz" stand out—but there were no pop hits. She married a Navy man named Marvin Gerber, settled down in Palo Alto, and birthed three children. Soon the Cow-Cow Boogie Girl was forgotten.

She came back in the fall of 1951, singing in West Coast clubs and recording for Capitol a strange mixture of pop, country, and black material: country songs such as "Tennessee Saturday Night," "A-Sleepin' at the Foot of the Bed," and "Big Mamou"; R&B songs such as "Greyhound" and "Smack Dab in the Middle." Her hungry-housewife voice was as strong and sultry as ever it had been—stronger perhaps, and more sultry—but no one seemed to understand what she was doing.

In 1954 Capitol released her startling LP *Barrelhouse, Boogie, and the Blues*, composed of her versions of recent R&B songs: the Ravens' "Rock Me All Night Long," the Drifters' "Money Honey," Bull Moose Jackson's "I Love You, Yes I Do," Ruth Brown's "Daddy, Daddy," and more. She sang magnificently, ruthlessly ("Rock Me All Night Long" emerged from her throat as not merely suggestive, but as sublimely and plainly lewd). But it was to be at least another year till the advent of Elvis and the appreciation of such things.

Ella Mae Morse withdrew again a few years later, and Capitol released her last record in 1957, when she was barely thirty-three. No one heard from her again until 1976, when she emerged for a

Autumn, 1943.

handful of club dates in the Los Angeles area. But it was over, and the tears of ancient hepsters fell as the lank lady stood onstage and sang "Feelings" and "Send in the Clowns." Someone had indeed, ahem, pulled the plug on the house of blue lights.

"They tell me," Ella Mae Morse recalled, "that I was the first gal singer to hit the big time with one record. It ['Cow-Cow Blues'] sold way over a million, I hear. I wasn't getting royalties. Man, I made thirty-five bucks on it. Isn't that the end!" Perhaps, my well-gartered girl; perhaps.

CECIL GANT

Owl Stew, and All That

Cecil Gant was born in Nashville, Tennessee, on April 4, 1913. His early years are a faded stain of which nothing is known, nor probably ever will be known.

Our first glimpse of him is in 1944: a small black soldier in a loud crowd at a wartime bond rally on the corner of Broadway and Ninth in Los Angeles. He approached the bandstand during an intermission and asked to play the piano. They let him. He went over so well that the local campaign committee sought and got permission from Gant's commanding officer for him to perform at all Treasury Bond rallies in the Los Angeles area.

Later that year, following one of his shows, Gant was offered a recording contract by Richard A. Nelson, who was on the verge of starting Gilt-Edge Records. Gant's first release was a slow thing called "I Wonder," a strong ballad sung from the viewpoint of a soldier abroad who torments himself with wonderings about whom his sweetheart is fucking back home. The flip side was a fast boogie-woogie rocker, "Cecil's Boogie." A review in the January 6, 1945, issue of *Billboard* said that the record sounded "like something picked up with a machine hidden under a table in a smoky back room." But, at that same time, "I Wonder" was heading fast up *Billboard*'s "Harlem Hit Parade" charts, and, in the end, it emerged as one of the great R&B successes of 1944–45.

"I Wonder" sold so well, in fact, that Gilt-Edge issued a special pressing of the disc, on which a smiling Cecil Gant, in the khaki shirt and tie of his buck-private wardrobe, could be seen sitting at the piano. It was the first rock 'n' roll picture disc.

Gant recorded prolifically for Gilt-Edge through 1946. All his releases bore the name "Pvt. Cecil Gant," and he was further billed as "The G.I. Sing-Sation." From early 1946 to 1949 Gant recorded for Bullet Records, in his hometown of Nashville. Jim Bulleit, who ran Bullet, and who now operates a candy company outside Nashville, told me in 1977 that he "never recorded a thing on him [Gant] that didn't sell and make money. It was just uncanny."

"He drank too much," Bulleit recalled on another occasion. "He would say, 'I want to do a session' when he ran out of money. We would get a bass-player and a guitarist and get him a piano, and I'd go sit in the control room, and he'd tinkle around on it, and then he'd say, 'I'm ready,' and tap that bottle; and if we didn't get it the first time, we didn't get it, 'cause he couldn't remember what he did. He'd dream up and write a song while he sat there, and he'd give me the title of it. And the uniqueness of the thing is that all of them sold."

In 1949 Gant returned to Los Angeles, recording there for the related Down Beat and Swing Time labels. After that, in early 1950, he cut two singles for Imperial in New Orleans. The following summer he began recording for Decca in New York.

Cecil Gant's last session was held on January 19, 1951. Not long after that, he was dead. Although the exact circumstances of his premature demise are unknown—beyond the fact that he died on February 4, 1951, at Hubbard Hospital in Nashville, ostensibly of pneumonia—it was generally believed that, like so many of these characters, he died from a surfeit of drink.

Gant's biggest hits—"I Wonder" (1944), "Another Day, Another Dollar" (1948), "I'm a Good Man, but a Poor Man" (1948), and so on—were slow, melancholy songs. His most remarkable stuff, however, was a group of fiery piano rockers with titles like "Nashville Jumps" (1946), "Ninth Street Jive" (1946), "We're Gonna Rock" (1950), "Owl Stew" (1951), and "Rock Little Baby" (1951).

Gant's deep swampish voice, which lent gravity and pathos to his slower, sadder songs, gave to his breakneck rockers a certain jarring audacity. In "Nashville Jumps" he rasped:

Seen ya goin' up Cedar Street hill,
I know you got your whiskey from Jack Daniel's still!
Nashville really jumps, really jumps all night long;
I'd rather be in Nashville than to be way back down at home.
Yeah, jump, Nashville!

Before the last stanza, Gant yelled, "Bring me another drink and I'll be all right!" (He shouted something similar in "Ninth Street Jive," but quickly amended the request to, "Call that waiter and tell him to bring me a *fifth*!")

On "We're Gonna Rock" he simply chanted, over and over, like some sort of manic, apocalyptic subhuman, pounding his piano with both fists:

> *We're gonna rock, we're gonna roll,*
> *We're gonna rock, we're gonna roll;*
> *We're gonna roll, we're gonna rock,*
> *We're gonna roll, we're gonna rock.*

His "Owl Stew" was a private tribute to a whorehouse on Fourth Avenue North in Nashville. "The stew in Nashville," he explained, one eye open, one eye shut, "it really is the best . . . the price is low; if you get it once, you gonna want some mo'."

Though he recorded for a mere seven years, Cecil Gant proved himself to be one of the great rockers of the late forties. He told his friends in Tennessee that all he really wanted to do was to play the piano and get drunk, laid, and rich. He succeeded in all but the last. Three out of four isn't bad at all.

AMOS MILBURN

The Chicken Shack Factor

"I practiced what I preached," Amos Milburn told me in July 1979, referring to his old hits—hits like "Bad, Bad Whiskey," "Let Me Go Home, Whiskey," and "One Scotch, One Bourbon, One Beer."

"I was a heavy drinker. I loved that scotch. And the Devil kept tellin' me: Go on, Amos, drink all you want to, it'll never hurt you none. I drank myself into two strokes." It was a low, faint voice that spoke. It bore little resemblance to that cool, tough Amos Milburn voice of twenty-five, thirty years ago, that voice that bespoke the ceaseless saxophones of salvation, the crossing and uncrossing of restless nylon knees, the eightfold path of the unfiltered Kool, and the miracle of Our Lady of the After-Hours Joint. But the party had been over for years now.

Amos Milburn was born in Houston, Texas, on April 1, 1927. He graduated from high school in 1942, at the age of fifteen. Lying about his age, he signed up with the Navy for the duration of World War Two, and served three years as a steward's mate aboard an infantry landing craft. During the course of his service, Milburn earned thirteen battle stars in engagements at Guadalcanal, Bougainville, and the Philippines. His boogie-woogie piano-playing was in demand at officers' clubs on islands everywhere. On May 5, 1945, eighteen-year-old Milburn was discharged. Returning home to Houston, he formed a small band and hit the clubs.

He was playing a joint in San Antonio in 1946. A woman named Lola Anne Cullum, wife of a Houston dentist, approached Amos and explained that she had recently started a booking and management agency in Houston. Not long after, the two got together in Houston. Lola Anne made some raw, paper-backed tapes of Milburn's songs and sent them to Aladdin Records in Los Angeles. In September of the same year, she and Milburn (along with Lightnin' Hopkins, another of Lola Anne's discoveries) traveled to the Coast. On September 12, Milburn cut his first sides, for Aladdin.

Milburn's third release, a version of the 1940 Don Raye hit, "Down the Road Apiece" (the same song that the Rolling Stones did on *The Rolling Stones, Now!*), was a minor hit, but it wasn't until 1948 that he had his first Number 1 R&B hit, with his own "Chicken Shack Boogie."

"Chicken Shack Boogie" was a hardrocker celebrating the countless after-hours joints hidden away on the outskirts of Texas towns, places where you could eat, drink, and often gamble until past the break of day. (Thirty-five years later, the chicken shacks are still rocking hard. Next time you're in Austin, find Webberville Road and follow it till it fades away into dirt: you'll be at Ernie's Chicken Shack. Just don't shoot dice.)

For more than ten years, from 1946 to 1957, Amos Milburn cut some of the toughest records in the history of rock 'n' roll, records built upon raw electric guitar, drunken tenor sax (usually played by the great Maxwell Davis), and Milburn's own piano and voice. In "Walking Blues" (1950) and "Roll Mr. Jelly" (1952), he bragged about what a great fuck he was. (In the first song, he sang of raising women from the dead merely by shaking his pecker at their corpses.) In "Let's Rock a While" (1951) and "Rock, Rock, Rock" (1952), he helped to define the classic rock 'n' roll lyric that was to eventually sweep the white folks off their feet a few years later. "Bad, Bad Whiskey" (1950), "Just One More Drink" (1951), "Let Me Go Home, Whiskey" (1953), "One Scotch, One Bourbon, One Beer" (1953), "Good, Good Whiskey" (1953), "Vicious, Vicious Vodka" (1954), and "Juice, Juice" (1956) all dealt with Milburn's demon, booze. (He even had a rocker about drying out, the 1954 "Milk and Water.")

After "One Scotch, One Bourbon, One Beer" in 1953, Amos Milburn never had another hit. Aladdin Records folded in the late fifties. In 1960 Milburn had a single released by King Records; then, in 1962, he signed with the new Motown label. One single and one album, *Blues Boss*, were released by Motown the following year, but nothing happened. There was just no room in soul music for Milburn's bad-ass chicken-shack music.

Milburn continued to perform until 1968. In 1969 he had his first stroke. In 1970, lying on a couch in Cleveland, watching a football game on television, he had his second stroke, and emerged an invalid. He quit drinking and returned to Houston.

"I still got my Kool Super Longs," he told me. "I got my ice water and my Coca-Cola. Don't allow no booze in my home, no sir. Somebody wanna visit me, they better leave their bottle at the door. I'm a Christian man now, and I leave it all up to the Lord. I figure if the Lord wanted me to quit these Kools, he'd let me know, like he let me know about the booze with them two strokes."

Four weeks before I talked with Amos, he had been on the operating table. "They took my leg off," he told me. "The one that used to stomp all that good rock 'n' roll, all that fine boogie woogie on the old piano. They cut it clean off."

And there he was. The first great rock 'n' roll piano man, living on Navy disability checks and Kool Super Longs. It had come to that.

Less than six months after I talked with him, I received word that Amos Milburn had died, on January 3, 1980.

Amos Milburn, back when a Kool was a Kool.

ROY BROWN

Good Rockin' Tonight

Roy Brown, the man who wrote and first cut "Good Rockin' Tonight," and who had rocked his way to the top and fallen to the bottom before Elvis had ever even gotten laid, saw it like this: "I remember Colonel Parker making the statement, 'I believe the white kids want to hear rock 'n' roll, but I'm gonna have a white boy do it.' In other words: If you want to hear 'Good Rockin' Tonight,' I'm gonna have Elvis Presley do it. A lot of those guys did those things and copied the arrangements note for note, but that way it was accepted."

Brown remembers Elvis, whom he met only once, in 1954, as an unknown cracker punk trying to sneak onto the stage at one of Brown's gigs: "We used to play for the high sheriff in Tupelo, Mississippi. My bandleader, my guitar player at that time was Edgar Blanchard, from New Orleans—he's dead now—he loved to drink. Elvis came around. He wanted to sing, but Edgar wouldn't let him on the bandstand. Elvis discovered that Edgar liked to drink, so he got him a big bottle of moonshine—Tupelo was a dry town—and when I came back from changing my clothes at the sheriff's house, there was Elvis. He was up there playing and singing with them, nobody paying any attention to him.

"On my West Coast tour a few months later, Tommy Shelvin, my bass-player, said, 'Hey, man, there's a hillbilly singing your song.' Sure 'nuff, Elvis was singing this song with a hillybilly band. But he never did sell, because he hadn't become Elvis yet, y'know. Yeah, they're both dead now, old Edgar and old Elvis."

It's wise when listening to these characters to keep in mind Shakespeare's warning about "old men of less truth than tongue." But nothing can shake the truth from the fact that, like many others, Roy Brown was an originator of that strange, exalted thing, rock 'n' roll, for which Elvis and a few other kids received the credit.

Roy Brown was born in New Orleans on September 10, 1925. His mama, True Love Brown, part Algonquin, part black, was a choir director and organist. His daddy, Yancy Brown, was a plasterer and bricklayer. As the old man followed work, the family moved through the towns of rural Louisiana. Roy worked for a while in the sugar cane fields of Morgan City and New Iberia. He didn't hear the blues there, only spirituals.

His mother died when he was fourteen. Three years later, after finishing high school, Roy moved to Los Angeles. He became a boxer, winning sixteen of his eighteen professional welterweight matches. But the sight of blood made him sick, and he was forced to quit the fight game.

In 1945, at the Million Dollar Theater in L.A., Brown won an amateur singing contest by imitating Bing Crosby's versions of "San Antonio Rose" and "I Got Spurs That Jingle Jangle Jingle." Crosby was Roy Brown's favorite singer, and he's not ashamed of it. He says he heard no blues until the early forties, when he heard Billy Eckstine sing "Jelly Jelly" and Ella Johnson sing "When My Man Comes Home."

Brown returned to Louisiana and got his first steady singing job, at Billy Riley's Palace Park in Shreveport. He sang stuff like "Stardust" and "Blue Hawaii." Looking back, he feels he got the job because he was a novelty, a colored guy who sounded white—sort of the Elvis syndrome in reverse.

From Shreveport he went to Galveston, Texas, where he wrote the song that made him famous. "I think we had the first black group on radio in that area," he says, again bringing to mind the words of Shakespeare's "Sonnet XVII." "My theme was 'There's No You,' a Crosby thing. But I wrote a tune called 'Good Rockin' Tonight.' We added a trumpet player to the group. His name was Wilbert Brown, and when we did our radio show on KGBC he sang 'Good Rockin' Tonight.'" One fateful day, Wilbert fell sick and Roy sang the song. The audience loved the way Roy sang it, and it became a local hit. While in Galveston, he made his first record, for Gold Star.

Brown fled Galveston after he was caught fucking the girlfriend of the club owner he was working for. In New Orleans he ran into Cecil Gant, a fellow unsung-hero-to-be. Gant heard Brown's "Good Rockin' Tonight" and brought him to Jules Braun, who owned DeLuxe Records. Brown's first DeLuxe release, "Good Rockin' Tonight," was issued in September 1947.

Roy continued to record for DeLuxe for three years. During those years, his voice grew tougher, wilder. He was no longer merely an exceptional pop singer—like Crosby, Sinatra, Prima, or Nat Cole—but one of the first real rock 'n' roll voices. By the time he cut "Hard Luck Blues"—the most morbid Number 1 hit in the history of the R&B charts—in 1950, Brown had achieved a low-down range and power in his voice that few other singers then or since could equal.

King Records bought out his contract in 1950, and Brown found himself screwed in the process. After he finally went to BMI and the musician's union to retrieve his rightful royalties from King, he was blackballed. Following his 1951 "Big Town," Brown continued to record for King, but the hits came to an end and so did the big-money dates.

He left King, belatedly, in 1955. For the next two years he recorded for Imperial. His versions of Buddy Knox's "Party Doll" and Fats Domino's "Let the Four Winds Blow" were minor pop hits in 1957, but by 1959 Brown was so desperate he returned to King for two sessions. In 1960 and 1961 he cut four singles for the Home of the Blues label in Memphis. As irony might have it, these ill-starred records were produced by former Elvis sideman Scotty Moore.

The sixties were slow for Roy Brown. There were a few sessions for fly-by-night labels like DRA and Connie and Mobile. Chess cut four sides on him in 1963, but never released them. He became a door-to-door salesman, easing himself into the homes of older blacks with autographed pictures of the former star that was him. "I sold a lot of encyclopedias that way," he recalled.

Brown started recording again in 1967. There was an album for Bluesway, *Hard Times*; singles for local L.A. labels—Gert, Summit —and his own Tru-Love and Friendship labels. In 1971, the year after his successful appearance with Johnny Otis at the Monterey Festival, there were a pair of singles on Mercury. Although much of this work was as fine as his work of twenty years before, it was less lucrative than selling encyclopedias. In 1978 he issued an album, *The Cheapest Price in Town*, on his own Faith label. It was one of

Roy Brown, dressed by himself, c. 1948.

the best and sleaziest albums of the year, but probably no more than a few hundred people heard it.

Roy Brown is still living in L.A., singing here and in Europe, trying to good-rock his way to a comeback. He's only just turned fifty-four, and he might have his way. If not, that's cool, too. As Mr. Brown says, "I drive a new Monte Carlo, my wife drives a Chevron. I'm very happy." Even Shakespeare would find no fault with that.

LOUIS PRIMA

Gleeby Rhythm Is Born

Louis Prima often spoke of writing a book about his life and times. Had he done so, his memory would not have to be contented with the few meager and hastily written paragraphs that follow. Indeed, were it not for the kindness of my own heart, his memory would have not even these.

Prima presaged the Rock 'n' Roll of the Ridiculous. He perceived and embraced, in all its tutti-frutti glory, the spirit of post-literate, made-for-television America. His was a brave new world of chrome, not gold; of Armstrong linoleum, not Carrara marble; of heptalk, not meaningful dialogue (what did words matter to Louis, when noise could be made instead?). It was a world in which everything came down to broads, booze, and money, with plenty of linguini on the side. It was the modern world, the senseless prefab Eden from which rock 'n' roll is in part descended and devolved. To hear Louis Prima sing is not only to begin to comprehend this world, but also to begin to comprehend why no one in a tweed suit ever got laid within ten miles of downtown Newark.

Eschewing cheap sensationalism, I make no mention of the filthy procreative deed which led to Mr. Prima's birth, but begin my account with the birth itself. He was born on December 7, 1910, in New Orleans. He studied the violin for seven years, and at the age of ten he won the first prize in an amateur fiddling contest. While still young and pure and incapable of the filthy deed, he put aside his violin and lifted to his lips a trumpet. By the time he was twelve, he and his fifteen-year-old brother, Leon, were leading their own band, playing at various functions throughout the Crescent City.

After graduating from the city's Jesuit high school, Louis and his band, which was then called the Collegiates, began performing regularly at the Saenger Theatre. When his brother opened up a night-club, the Beverly Gardens, Louis was the first act Leon hired, and until 1930 the young man with a horn trod regularly between the Saenger Theatre and the Beverly Gardens.

His innocence was behind him now. Soon he married a young lady named Louise Polizzi. What happened on their wedding night I leave to your imagination. His hometown was no longer enough. He had a lot of living to do.

In 1932 Prima traveled to Cleveland, where he played for a brief time with Red Nichols. In September 1933 he went to Chicago, where he and two other musicians recorded two songs for the Blue-bird label. These recordings, hot versions of "Chinatown" and "Dinah," were released under the fitting name of the Hotcha Trio.

In August 1934 Prima moved to New York, where he organized a seven-piece band, Louis Prima and His New Orleans Gang. They began recording for Brunswick-Vocalion in September of that year. By March 1935 they were playing regularly at the new Famous Door on 52nd Street, one of the most prestigious jazz clubs in town.

In 1936 he traveled west to Los Angeles, where he successfully exploited his musical talents and *faccia bruta* in a series of films. First was the RKO short *Swing It*, followed by several full-length features: *Rhythm on the Range* (1936); *You Can't Have Everything* (1939); *Start Cheering*, with Broderick Crawford and the Three Stooges (1938); and *Rose of Washington Square*, with Tyrone Power and Al Jolson (1939). It was while in California, in 1936, that Prima wrote and introduced the song "Sing, Sing, Sing," which Benny Goodman cut and made famous the following year.

Returning to New York, Prima began recording for the Varsity label in January 1940. By now he had mastered a singing style the likes of which the world had never heard. It was, like his music itself, jazz-influenced, yet it struck one's ears as decidedly strange. He sang in English, granted; but it was an English heavily interlaced with the Neapolitan slang of his greaseball roots. When all else failed, he simply commenced making odd sounds. Long before there was a Little Richard, there were people sitting around listening to Louis Prima records, asking one another, "What was that? What did he say?"

When he recorded for Varsity, he rechristened his band Louis Prima and His Gleeby Rhythm Orchestra. Suitably, the first song he recorded under this new name was the mysterious "Gleeby Rhythm Is Born."

Gleeby rhythm is born.
Gleeby rhythm is born;
Gleeby rhythm comes on,
Gleeby rhythm comes on;
Oh, gleeby rhythm is born.
The gleebs are rompin',
The gleebs are stompin';
Oh, gleeby rhythm is born.

Most men would rest upon their laurels after such an achievement. But not Louis. Onward he blew and howled, towards the rhythm beyond gleeb. He went through record companies like they were candy. Leaving Varsity in 1941 he signed with Okeh. Then came Hit, then Majestic, then RCA-Victor, then Robin Hood. He had a hit or two with each of these labels, then moved on. Nothing, it seemed, could contain him. (He went through wives fairly well, too. After divorcing La Polizzi, he married an Alma Raase. Divorcing her, he married Tracelene Barrett, a twenty-one-year-old secretary, in June 1948. Perhaps the procreative deed is addictive to some of us. But, alas, we have no time here to pause and ponder, nor to weep. Like the man whom we honor, we must move on.)

In October 1951 Prima signed with Columbia Records, for which he recorded some of his most outstanding and intriguing work, such as "The Bigger the Figure" (1952), a salacious homage to fat broads based on the "Largo al Factotum" aria from Rossini's *Barber of Seville*. (The flip side, "Boney Bones," dealt with a lady of leaner dimensions.) It was also in 1952 that Prima married his fourth wife, twenty-year-old Dorothy Keely Smith, a Virginia girl who had been working with Louis since 1948. (Keely Smith was not the first female vocalist that Prima employed. As early as 1939 he had been performing duets with Lily Ann Carol, who was billed as Miss Personality of Song.)

Prima stayed with Columbia for a year, but there were no hits. This mattered little, however, for by 1954 Louis Prima and Keely Smith were one of the most popular acts in Las Vegas, commanding nearly $10,000 per week for their shows at the Sahara. (A full-page ad run by the Sahara in a December 1955 issue of *Variety* quoted none other than Howard Hughes on the subject of Prima and Smith: "The more I see them, the more I enjoy them." What a way with words.)

An interesting little story concerning Louis Prima in Las Vegas

Louis Prima and Keely Smith regard the big come-si-chiama *in the darkling Nevada sky, a year before the divorce.*

was told in Ovid Demaris's 1981 book, *The Last Mafioso: The Treacherous World of Jimmy Fratianno*. The man being quoted here was Fratianno's associate John Roselli: "'Now this really kills me. One day Beldon sees this dealer with a black eye and the guy tells him he's fucking Keely in the dressing room when suddenly he feels someone licking his balls. He jumps up and Louie punches him in the eye.'"

After Columbia, Prima went to Jubilee, then Decca. Towards the end of 1956, he signed with Capitol. Singing a Son-of-Sam version of "That Old Black Magic" with Keely Smith in 1958, he had his first hit since 1950. One more Capitol hit followed, "I've Got You Under My Skin" (1959); then the couple switched to Dot Records.

While at Dot, Louis had the worst hit of his career, "Wonderland by Night" (1960). Indeed, now, at the age of fifty, Louis seemed to be losing the powers he had once possessed. Gleeby rhythm was nearly dead.

The Prima-Smith act broke up in October 1961, when Keely filed for divorce on the grounds of "extreme mental cruelty." Prima's comment was terse: "Eh, fucka the Irish *troia*, eh?"

He returned to his roots, performing in March 1962 at the old Saenger Theatre in New Orleans. Signing again with Capitol, he made the last great album of his life, *The Wildest Comes Home*, released in June of the same year. But there were no more hits, and slowly Mr. Prima became naught but a memory except among the faithful who gathered before him in Vegas and Tahoe to hear him sing his words of magic.

> *I got a gal, she's six an' a half feet tall;*
> *Y'oughta see my baby, she's six an' a half feet tall;*
> *She sleeps wit' her head in the bed an' her—ooo—*
> come-si-chiama *in the hall.*

In 1965 he took on a new wife and vocalist, Gia Maione, with whom he performed the deed. The next ten years passed as in a dream, the great man being reduced to deeds such as supplying the voice for King Louis, the cartoon orangutan in Walt Disney's 1969 *Jungle Book*. In October 1975 his head was opened for the purpose of removing a brain tumor. He fell into a coma, and he lay in stillness in a New Orleans nursing home. On the bright, hot day of August 24, 1978, he died. And with him, not only gleeby rhythm but much, much else besides.

THE TRENIERS

Their God Wore Shades

The Trenier twins, Claude and Clifford, were born in Mobile, Alabama, on July 14, 1919, the third and fourth children brought into this vale of jive by Denny and Olivia Trenier, whose spawn eventually numbered ten. It was a musical family. Denny Trenier, in between ejaculations, played the baritone horn with the Excelsior Band, one of the legendary marching and funerary brass groups in the deep South; Olivia played piano; and their children took to the rhythm at a tender age.

In the fall of 1939 Claude and Clifford went north to Alabama State College, in Montgomery. Ostensibly, the twins were pursuing the study of education, preparing for careers in teaching.

"But, really, we weren't studyin' nothin'," Claude told me when I tracked him down in Atlantic City in August 1982. "We were there for the music. Our older brother Buddy had been doing some singing in little clubs around Mobile, and we saw that he had a lot of girls. It looked good to us.

"Alabama State at that time had some fine musicians. Erskine Hawkins had come out of there with a band, the 'Bama State Collegians, in '36. We hooked up with a few guys who were also studyin' nothin' at the time: Sonny Stitt, who went on to make quite a name for himself in jazz; Joe Newman, the trumpet-player, who connected with Lionel Hampton and Wynonie Harris a few years later; Gene Gilbeaux, who played piano; and Don Hill, who's been playin' alto sax with us ever since.

"When they threw Cliff and me out of college in 1941, we took the band with us. But it wasn't long before the World War II draft busted things up."

In 1944 Jimmie Lunceford, whose music the Trenier twins had been listening to since their early teens, hired Claude as his vocalist. And on December 27 of that year, in New York, he cut his first record, singing "I'm Gonna See My Baby" and "That Someone Must Be You" with the Jimmie Lunceford Orchestra. Soon after the record was released, Lunceford also hired Cliff Trenier. On February 27, 1945, in New York, the twins sang together on record for the first time, on Lunceford's recording of "Buzz Buzz Buzz." (This record, however, was not released until 1949.)

Towards the end of 1945 Cliff returned to Mobile, and Claude, leaving the Jimmie Lunceford Orchestra, settled in Los Angeles, where, on January 29, 1946, he recorded "Young Man's Blues" (which Wynonie Harris had cut for Apollo the previous summer) with the Barney Bigard Quintet for Lamplighter Records. Soon after this came another single, "Weird Nightmare," with Charlie Mingus & His Orchestra, on the Excelsior label.

Claude found work singing for $25 a night with Joe Liggins and His Honeydrippers at the Casablanca, an after-hours joint on San Pedro Street. From there he moved across the street to Cafe Society, another after-hours club. When Wynonie Harris was fired from the Club Alabam for cussing out the audience, Claude took his place. Finally he got his first big booking—at the Melody Club— where he stayed for over a year, his pay rising to $1200 a week.

In 1947 Claude brought Cliff, Don Hill, and Gene Gilbeaux out to the coast. Picking up a drummer and a bass-player, they hit the road, billed first as the Trenier Twins & the Gene Gilbeaux Quartet, then simply as the Trenier Twins. By the time that the Trenier Twins signed their first recording deal—with Mercury, late in 1947—they had developed a unique sound, derived somewhat from Jimmie Lunceford's 2/4 and Louis Jordan's shuffle; more so from the sort of ineffable knowledge that can be had only by long years of studyin' nothin'; and, just as important, a style of performance—involving everything from a cappella shrieking to acrobatics to football formations—the likes of which had not been known. ("When we used to jam at Billy Berg's club in Hollywood," Claude recalled, "all those bebop musicians would shy away from us. They thought we weren't cool because we jumped around and shouted and all that.") It was the owner of a Chicago jazz club, the Blue Note, who first thought to bill them as "The Rockin' Rollin' Treniers" in the summer of 1949 (not long after their older brother Buddy had joined them).

*Claude and Cliff Trenier, seated, with Johnny Otis and his
Orchestra.*

The Trenier Twins stayed with Mercury until 1950, putting out
five records in all. After one single for London ("Why Did You Get
So High, Shorty?"), the Treniers, as they now called themselves,
were signed to a long-term contract with Okeh by Danny Kessler,
who had been put in charge of that reactivated label's R&B product.
By then their younger brother Milt, who had been singing in Oklahoma, had also become part of the group.

Their first Okeh release, cut on May 21, 1951, was "Go! Go! Go!,"
one of the first real rock 'n' roll records to come out of New York,
and "Plenty of Money," a slow city blues sung by Claude in the
voice that had prompted Jimmie Lunceford to call him the Sepia
Sinatra.

The Treniers' Okeh records contained some of the best rock 'n' roll to be heard in the early fifties: "Old Woman Blues" (1951), "Hadacol, That's All" (1952), "Rockin' on Saturday Night" (1952), "Rockin' Is Our Business" (1953), "Rock-a-Beatin' Boogie" (1954), "Get Out the Car" (1955), and more. (Nothing to write home about in terms of music, but of no mean interest to serious students of nothin' is "Say Hey," which they made with Willie Mays in 1954, the summer Mays was voted National League MVP. In any case, it beats hell out of Mickey Mantle and Teresa Brewer.) The best record of them all was the two-sided affront to decorum which the Treniers cut in Chicago towards the end of 1952.

> *I don't wanna eat and I don't wanna sleep;*
> *I got a yen that I'm dyin' to please,*
> *Till I get weak in the knees—*
> *Gonna get me that poon-tang!*
> *Poon-tang, poon-tang, poon-tang . . .*

So went the plaintive "Poon-Tang!" The flip-side, "Hi-Yo, Silver," all drums and saxophone and chanting, seemed to invoke not so much the Lone Ranger as it did that most exalted turbaned lord on high Dooji Wooji.

> *Hi-yo, hi-yo, Silver, ride;*
> *Hi-yo, hi-yo, Silver, ride.*
> *Hi-yo, hi-yo, Silver, ride;*
> *Hi-yo, hi-yo, Silver, ride.*
> *Now, I'm the lone stranger*
> *from across the tracks;*
> *I got a pocketful of money*
> *and a Cadillac.*
>
> *Just sit in the saddle*
> *and hold on tight*
> *'Cause, baby, we're really*
> *gonna rock tonight.*

The Treniers stayed with Okeh till 1955, when Columbia retired the label. Four singles followed on Epic along with an album, *The Treniers on TV*, released in the summer of 1955. Although a few of their records had sold well—"Go! Go! Go!," "Hadacol, That's All,"

"Get Out the Car"—none of them had been hits. The trouble, in Claude Trenier's opinion, was that the Treniers were basically a live act. Entering a studio, much of the fire and madness died. On stage the Treniers could stop in the middle of "Hi-Yo, Silver" and go into a parody of the Julius La Rosa hit "Eh Cumpari," transforming it into "Eh Cumpari, You Ain't Nothin' but a Hound Dog," then go back into "Hi-Yo, Silver"—as they often did in their 1953 performances. But this wasn't the sort of thing that could be transferred well to recording.

In 1956 the group cut two singles for Vik; three for Brunswick in 1957. In 1958 there were a pair of lackluster singles and an album, *The Treniers Souvenir Album*, on Dot. (It was also in 1958 that the Treniers accompanied Jerry Lee Lewis to England as the opening act of that disastrous tour.) There was a single for the DOM label in 1959. Four years later there was an embarrassing "After Hours Bossa Nova" on Hermitage; then, in 1964, one last single, on Ronn.

But that wasn't the end. Guys who really know the ins and outs of nothin' are hard to keep down. The Treniers kept rocking the clubs, and they kept making money, mostly in Vegas, the Caribbean, and Atlantic City. In the mid-seventies they put out two albums on their own Mobile label, *The Treniers Live and Wild at the Flamingo* and *The Fabulous Treniers*, both of which hold up better than many records of that silly and unmissed decade.

The group today consists of Claude and Cliff, Buddy, and their nephew Skip (Milt left to open a club in Chicago), all of whom sing; Don Hill, the alto sax man from way back when; Jack Holland on piano; Stan Richards on guitar; Chip Cole on bass; and Dave Akins on drums. When Don Hill sat down to do his income tax in 1982, he discovered that the Treniers had played 355 nights in 1981. And the night before I spoke with Claude, the Treniers had them packed six deep at the bar at Resorts International.

At the age of sixty-three, Claude Trenier feels that he and his brothers will be rocking for another ten years before they call it quits. Looking back, he is well aware that the Treniers were making rock 'n' roll long before most people knew what to call it.

"I remember we were playing the Riptide in Wildwood, New Jersey, in the summer of 1950. Bill Haley had a cowboy band, the Saddlemen, that played right across the street from us. He used to come in and watch us. He asked us what we called the music we were playing. And we told him. Hell, we told him."

STICK McGHEE

Spo-Dee-O-Dee: How to Get It, How to Use It

In life, one encounters very few truths of the absolute sort. The sages of Hellas enumerate but three. The first: Everything flows, nothing abides. The second: Give them an inch, they'll take a mile. The third: All things can be reduced to moisture, whence they came. A fourth truth has been often attributed to Thales of Miletus. Whether this attribution is valid or not is of little matter since the alleged truth was disproven two years ago by several brave women wearing Undie-Leggs. I, for one, applaud them.

But the sages of Hellas knew nothing of the song whose title is "Drinkin' Wine, Spo-Dee-O-Dee"; nor did they know that this song inspired more great recordings than any other song in the history of what people on television refer to as the rock 'n' roll field. We must excuse the sages, for they passed on long before the song we speak of; long, even, before television itself.

Granville McGhee, the author of "Drinkin' Wine, Spo-Dee-O-Dee" and much else, was born on March 23, 1917, in Knoxville, Tennessee. His elder, more famous, and less gifted brother, Brownie McGhee, was stricken with polio as a child. To get around, young Brownie built a wooden cart with wheels, and assigned his little brother the duty of pushing him along by means of a stick. Granville took to carrying the stick with him at all times, and thus became known as Stick McGhee. Already this story is interesting.

Stick began to play the guitar when he was about thirteen. He quit high school after his freshman year and took a job at Eastman Kodak, where his dad worked. He left that job about 1940, traveling to Portsmouth, Virginia, and then to New York, where he joined the Army soon after the United States declared war on Japan in 1941.

Driving a truck in a laundry unit, Stick was wounded in the Pacific. After further service in Japan and Korea, he returned home, a hero. This and a nickel enabled him to use a pay phone.

In the army, Stick's colored drinking buddies had a song they would sing towards the close of their periodic excesses:

> *Drinkin' that mess is our delight,*
> *And when we get drunk, start fightin' all night.*
> *Knockin' out windows and tearin' down doors,*
> *Drinkin' half-gallons and callin' for more.*
> *Drinkin' wine, motherfucker, drinkin' wine!*
> * Goddam!*
> *Drinkin' wine, motherfucker, drinkin' wine!*
> * Goddam!*
> *Drinkin' wine, motherfucker, drinkin' wine!*
> * Goddam!*
> *Pass that bottle to me!*

And so forth. In 1946, after the war, Stick and his brother Brownie, who had been making records since 1944, got together to cut a version of this cherished drinking song for Harlem Records in New York. Stick cleaned the song up a bit and called it "Drinkin' Wine, Spo-Dee-O-Dee." (Sam Theard, the black comedian and co-author of "Let the Good Times Roll," had been using Spo-Dee-O-Dee as a stage name since the thirties and had made a record called "Spo-Dee-O-Dee" for Vocalion in 1937.)

Stick's record went nowhere, but on February 14, 1949, he remade "Drinkin' Wine, Spo-Dee-O-Dee" for Atlantic. The record hit the R&B charts the following month and eventually rose to Number 3.

The first cover version of Stick's record was by Lionel Hampton, featuring the great blues shouter Sonny Parker, on Decca. (Decca also bought Stick's original 1946 recording from Harlem and issued that.) Next came a version by Wynonie Harris, recorded for King on the 13th of April. The third cover was a hillbilly bop rendition by Loy Gordon & His Pleasant Valley Boys, cut on August 23 for Stick's label, Atlantic. "Drinkin' Wine, Spo-Dee-O-Dee" continued to be cut throughout the fifties: by Malcolm Yelvington, for Sun, in 1954; by Johnny Burnette, for Coral, in 1957; by Jerry Lee Lewis, for Sun, in 1959. (Jerry Lee cut the song again, for Smash, in 1964, and for Mercury, in 1973.)

Although only two of these many versions—Wynonie Harris's 1949 cover and Jerry Lee's 1973 recording—achieved anything like the commercial success of the original, the odd thing is that they're all magnificent; I can't think of another song that exists in so many great varieties. And don't give me any of that Hank Williams shit, either, because I don't want to hear it.

Stick McGhee continued to make records for Atlantic, but his only other hit was an instrumental cover of the 1951 country hit "Tennessee Waltz," to which title he affixed the word "Blues." There were some hot ones—"Drank Up All the Wine Last Night" and "Venus Blues" in 1950; "Let's Do It" and "One Monkey Don't Stop No Show" in 1951—but they didn't pay the bills. He cut a record for London in early 1951. That failed, too.

In 1952 Stick moved from Atlantic to Essex for one miserable, failed record ("My Little Rose")"; then, in 1953, to King, where he made a lot of great rock 'n' roll—"Whiskey, Women and Loaded Dice," "Dealin' from the Bottom," "Jungle Juice," "Double Crossin' Liquor," "Get Your Mind Out of the Gutter"—but very little money. Leaving King, he cut a record for Savoy in 1955; but his heart was no longer in it.

Stick retired from the music business, but not from drink. In 1960 his brother convinced him to cut a record for Herald in New York. While both sides of that record, "Money Fever" and "Sleep-in Job," were as nasty and fine as anything to be heard that year, they didn't happen. Stick went back into retirement. Further back this time.

Stick McGhee died in the Bronx V.A. Hospital on August 15, 1961, of cancer. He was barely forty-four years old. He didn't have much when he went, but what he had he left to Brownie's son. It was an old guitar, and within its chords and creaks and resonances, somewhere, lay the power of spo-dee-o-dee. That's a fact.

YOUNG BILL HALEY

The Lounge Act That Transcendeth All Knowing

Bill Haley's "Rock Around the Clock" is the biggest hit in the history of rock 'n' roll. It has sold more copies—over 25 million, according to the *Guinness Book of World Records*—than any other rock record, and has been the popular anthem of the fifties for a quarter of a century now, from *The Blackboard Jungle* to *Happy Days*. In light of this, it might seem odd to describe Bill Haley as an unsung hero of rock 'n' roll, but the truth is that it is what Bill Haley did before "Rock Around the Clock," rather than that silly song itself, that deserves recognition.

William John Clifton Haley was born on July 6, 1925, in Highland Park, Michigan. When he was seven, he moved with his family to Wilmington, Delaware. Not long after, Haley built and began to play a homemade guitar. At the age of thirteen he got his first paying job, performing at a local auction for a dollar a night. Two years later he left home and picked up work as a hillbilly singer with various bands in rural Pennsylvania.

In Hartford, Connecticut, Haley met up with a country band called the Downhomers, who had recently lost a member, Kenny Roberts, to the draft army. Haley replaced Roberts, and when the Downhomers cut a record called "We're Recruiting" for Vogue in 1944, he finally had something to call home about.

After parting with the Downhomers, Haley got a job as a disc-jockey at WSNJ in Bridgeport, New Jersey, where he was often known as Yodeling Bill Haley. In 1948 Haley moved across the Delaware River to station WPWA in Chester, Pennsylvania, where he remained as musical director until 1954. Bill Haley & the Four Aces of Western Swing, the band Haley formed after moving to

Chester, cut their first records, for the local Cowboy label, in 1948. These records were mostly cover versions of recent country bits, such as George Morgan's "Candy Kisses," Red Foley's "Tennessee Border," and Hank Williams's "Too Many Parties, Too Many Pals."

Late in 1949, after cutting one record for Center (another local label), Haley renamed his group Bill Haley & the Saddlemen. In late 1949 this group cut two records for the Keystone label. In September of that year Haley succeeded in selling masters to Atlantic Records in New York, which released his "Why Do I Cry Over You" and "I'm Gonna Dry Ev'ry Tear with a Kiss" with little promotion and little success.

All of Haley's recordings through 1950 were common country records with their roots in slick Western swing. But by 1951 Haley had begun to forsake country music. He took off the cowboy hat he had worn since his Yodeling Bill Haley days, and began to cultivate the appearance of a hepcat—or, more precisely, the appearance of a hepcat who resided in Chester, Pennsylvania. He fashioned a spit curl upon his forehead. He put on a garish dinner jacket. He beheld himself and saw that it was good.

When Bill Haley & the Saddlemen signed with Holiday, a Philadelphia label operated by Dave Miller, in 1951, the first record they cut was a version of the outlandishly tough "Rocket '88'," which had been a Number 1 R&B hit earlier that year for Jackie Brenston and His Delta Cats. (Years later Sam Phillips, who produced the Brenston record and leased it to Chess, reflected that "Rocket '88'" was the first true rock 'n' roll hit.)

Although some of his Holiday recordings leaned more heavily on country music than on R&B—such as the 1952 "Jukebox Cannonball," which fit hepster lyrics, not too successfully, to Roy Acuff's "Wabash Cannonball"—most of Haley's efforts throughout 1951–52 were inspired by the R&B charts. In 1951, with a female voice identified only as Loretta, he cut duet versions of the Griffin Brothers' "Pretty Baby" and Memphis Slim's "I'm Crying." Both songs continue to stand as examples of his best work.

Haley began recording for Essex, another Dave Miller label in Philadelphia, in 1952. It was then that he began calling his group Bill Haley and His Comets, or, on a handful of Essex records, Bill Haley with Haley's Comets (just, one presumes, to be sure you didn't miss the point).

The first Essex release was "Icy Heart," obviously inspired by

"Cold, Cold Heart," the Hank Williams hit of the previous year. But the flip side of "Icy Heart" was "Rock the Joint," a wild, fiery rocker—not merely a cover of an R&B hit (Jimmy Preston's 1949 original was on Gotham, another Philadelphia independent), but one of the first instances of a white boy really getting down to the heart of hep.

Bill Haley's first hit came in the spring of 1953. "Crazy, Man, Crazy" rose to Number 15 on the pop charts at a time when "Song from Moulin Rouge" by Percy Faith was Number 1. There had been rock 'n' roll records on the pop charts before, going back to 1951 and "Sixty-Minute Man" by the Dominoes; but "Crazy, Man, Crazy" was the first white rock hit. The trouble was—and is—that it

Young Bill Haley, second from left, in a group called the Range Drifters, c. 1948.

was nowhere near as good, as heartfelt, as "Rock the Joint." Within a year, Bill Haley had gone from being one of the first blue-eyed rockers to the first decadent show-biz rocker. In other words, he had played out the entire history of rock 'n' roll about two years before anybody ever heard of rock 'n' roll.

Largely on the basis of "Crazy, Man, Crazy," Haley was signed by Decca in 1954. On April 12 of that year, in New York, Bill Haley and the Comets cut "(We're Gonna) Rock Around the Clock." The song had been written in 1953 by two Tin Pan Alley veterans, lyricist Max Freedman and composer Jimmy DeKnight. Freedman, born in 1895, had written "Sioux City Sue" and "Song of India." DeKnight was really James Myers of Myers Music, a New York publishing firm. Haley had known DeKnight since the late forties, and had cut several of his songs back in those early days. "(We're Gonna) Rock Around the Clock" was released as the flip side of "Thirteen Women" in May 1954. Despite a full-page ad in *Billboard*, the record went unnoticed.

Haley went back into the studio and cut a cover of Joe Turner's "Shake, Rattle and Roll," which had been issued in April and was now heading fast up the R&B charts. Haley's "Shake, Rattle and Roll" was released in June of 1954. The August 7 issue of *Billboard* carried an ad for the record, in which Decca billed Haley and the Comets as "The Nation's 'Rockingest' Rhythm Group." (This same issue of *Billboard* also carried the first review of Elvis's first single, which had been recorded the month before.) "Shake, Rattle and Roll" broke into the Top Ten, but that didn't alter the fact that it was an inferior record. The way Haley and the Decca boys had censored the original sexy lyrics was shameful.

Haley's next two singles, "Dim, Dim the Lights" and "Birth of the Boogie," were Top Twenty hits. When Evan Hunter's 1954 novel, *The Blackboard Jungle*, was made into a movie, Jimmy DeKnight was chosen as the film's technical advisor. He dug up the failed "Rock Around the Clock" for the movie's central song. The movie was released in March 1955, and the rest is history, of a sort.

Bill Haley continued to have very minor hits with Decca until 1960, when he went to Warner Brothers, sundry other labels, and oblivion. Plainly, by the end of 1955 he had been superceded by Elvis Presley, whose fame continued to rise throughout the late fifties as Haley's fell. This is the way it should have been. He died, out of his mind, on February 9, 1981.

"We use country and Western instruments," Haley was quoted as saying in a 1955 collection of sheet music, "play rhythm and blues tunes and the result is"—hold your breath—"pop music." He didn't even know what to call it, for the love of Christ.

But the fact remains: Bill Haley was there first, and he helped set the stage for Elvis and all that came in his wake. For that, Bill Haley, who walked among us, deserves, as do all things hep, to be honored.

ROY HALL

See, We Was All Drunk

Roy Hall was born on May 7, 1922, in Big Stone Gap, Virginia, a backwoods town about twenty miles from the Tennessee line, near the foothills of the Appalachian Mountains. An old colored man taught him to play piano, and to drink. By the time Roy turned twenty-one, he knew that he was the best drunken piano-player in Big Stone Gap, and armed with the pride and confidence that this knowledge gave him, he departed the town of his birth to seek fame in those dreamed-of places beyond: Jasper, Slant, Nicklesville, Weber City, and Bristol.

Roy made it to Bristol and farther, pumping boogie woogie in every Virginia, Tennessee, or Alabama beer-joint that had a piano. He played those pianos fast and hard and sinful, like that colored man who had taught him back in Big Stone Gap; but he sang like the hillbilly that he was. Wherever he went, the people told him they had never heard a country singer quite like him, and they bought him drinks and gave him silver coins towards closing time.

He organized his own band, Roy Hall and His Cohutta Mountain Boys (Cohutta was part of the Appalachians, in the shadows of whose foothills he had been raised up). It was a five-piece band, with Tommy Odum on lead guitar, Bud White on rhythm guitar, Flash Griner on bass, and Frankie Brumbalough on fiddle. Roy pounded the piano and did most of the singing; but everybody else in the band sang, too, especially the rhythm guitarist and the fiddler.

In the late forties Roy Hall and His Cohutta Mountain Boys headed north, through West Virginia, through Ohio, into Michigan. In 1949 Roy and the band cut their first records, for Fortune, a small, independent label located on 12th Street in Detroit. Over the next year Fortune released six sides by Roy Hall: "Dirty Boogie," "Okee Doaks," "Never Marry a Tennessee Girl," "We Never Get Too Big to Cry," "Five Years in Prison," and "My Freckle Face Gal." Most of these recordings were slick hillbilly blues, similar to the sort of music with which Hank Williams had recently risen to fame. But the most successful of the bunch, "Dirty Boogie"—the closest that Fortune came to a C&W hit—was a wild, nasty rocker which foreshadowed much of what was to come to be musically in the South during the next few years.

In 1950 Roy traveled to Nashville, leaving the Cohutta Mountain Boys to fend for themselves in the wicked North. He cut two records there that year for Bullet, one of Nashville's most active independent labels. Both of these Bullet singles, "Mule Boogie" and "Ain't You Afraid," were fine hard-driving things, but they failed to sell. After Bullet, he recorded for Tennessee, a small local company that had a national hit in 1951 with Del Wood's piano instrumental "Down Yonder;" but Roy Hall's piano brought no hits.

He opened an after-hours joint on Commerce Street in downtown Nashville called the Music Box (later renamed the Musicians' Hideway). There he played piano and drank, and, for a sweet change, made money doing so. In addition to liquor and music, Roy's club also featured blackjack and roulette, towards which diversions many of the Grand Ole Opry's most revered stars directed with moist and shaking hands their many-zeroed royalty checks.

One of Roy Hall's most loyal customers was Webb Pierce, who, following Hank Williams's death on New Year's Day 1953, became the undisputed king of the country singers. Pierce hired Roy as his piano-player, using him on most of his recordings in 1954–55. During this time, Roy also recorded with Marty Robbins and Hawkshaw Hawkins, a couple of successful cornballs whose music gave him even less room to move around in than Pierce's.

In the summer of 1954 Elvis Presley came to Roy Hall's club looking for work. "I was drunk that night, didn't feel like playin' piano, so I told 'im to git up there an' start doin' whatever in hell it was that he did," Roy recalled to me in the spring of 1981. "I fired 'im after just that one night. He weren't no damn good."

Towards the end of that same year another young man came to the club looking for work. He was Jerry Lee Lewis, and Roy kept him on for a few weeks, until Jerry Lee decided to return home to his wife and son in Louisiana.

"I hired 'im for $15 a night. He'd play that damned piano from one in the mornin' till daylight. We did a lotta duets together. He was still a teenager, and ever'body figured that when we got busted he'd be the one that the cops would let go; so ever'body gave 'em their watches an' jewelry to hold for 'em, case the cops came. We got hit one night, he musta had fifteen wristwatches on his arms. Sure enough he was the only one didn't git searched."

It was also in 1954 that Roy Hall and a black musician named Dave Williams took a trip to the Everglades that resulted in one of the classic rock 'n' roll songs.

"We was down in Pahokee, on Lake Okeechobee. We was down there, out on a damn pond, fishin' an' milkin' snakes. Drinkin' wine, mostly. There was a bunch of us down there.

"See, this guy down there had a big bell that he'd ring to git us all to come in to dinner; an' I call over there to th'other part of th'island, I say, 'What's goin' on?' Colored guy said, 'We got twen'y-one drums'—see, we was all drunk—'we got an ol' bass horn an' they even keepin' time on a ding-dong.' See, that was the big bell they'd ring to git us t'come in."

Out of this legless colloquy came a song that began:

> Twenty-one drums and an ol' bass horn,
> Somebody beatin' on a ding-dong.
> Come on over, baby, whole lotta shakin' goin' on;
> Come on over, baby; baby, you can't go wrong.
> There ain't no fakin', whole lotta shakin' goin' on.

Webb Pierce arranged for Hall to sign a contract with Decca, and on September 15, 1955, Hall went into the studio and cut three songs for the label, including "Whole Lotta Shakin' Goin' On." The record was released three weeks later, coupled with a cover version of Fats Domino's "All by Myself." In its review of "Whole Lotta Shakin' Goin' On," *Billboard* said, "Webb Pierce's pianist takes a stab in the vocal field and shows a highly distinctive, flavorsome voice." But the stab did not result in a hit.

Roy Hall continued to record for Decca until the summer of 1956. While a few of these recordings, such as his cover of Carl Perkins's "Blue Suede Shoes," were plainly uninspired, most of them were among the most fiery rockabilly records of the mid-fifties. His "Diggin' the Boogie" contained one of the toughest and most unrelenting rhythms that had ever been recorded in the South. But none of this amounted to a hit record.

Roy Hall, 1955.

Bad luck seemed to follow Roy Hall. "Whole Lotta Shakin' Goin' On," which he had co-written under the pseudonym of Sunny David ("I was tryin' to git away from the income tax. They finally caught my ass, too"), became a huge hit for Jerry Lee Lewis, Roy's ex-employee, in 1957, and Roy stood to make a good deal of money in royalties. But when the time came to collect he was sued by his ex-wife, and the court awarded her his share of the royalties from the song. "And," Roy said, "Paul Cohen, who was the head of

Decca, got me to sign a buncha papers when I was drunk, one o' them kinda deals, and I lost out that way. I worked for Webb Pierce for six years, an' he did the trick to me, too."

But Roy Hall kept on pumping his rockabilly music, and he is still playing around Nashville and wherever else he can find a piano and a paycheck.

"I quit drinkin' in 1972," he told me, "an' I play rock 'n' roll better'n I did twenty-five years ago. Ain't none of these young fellas got nothin' on me when it comes to rockin' out, nosir. You git me a date somewhere, transportation an' a few bucks, an' I'll put out some good ol' rockabilly, knock 'em dead."

A few years later, James Faye "Roy" Hall was no longer one to do the knocking. He went for the big drink on March 2, 1984, in Nashville. He was sixty-one years old.

For him, if for no other reason, Big Stone Gap shall stand tall forever in a purple girdle of pride.

HARDROCK GUNTER

The Mysterious Pig-Iron Man

Unlike the Bohemian culture of Paris in the twenties and thirties, that of Birmingham, Alabama, bespoke itself not through painting and literature, but through music. Its voice was not that of the sissy expatriates who had left their country to dwell with the ignoble Frog, but rather that of men—*men*—who stayed right where they belonged.

Most of these men earned their daily bread working in the mines from which were wrested iron ore, coal, and limestone, or in the mills where those wrested things were transformed into steel. The music of these men depended usually upon the color of their skin. Both country music and the blues had flourished in Birmingham since the late nineteenth century, but in the years after World War One, the true music of Birmingham was the boogie.

The first and most famous of the Alabama boogie men was Pinetop Smith, who had moved to Birmingham as a teenager. It was there that he learned to play piano, and it was there that he recorded "Pinetop's Boogie Woogie" for Brunswick in 1928. (Three months after he made the record, Pinetop was killed by a stray bullet while attending a party at the Odd Fellows Lounge in Chicago. By then the strange new phrase in the title of his record had begun to be heard wherever the hep argot was spoken.) Other pianists, such as Robert McCoy and Pinetop's friend Cow Cow Davenport, also contributed to the boogie fever that swept Birmingham in the twenties and thirties. From the forbidden North Side it spread like a wicked thing throughout that city of steel and of the Holy Spirit; it spread until even the noble white man stomped in sublime fealty to it. And one of those noble white men was a young clay-eater named Sidney Louie Gunter.

He had been born on September 18, 1918, in a workman's barracks on the outskirts of town. After dropping out of high school in the early thirties, he took a job in the mines. In his off-hours he played guitar and sang in local beer-joints. The music that he made was hillbilly music, but it was hillbilly music with a boogie-woogie bent. No one in Birmingham had ever heard anything quite like it.

All those men and boys who, like Sid Gunter, worked with pickaxes were referred to as hardrock miners, or, simply, as hardrocks. In 1939, when Gunter quit the mines and took a job as a singing disc-jockey at Birmingham's oldest radio station, WAPI ("The Voice of Alabama"), he carried that epithet with him and came to be known then, if not quite forevermore, as Hardrock Gunter.

At WAPI Gunter worked as a solo performer and at times as a member of Happy Wilson's Golden River Boys. He eventually formed his own six-piece band, consisting of himself, a fiddler, a steel-guitarist, a bass-player, a drummer, and a boogie-woogie piano man. They were known throughout Birmingham, and as far as the mighty Voice of Alabama could be heard, as Hardrock Gunter and the Pebbles.

In 1949 Gunter wrote a song called "Birmingham Bounce." It was a cut-time boogie that made frequent use of the word "rockin'," and it became a local sensation. Early in 1950 he and his band recorded the song for Bama Records, a small label which operated out of Room 905 in the Bankhead Hotel. The record was quickly covered by the Decca country singer Red Foley. Foley's record hit the country charts in early May, and by the end of the month it had risen to Number 1, beating out Hank Williams's latest record, "Long Gone Lonesome Blues." Gunter's song continued to be covered, by slick hillbillies such as Tex Williams and Pee Wee King, by black singers such as Amos Milburn and Lionel Hampton. By summer's end "Birmingham Bounce" was one of the best-known songs in the country, and the sudden anthem of Southern hep.

Hardrock Gunter's second record for Bama, released in July 1950, was a song called "Gonna Dance All Night." This new record was even more emphatically frenzied than its predecessor. Again and again throughout the song Gunter half-drawled, half-growled, "We're gonna rock 'n' roll." The record did not sell, not in Birmingham or anywhere else. Nor did his third and last Bama release, a nasty jump song called "Lonesome Blues." (The flip side of "Lonesome Blues" was a wonderful indictment of hillbilly music, "Dad Gave My Hog Away.") By then Gunter was appearing regularly on Happy Wilson's new WAFM television show, "The Happiness Boys."

Towards the end of 1950, Hardrock Gunter and the Pebbles recorded for Bullet Records in Nashville. "My Bucket's Been Fixed," released in December 1950, was Gunter's answer to Hank Williams's 1949 hit, "My Bucket's Got a Hole in It."

Hardrock Gunter, in matching tie and boxer shorts, looks to the West and digs it.

Gunter was signed by Decca in early 1951. "Boogie Woogie on Saturday Night," recorded, like most of Decca's country records, at the Tulane Hotel in Nashville, was released in March. It was a fine rockabilly record, but it failed to sell, as did its successor, "I've Done Gone Hog Wild." His third release for Decca, cut in the summer of 1951, was stranger by far than anything preceding it: a country version of "Sixty-Minute Man," the Dominoes' recent R&B hit about Lovin' Dan, the hepster who could fuck for an hour without missing a stroke. As if this were not enough, Gunter recorded the song as a duet with smut-voiced Roberta Lee. (Now signed to Decca, Roberta Lee was a young lady from Dayton, Ohio, who was known in the late forties, when she had recorded for Tempo, as "The Girl with the Anfractuous Voice.")

Decca continued to release the recordings that Gunter made, but his days as a Decca act were numbered. In September 1951 the thirty-three-year-old singer, perhaps fearing a Chinese takeover of his beloved Alabama, joined the Army. He got no closer to Korea than Fort Jackson, South Carolina, where he became a first lieutenant in the 167th Infantry Regiment.

In 1953 Gunter headed north, where he began work at the WWVA "Jamboree" in Wheeling, West Virginia. He recorded for MGM that spring. By the end of the summer he had gone back to Birmingham, where he began broadcasting a daily four-hour show at radio station WJLD. In April 1954, while in Birmingham, Gunter cut a new version of "Gonna Dance All Night" and leased it to Sun Records in Memphis. The Sun record was released in May, and it sold as poorly as the Bama recording of it had sold four years earlier. A few months later Sun released a more accessible rockabilly record by a young man named Elvis Presley.

Later in the year, he returned to WWVA in Wheeling. Throughout 1954–55 he made records for King, which was located not too far away, in Cincinnati. The best of his King releases was a double-sided rocker, "I'll Give 'Em Rhythm" and "I Put My Britches On Just Like Everybody Else"; but the record failed to receive airplay.

Gunter leased another recording to Sun in the spring of 1956: "Jukebox, Help Me Find My Baby," which he had cut in Wheeling. Even though it was a bad record, it failed to sell.

Hardrock Gunter began to fade. He was forty years old now, and rock 'n' roll, which he had helped to bring into being, had passed him by without so much as a cursory tip of the bebop hat. He continued to make records, bad records, for his own labels, such as

Emperor ("Whoo! I Mean Whee!", 1957), Cross Country ("Let Me Be a Fool," 1958), and Cullman ("Is It Too Late," 1959); but nothing could stay the fading.

Early in 1962 he cut a record for Starday. It was an atrocity, a truly singular one, called "Hillbilly Twist." The Lord, who had taken a great liking to Hardrock's records of ten years past, mercifully delivered "Hillbilly Twist" to a fast darkness. Not long after this, Hardrock Gunter quit the WWVA "Jamboree" and announced that he was retiring to Golden, Colorado.

In the sixties he put out an album called *Songs They Censored in the Hills*. In 1972—by now he was called simply Rock Gunter—he made an album consisting of guitar renditions of a dozen Hank Williams songs. After that he ceased to be heard from.

MERRILL MOORE

The Saddle,
Rock & Rhythm Man

Merrill E. Moore was born in Algona, on the eastern shore of the Des Moines River, in northern Iowa, on September 26, 1923. He began playing piano at about the age of seven, picking out the melodies of the hymns he heard at the Methodist church his parents dragged him to on Sundays. When he was eight he made his debut on WHO.

Then came Mrs. Gunn, a piano teacher, a fancy lady from the Oberlin Conservatory in Ohio. And what of her breasts? Did they linger, warm and rife, against the nape of young Merrill's neck, fill his tender being with the intoxicating liquor of their perfume, as she bent over his shoulder to guide his hands across the keys? Mr. Moore makes no mention of this. Yet, one wonders at the sins which might—might, I say—cause a woman to flee in shame from the Oberlin Conservatory, across the endless desolate miles of Indiana and Illinois, to seek unholy sanctuary in Algona, Iowa. But let us speak no more of this woman, who in fact may have done no wrong. She is departed now. Let her Maker alone be judge.

While in high school, Merrill discovered boogie woogie through the records of Meade Lux Lewis, Albert Ammons, Pete Johnson, and Freddie Slack, who was then playing piano in Will Bradley's Orchestra. "Those were the cats that really laid it down for me," he told me.

After high school Merrill enlisted in the Navy to fight the war. He won. In 1945 he married, moved to Tucson, and took a job playing at the Santa Rita Hotel. Three years later he moved to San Diego. Playing a mixture of boogie woogie and Western swing, Merrill found steady work in various local bands. But both types of music were dying fast. Soon they would be completely dead, even in San Diego.

In 1950 Merrill Moore formed a band of his own. It looked like a country band: piano, guitar, bass, steel, and fiddle. It didn't sound like one, however. And while Merrill continued to pump boogie-woogie bass lines with his left hand, his right hand was up to something altogether different. He didn't really have a name for the new type of music he was playing, but he had a name for his band: the Saddle, Rock & Rhythm Boys.

Early in 1952 Ken Nelson signed Merrill Moore and his Saddle, Rock & Rhythm Boys to Capitol. On May 12, 1952, in Los Angeles, Merrill cut his first record.

Capitol didn't release anything by him until the latter part of 1952, when his recording of "Corrine, Corrina" was issued. Although he didn't have a hit, Merrill continued to make records for Capitol, and Capitol continued to release them, until 1958.

Merrill made some hot ones. His "Fly Right Boogie" (1954) recounted, at a dangerously fast speed, his doctor's warnings about the wages of living on a sustained second wind. His original "Buttermilk Baby" (1957) was about the pleasures of fat broads. More often, Merrill looked elsewhere for his material. He reworked country songs such as "Bartender's Blues," "Barrel House Bessie," and "Snatchin' and Grabbin'." From Western swing he took Bob Wills's "She's Gone" and Hank Thompson's "Doggie House Boogie." He played with boogie-woogie classics such as the 1940 "Down the Road a Piece" and the 1946 "House of Blue Lights." Sometimes he reached even further back, to Jelly Roll Morton's "King Porter Stomp," to "Five Foot Two, Eyes of Blue," or even to Felix Arndt's 1915 "Nola."

His best work, such as "House of Blue Lights" (1953), "Down the Road a Piece" (1955), and "Rock-Rockola" (1955; a tribute to the Rockola jukebox), represents some of the finest, most raucous rockabilly to be heard on record, a wedding of hillbilly boogie and R&B that would not be bettered until the coming of Jerry Lee Lewis.

Although Merrill, like everyone else, did not hear the word "rockabilly" until 1954 or so, there was pride in his broad Midwestern voice when he recalled, "We were doing that—rockabilly—before I ever heard of Bill Haley. I never knew those guys until later. But we were doin' that in 1948, yessir. 'House of Blue Lights,' 'Down the Road a Piece,' 'Red Light.' And I tell ya what, we'd take a buncha Hank Williams tunes and do the boogie-woogie to 'em. Yessir."

"House of Blue Lights," "Down the Road a Piece," and "Red Light" were Merrill's three best-selling records. But in all his years with Capitol he never had a national hit, and he never made the charts. Capitol simply didn't know how to sell him, or to whom.

"I always thought that they were kind of in the wrong category. I never was country. I was more boogie-woogie and rockabilly, that kind of stuff. So I think they categorized it a little bit wrong there."

After Capitol dropped him in 1958, Merrill Moore didn't record again until 1969, when he cut an album for release in Great Britain by BMC Records. (Like most obscure rockabilly heroes, Merrill is better known abroad than in his native land. In 1967 Ember Records in London issued an anthology of Capitol sides, *Bellyful of Blue Thunder*. A second collection, called *Rough-House 88*, followed in 1969.)

Merrill was still performing regularly in San Diego when I spoke with him, and was quick to say, "We play that stuff better today than we did back then. Yes sir."

As the philosophers tell us, it's a long way from Algona to San Diego. But now that Merrill Moore's made it, he's not looking back. Nosir.

Merrill Moore, winsome in the West.

SKEETS McDONALD

Whom in the End the Tattooed Lady Slew

Enos William McDonald was born on October 1, 1915, on a small farm near Greenway, Arkansas. He took to music and to female flesh at an early age. Humble tillers of the soil that they were, his parents, Sam and Ethel, could not afford to buy their son a maiden, but they did purchase for him a guitar. After finishing high school in 1932, young Skeets—such was the odd name by which our hero would thenceforth till the end of his days be known—bade farewell to his Arkansas home and traveled north, to Michigan, where cars and dreams are made.

With the help of several other displaced rednecks, which were plentiful in that land, Skeets formed his own hillbilly boogie band, the Lonesome Cowboys. By 1937 the Lonesome Cowboys had found steady work with WXEL in Royal Oak. From WXEL the band moved to WFDF in Flint, then to WCAR in Pontiac; but by then, 1943, the world was at war. In April of that year Skeets joined the Army and, loins girt, shipped out to help save hillbilly boogie from the iron talons of fascism. He returned to Michigan from the Pacific in 1946 and, wearing now a bronze battle star, took up where he had left off.

As the featured vocalist in a five-man group called Johnny White and His Rhythm Riders, Skeets recorded in the summer of 1950 for Fortune Records in Detroit. Skeets had written both sides of the record, and the songs were expressions of his curious devotion to the flesh of the lesser sex.

> *She had a face like a groundhog,*
> *Long, shaggy hair like an ape;*

But I loved that woman,
I loved her for her lovely shape.

Such was his "Mean and Evil Blues." Far more interesting was
"The Tattooed Lady, " which, in the splendor of its belabored meta-
phor, is, among all portraits of wondrous Gaea, surpassed only by
that in Hesiod's *Theogeny*.

Once I married a tattooed lady;
It was a cold and winter day.
And tattooed all around her body
Was the map of the good old USA;
And every night before I'd go to sleep,
I'd jerk down the quilt and I'd take a peep:
Upon her butt was West Virginny;
Through them hills I just love to roam.
But when the moon begins to shine down her Wabash,
That's when I remember my Indiana home.

Skeets McDonald moved west to Los Angeles in February 1951.
He called at the office of Cliffie Stone, an ersatz hillbilly who ran the
"Hometown Jamboree" show at KXLA in Pasadena. Stone signed
him to perform on the show, then recommended him to Ken Nelson
of Capitol Records. Within two weeks Skeets was signed to the
label.

His first record for Capitol, "Scoot, Git and Begone," was released in May of 1951. It did not sell well, nor did its successors:
"Today I'm Movin' Out," "Ridin' with the Blues," "Fuss and Fight."
The trouble was, these records were not quite like the records being
made by the other hillbillies who recorded for Capitol, and the
company did not really know what to do with them.

In early 1952 Skeets took a break from recording to appear as
Johnny Mack Brown's singing sidekick in the Monogram movie
Smokeless Powder. Returning to the studio, he cut a song called
"Don't Let the Stars Get in Your Eyes," written and first cut by Slim
Willet. The record hit the country charts in October, and it eventu-
ally rose to Number 2. Since it was a straight, mawkish record that
Skeets had now hit with, Capitol was very reluctant to allow him to
return to that stranger, louder, and more rhythmic music that he
had been recording.

Skeets went through the motions, but there were no more hits, and the singer seemed to come alive only occasionally, as in 1954, when he was permitted to record "Your Love Is Like a Faucet." But by 1956 the Capitol people, like those throughout the industry, were becoming aware of Elvis Presley and Carl Perkins and something called rock 'n' roll. As they became aware of these things, they began to recall those strange records Skeets McDonald had been making for them back in 1951, and they untethered him. The result was that in 1956 Skeets made some of the best rockabilly records to be heard: "I Got a New Field to Plow" (eat your heart out, Hesiod), "You Oughta See Grandma Rock," and especially "Heart-Breakin' Mama."

But there was a problem. Skeets was now forty years old, overweight, and balding. Capitol signed Gene Vincent, and Skeets McDonald hit the streets.

Late in 1959, after appearing as a regular on "Town Hall Party," broadcast from Compton, California, by KTTV, Skeets got a contract with Columbia Records in Nashville. What ensued was a series of pleasant but unexceptional country records, a notch or two above the usual middle-of-the-road Nashville stuff. A few of these Columbia records were successful in a small way: "This Old Heart" (1960), "Call Me Mr. Brown" (1963), "Big Chief Buffalo Nickel" (1965), and "Mabel" (1967) were minor country hits. Another few of them were actually quite good: "You're Not Wicked, You're Just Weak" (1961), "Chin Up, Chest Out" and "Fast Company" (from the 1964 album *Call Me Skeets!*). But 1956, let alone 1951, was a long time done.

Columbia dropped Skeets in 1967. He made one more record. "It's Genuine," which was released by Uni in early 1968. It was over, all of it, over the lea. The tattooed lady beckoned, but she did not smile.

His heart ceased, and he died, on March 31, 1968. Please, wherever you are, bow your heads for ten minutes of silent prayer.

Skeets McDonald, in the boots that only he could fill.

THE CLOVERS

Absalom, Absalom!
Doo-Wah, Doo-Wah!

Descended musically from the Mills Brothers and the Ink Spots, both of which groups had been making records since the early 1930s, and from the urban gospel groups such as the Swan Silverstone Singers ("Jesus Hits Like the Atom Bomb") that flourished during the war years, the young black vocal groups that ascended in Eastern cities—New York, Detroit, Washington, D.C.—in the late 1940s were a parallel development to the jump-blues bands that thrived on the West Coast. Together they were the main black vectors of rock 'n' roll.

First came the Ravens, the quartet organized by bass singer Jimmy Ricks in the spring of 1946. They made their debut at the Club Baron in Harlem, and their first records, for Hub, that same spring. Next came the Orioles quintet, who cut their first record in the summer of 1948, for It's a Natural (which, after this first Orioles release, became Jubilee Records). These earliest of the R&B vocal groups were rather conservative in both their style of singing and their choice of material. (That first Ravens record, for example, was a version of the popular ersatz Yiddish ditty "Mahzel." This was followed by a coupling of "Ol' Man River" and "Would You Believe Me," a piece of corn from the insipid 1947 Warner Brothers picture *Love and Learn*.)

Then came the Clovers. Lead singer Harold Lucas, bass singer Billy Shelton, and tenor Thomas Woods began performing as a trio in 1947, while they were still attending Armstrong High School in Washington, D.C. Lucas chose the name of the Clovers because he thought it would lend good luck to their musical undertaking. (*The Lucky Star Dream Book* concurs: "CLOVER—Denotes riches in abundance. This is an excellent dream for all. 929.") In time, John "Buddy" Bailey joined the group as the lead, with Lucas switching to baritone. Second tenor Matthew McQuater replaced Thomas Woods, and bass Harold Winley replaced Billy Shelton, in 1948. In 1949 the group took on guitarist Bill Harris. They were ready to box their dream.

In the beginning, the Clovers were not much more daring than the Ravens or the Orioles, whose material, along with that of the older Charioteers, formed a large part of the Clovers' early repertoire. By the end of the decade, however, the Clovers had begun to rasp the glossy polish from their music's edge, and to perform in a less refined, more vulgar manner. They became the first of the traditionally borne vocal groups to make the leap across the Jordan to the chicken shack that transcends all knowing.

Working at the Rose Club in Washington, D.C., in 1950, they made the acquaintance of Lou Krefetz, who was to become their manager through all the golden years. (To quote again from *The Lucky Star Dream Book*: "JEW—To dream that you speak to a jew denotes business success. It also indicates profitable employment. 990.") Krefetz brought the Clovers to New York, where late in 1950 they made their first record, for Eddie Heller's little Rainbow label. It was a rather timid debut, an innocuous version of the 1925 hit "Yes Sir, That's My Baby," in which the Clovers reverted to their tamer, earlier style. But what soon followed was anything but timid.

During Christmastide, Krefetz negotiated a deal with Herb Abramson and Ahmet Ertegun, the bosses of the three-year-old Atlantic label. On February 22, 1951, the Clovers went into the Apex studio in midtown Manhattan. They came out with one of the biggest R&B hits of 1951, "Don't You Know I Love You."

As their first Atlantic release was reaching Number 1 on the R&B charts in the summer of 1951, the Clovers cut "Fool, Fool, Fool." This, their second Atlantic release, hit Number 1 in the fall, emerging after "Don't You Know I Love You" as one of the best-selling R&B records of the year. (The only vocal group to surpass them in 1951 were the Dominoes, whose "Sixty-Minute Man" had somehow crossed over from the R&B to the pop charts.)

Their third release, Rudy Toombs's wonderful low-rent morality tale "One Mint Julep," recorded on December 17, hit the R&B charts in April. Their biggest hit of 1952 came in the summer, "Ting-A-Ling." After that came the two-sided hit, "Hey, Miss Fannie" (written by Ahmet Ertegun under his backwards-spelt nom de plume "Nugetre") and "I Played the Fool." After their next hit, "Crawlin'," was recorded on August 7, lead singer Buddy Bailey was drafted, and John Philip, who had previously performed as a solo, took Bailey's place through early 1953, during which time the Clovers did not record. By March, when they cut "Good Lovin'," a new lead singer had been found, Charlie White of the original Dominoes. White remained with the group for a year—it was him on "Lovey Dovey"—then was replaced in early 1954 by Billy Mitchell, who had sung on a few of Joe Morris's Atlantic releases (including the unforgettable "Bald Head Woman" of 1951). It was Billy Mitchell whose deep, wildly slurring cottonmouthed voice brought off the song, cut in April 1954, that stands as the Clovers' masterpiece, "Your Cash Ain't Nothin' but Trash," written by the great Jesse Stone (doing business as Charles Calhoun). Though one of the immortal rock 'n' roll records, it reached only as far as Number 9 on the R&B charts. (That summer of 1954 was dominated by Atlantic's new group, the Drifters.) The Clovers did, however, get to perform the song in living, lurid color in the 1955 Studio Films featurette *Rock 'n' Roll Revue*, which behooves beholding.

When Buddy Bailey returned to civilian life and to the Clovers, Billy Mitchell stayed on, and the two singers alternated in the lead. But after 1955 there was not all that much to alternate on. "Devil or Angel," which hit the charts in January 1956, was the group's last Top Ten R&B success. "Love, Love, Love," which followed it, was the first Clovers record to cross over to the pop charts—it reached Number 30 in the summer of 1956—but it did so only by diluting and sweetening the group's true sound. There were half a dozen more Clover records released by Atlantic through the spring of 1958. One of these, "Down in the Alley" (1957), was quite good; but none of them, good or bad, met with any success. Things had changed. Newer, younger groups—the Drifters, the Coasters, both of whom managed Number 1 pop as well as Number 1 R&B hits— had come along and taken up where the Clovers had left off. The big crossover Coasters hits—"Searchin'," "Yakety Yak," "Charlie Brown," and the rest—were really nothing more than cleaned-up, deconked reflections of the earlier Clovers sound. But, as it is writ: everything changes, nothing abides.

After Atlantic, the Clovers cut two unremarkable singles and an album, *The Clovers in Clover*, for Lou Krefetz's Poplar Records in 1958. Later that year they signed with United Artists. Six singles by the group were released by that company from 1959 to 1961. One of

The Clovers, before discovering that fame was a cut number. Left to right: Harold Lucas, Matthew McQuater, John Bailey, Harold Winley, Bill Harris.

them, "Love Potion No. 9," issued in the late summer of 1959, was the Clovers' last hit record, reaching Number 23 on both the pop and the R&B charts. In late 1961 the group returned to make one more record for Atlantic, "The Bootie Green," a godawful attempt to horn in on the Twist craze.

The Clovers broke apart at the end of 1961. Harold Lucas and Buddy Bailey put together another group called the Clovers, and they made a record for the Port label. After that, Lucas and Bailey went separate ways, each of them forming his own Clovers. Bailey's group made a few records for the Winley (owned by bass singer Harold Winley's brother Paul) and Porwin labels; Lucas's put out a record on Brunswick and one on Tiger.

In December 1964, thirteen Christmases since Lou Krefetz (who had split in 1958) had brought them to New York, Harold Lucas, Buddy Bailey, and Harold Winley held a Clovers reunion at the Apollo Theatre in Harlem. Then everybody looked round and faced facts.

"Where there were hills long ago," states the venerable Professor Konje in the Introduction to *The Lucky Star Dream Book*, "there are now streams. So the meaning of dreams changes likewise." Think about it.

THE DOMINOES

The Glory of Bubbonia

The Dominoes were, I think, the most brilliant, and the classiest, of the rock 'n' roll vocal groups. The Clovers and the Midnighters ruled the alley, but the Dominoes ordered from the top shelf and kept their pinkies pointed towards the morning star. Their music possessed power of a different sort. Their mastery of rhythm and meter, their subtle interweaving of the coarse and the sublime, their lyrics which seemed never to rhyme for the sake of rhyme alone—these are qualities so rare and so close to poetry's edge that one is almost tempted to bring that inescapable little gray mouse of a word, "art," into play. But don't worry; I wouldn't spring that one on you at this advanced point.

The founder and leader of the Dominoes was a man named Billy Ward. Born in Los Angeles on September 19, 1921, Ward was a classically trained child soprano who sang in concert at the age of six. In his years before high school, he studied piano, organ, and harmony. He began composing when he was fourteen. He was a Golden Gloves champion, and in the years after that he was a soldier, a journalist, and a voice coach at Carnegie Hall. It was in New York, in 1950, that he formed the Dominoes.

Ward recruited Clyde McPhatter, another former boy soprano who had become a high-placed tenor. McPhatter had been a choir-boy at Mt. Calvary Baptist Church in Durham, North Carolina. Moving to New York with his family when he was twelve, Clyde had adhered to the belief that his voice was something with which to serve the Lord. Persuading him to join in Billy Ward's worldly enterprise was not an easy task, but Ward succeeded. The others whom Ward brought in were Charlie White, second tenor, Joe Lamont, baritone, and Billy Brown, bass.

In November 1950 the Dominoes signed with King. They were to be the first act on King's new Federal label. In December the group appeared on "Arthur Godfrey's Talent Scouts," the popular Monday night CBS television show. At the end of the month their first record, "Do Something for Me," was released by Federal. It hit the R&B charts a month later, and it eventually rose to Number 6.

Variety has always been the most informed and most astute of the publications that cover popular culture. The weekly's comments concerning the Dominoes cut right to the heart of the group's singularity. Reviewing their recent show at the Apollo Theatre, *Variety* remarked in its issue of February 4, 1951, that the Dominoes' "unusual style" was in essence "an application of spiritual characteristics to pop song delivery." And by the word "spiritual" was meant all-out, sanctified, Holy Ghost fervency.

Nowhere was that fervency better illustrated than in the Dominoes' great hit of 1952, "Have Mercy Baby." From its first hard saxophone blast to its howling-and-hand-jive interlude to the brutally sarcastic rhythmic sobbing of its fade-out, "Have Mercy Baby" was the Dominoes' masterpiece, a perfect rock 'n' roll record, and one of the very few that really deserves to be played loud.

> *I've been a good-for-nothin',*
> *I've lied and cheated, too;*
> *But I've reaped it all, my darlin',*
> *And I don't know what to do.*

Less remarkable a piece of work, but more important as history was their 1951 hit about Lovin' Dan's powers of sexual endurance. Like most of the Dominoes' songs, it was written by Billy Ward and his manager, Rose Marks.

> *Lookee here, girls, I'm tellin' you now,*
> *They call me Lovin' Dan;*
> *I rock 'em, roll 'em all night long;*
> *I'm a sixty-minute man.*

Delivered in a manner of perfect on-the-nod composure, "Sixty-Minute Man" was the rage of 1951, the biggest R&B hit of the year. But what made "Sixty-Minute Man" important in terms of the

Billy Ward, with itchy palms, and the Dominoes, c. 1952.

history of rock 'n' roll was the fact that in August 1951, a little less than three months after it had hit the R&B charts, it crossed over to the mainstream pop charts. "Sixty-Minute Man" thus became the first record by a black rock 'n' roll group to become a pop hit. It was surprising in light of the song's subject matter. At the time, Rosemary Clooney's "Come On-a My House" was at the top of the pop charts. It is curious to think of Lovin' Dan taking her up on her offer.

That "Sixty-Minute Man" reached only as high as Number 23 on the pop charts mattered little. What really mattered was that it had reached the pop charts at all. It set the precedent for things to come. During the next few years, other black rock 'n' roll groups crossed over to the pop charts—in 1953, the Orioles with "Crying in the Chapel"; in 1954, the Crows with "Gee," the Chords with "Sh-Boom," the Charms with "Hearts of Stone," and the Five Keys with "Ling, Ting, Tong"—but none of these ensuing crossover hits was as exciting or as good as "Sixty-Minute Man."

The group underwent drastic changes in 1952. Charlie White, the second tenor, was replaced by James Van Loan. Billy Brown, the bass man, was replaced by David McNeil. In May 1953 came the change that truly altered the course of the group. Clyde McPhatter was apparently no longer worrying about whom he was to serve. He quit the Dominoes, formed his own group, the Drifters, and signed with Atlantic Records. (The immense success of the Drifters' first record, "Money Honey," released in August, proved that McPhatter had made no mistake.) Billy Ward replaced McPhatter with another singer who would find fame on his own in a few years' time, Jackie Wilson.

The new group, billed now as Billy Ward and His Dominoes, continued to have hits throughout 1953. But they were decidedly minor hits, and they were not achieved with songs written by Ward, but rather with a rendition of the standard "These Foolish Things Remind Me of You" and a cover version of Tony Bennett's hit "Rags to Riches." An attempt to capitalize on that year's 3-D movie craze with a single called "My Baby's 3-D" failed.

Ward and the Dominoes left Federal and signed with Jubilee Records in September 1954. In the spring of 1956 they moved to Decca. Their first Decca single, released that May, was "St. Therese of the Roses." This was indeed a far cry from "Sixty-Minute Man" and "Have Mercy Baby," but it succeeded in bringing the group to the pop charts. (St. Therese, however, did not make it as far up those charts as Lovin' Dan had made it.) In the following spring they signed with Liberty. Their first release on that label, a version of "Star Dust," was a minor hit in both the R&B and pop markets. Two more small pop hits followed on Liberty, "Deep Purple" in the fall of 1957 (by then Jackie Wilson had left and signed with Brunswick) and "Jennie Lee" in the spring of 1958. In the summer of 1960 they made a handful of recordings for ABC-Paramount, among them the most torpid rendition of "The World Is Waiting for the

Sunrise" that had been heard since 1919. It had been a long, a very long ten years since 1950.

Lovin' Dan, of course, had seen it all coming. In 1954, at one of their last worthy sessions, the Dominoes had recorded a song called "Can't Do Sixty No More." As Frank Costello once observed, there's only so many bullets in that gun. Have mercy, baby, and pass the *TV Guide*.

JACKIE BRENSTON

To the Package Store in Style

The exemplary Christian capitalist Sam C. Phillips, founding father of those great Memphis institutions of the 1950s, Sun Records and Holiday Inns, is said to have expressed the view that a certain 1951 recording (which, as coincidence has it, was produced by him) was the first true rock 'n' roll record ever made; and this notion from on high has been echoed by others. While it certainly is not the case—there being no first rock 'n' roll record any more than there is any first modern novel—the fact remains that the record in question was possessed of a sound and a fury the sheer, utter newness of which set it apart from what had come before. In a way, it can be seen as a turning point, an embarking from the rock 'n' roll of the 1940s towards a brave new world of pegged pants, filtered cigarettes, and Medalo Bops: "Rocket '88' " by Jackie Brenston and His Delta Cats.

Jackie Brenston was born on August 15, 1930, in Clarksdale, Mississippi, the delta town where Highway 49 meets Highway 61. Since early in the century Clarksdale had been one of the most musically fertile places in the South. It was where Son House, Charley Patton, and Robert Johnson worked their wicked magic in juke joints at the outskirts of town. (And where, according to House, Johnson literally sold his soul to the Devil one night, standing at the crossroad.) It was where Muddy Waters, who had grown up listening to and learning from those men, made some of his first recordings. It was where John Lee Hooker and Eddie Boyd were born.

Falsifying the date of his birth, Brenston enlisted in the Army in 1944. Returning to civilian life, and to Clarksdale (indeed, who, though he may travel the wide world over, can resist the allure of Fourth Street?), in 1947, he fell in with a local character named

Jesse Flowers, who drank and played the saxophone. It was Flowers who aided Brenston in his quest to discover that instrument's most degraded possibilities. By the close of the decade Brenston, the proud owner of the shiniest secondhand saxophone in all of Coahoma County, had succeeded.

Entering at this point into the scheme of things was Isaiah Turner, an eighteen-year-old disc-jockey who had the shiniest suits in Clarksdale. He also had a band, in which he played piano and sometimes sang. He had seen Muddy Waters get out of Coahoma County and go on to make records—one of which, "Louisiana Blues," was now becoming a hit—for Chess. He saw no reason why he, a far sharper dresser than that former cotton-picker, should not do the same. As 1950 became 1951, Ike Turner was ready to start making records. There was only one problem. His lead singer, Johnny O'Neal, had recently been signed by King Records, and he had run off, leaving the rest of the band to stand around picking lint from their suits on the corner of Fourth Street. Ike looked, and he found Jackie Brenston. He told him to buy a shiny suit and write some songs; they were going to be stars.

They traveled north on Highway 61 to Memphis in the last, chilly days of February 1951. There were five of them: Ike Turner, guitarist Willie Kizart, tenor saxophone-player Raymond Hill, drummer Willie Sims, and the new guy, Jackie Brenston.

Twenty-eight-year-old Sam Phillips had not yet begun his Sun Records Company; another year would pass before the first Sun record would be made. But he had been operating a recording studio, making and leasing recordings, for almost a year. It was to that studio, at 706 Union Avenue, that Ike Turner and his band went; and it was there, on March 3, that "Rocket '88'" was made.

It was Jackie Brenston's song, but he had derived it from a song in the band's repertoire—"Cadillac Boogie," which Jimmy Liggins had cut for Specialty in 1947. Instead of the Cadillac, Brenston used the new Oldsmobile Rocket Hydra-Matic "88" as his symbol of the do-rag godhead. Far from hiding this unoriginality, Brenston openly admitted it. Many years later, he told Jim O'Neal of *Living Blues* magazine that "if you listen to the two [songs], you'll find out they're both basically the same. The words are just changed."

While the song itself may not have been original, its performance surely was. The overcharged amplification of Willie Kizart's electric guitar, the careening glissandi and manic triplets issuing from Ike Turner's piano (it is not improbable that six years later, when he came upon Jerry Lee Lewis, Sam Phillips, whose Christian-capitalist eyes had seen in Elvis a white boy who sang like a black, saw in Jerry Lee a white boy who played piano like the odd, intense colored fellow, Ike Turner, whom he had witnessed this cold March day), Raymond Hill's post-melodic saxophone shriekings, Willie Sims's trash-can drumming, and the raw, heartfelt degeneracy of Jackie Brenston's singing, shouting, and yelping—the whole of these parts was a sound so loudly and luridly shocking, so preposterous in its celebration of booze, broads, and unrepossessed cars, that it was difficult to perceive where its brilliance ended and its lunacy began.

The band made four more recordings that day, with Ike Turner singing on two of them while Brenston stood back on second tenor sax. Sam Phillips wasted no time. He sold the recordings to Chess Records in Chicago, and Chess released two singles by the group in mid-April. The coupled sides that featured Turner's voice bore on their labels the credit Ike Turner and His Kings of Rhythm. This was how it should have been, and Ike was pleased. The other single, however, was credited to Jackie Brenston and his Delta Cats. This, in the eyes of Ike Turner, known no more then than now for his magnanimity and humility, was not how it should have been, and he was displeased. His displeasure grew more pronounced as it became apparent that the single that bore Brenston's name, rather than the one that bore his own, was going to be a hit.

"Rocket '88'" entered the R&B charts at the end of April. It rose to Number 1, and in the end emerged as one of the best-selling R&B records of 1951. The success of "Rocket '88'" had far-reaching effects. It heralded a new and wilder wave of rock 'n' roll. It stirred Sam Phillips's determination to found Sun, as he realized that the large profits from the recording he had produced could have been his rather than the Chess brothers'. And it caused Ike Turner and Jackie Brenston to part company after one more session (at which only one recording was made, "My Real Gone Rocket," the follow-up to "Rocket '88'"), in the summer of 1951. As time went on, Turner stepped forward from piano to guitar, allowing there to be no mistaking who the leader of his band was.

"My Real Gone Rocket" was released by Chess at the end of June. For whatever reason—perhaps it was *too* much like its antecedent—it failed to sell. Brenston's next single, "Independent Woman," the remaining recording from the first session, was put out in July. (The flip side of this record, "Juiced," was also credited to Jackie Brenston and His Delta Cats; but there are reasons to

Jackie Brenston, near where the road ended.

believe that it was actually by Billy Love, another R&B singer whose work Phillips leased to Chess.) Though it was quite different from the failed follow-up to "Rocket '88,'" the slower, more lyrically subtle "Independent Woman" faded into oblivion with like celerity.

"Hi Ho Baby," Brenston's duet with Edna McCraney, was released by Chess in January 1952. "Starvation," a last Chess single, came in 1953. Then, little more than a year after it had begun, it was over. "I was a greenhorn," Brenston later reflected, "I had a hit record and no sense."

He took a job playing saxophone with Lowell Fulson's band in 1953, and he stayed with Fulson, on and off, through 1955. Then, humbled and weary, he was taken back into the fold by Ike Turner, who still had not managed to come up with a hit record. He remained with Turner until the early 1960s. Though he recorded with Turner's Kings of Rhythm throughout those years, Brenston's voice, which had once shaken the cool world, was heard on only two of the many singles that the band had out during that time. He was reduced to being Ike Turner's baritone sax-player. Turner allowed Brenston to sing a few songs when the band performed in public, but he forbade him to sing "Rocket '88.'"

One of Brenston's most spirited couplets in "Rocket '88'" had been near the song's closing: "Goin' round the corner and get a fifth," he had sung; "Everybody in my car's gonna take a little nip." He no longer had the car, so to speak, but he was still going round the corner for fifths. Singer Jimmy Thomas, who joined Turner's band in 1958, said in a 1980 interview for *Blues Unlimited* of London that he remembered Brenston and tenor sax-player Raymond Hill being more or less drunk throughout the late fifties, even though Turner fined them for drinking. "They was drinking that really bad shit, boy," Thomas recalled. "That stuff they used to drink you probably wouldn't allow it in your house. Not even to wash the floor. I'm telling you, man, it's really amazing . . . them cats, they could put away some alcohol, man."

In the summer of 1960 Ike Turner, with the help of Tina Turner, finally got his hit record, "A Fool in Love," the first of several for the Sue label. In New York that same summer Brenston cut a single of his own for Sue, "Trouble Up the Road" and "You Ain't the One," which was released during the Christmas season.

Brenston and Turner parted again, for the last time, in 1962, when Turner finished with Sue Records. Brenston got a job working in a band with a guy named Sid Wallace. "The only thing he was basically concerned about then," Wallace recalled of Brenston, "was a bottle of wine. And he'd play all night if he got that wine, and didn't worry about whether we made anything. But he pulled himself back up."

Before pulling himself back up, Jackie Brenston made one more record, "Want You to Rock Me" and "Down in My Heart." He cut it in Chicago with Earl Hooker's band, and it was put out on Mel London's Mel-Lon label in 1963. That was it. He returned to Clarksdale, to fabled Fourth Street. He wrung out his brain and sized up what was left. Years passed. The saxophone was no longer shiny. People in the street looked at him sideways, for he dressed in a manner that might best be described as futuristic and his behavior was erratic at times. They did not know, these people, what can happen to a man when his dreams of riding in style are repossessed; they did not know. He took a drink, he took another. The warm days ended, the cold days came. He awoke in a room at the Kennedy V.A. Hospital in Memphis. The Army, at least, had been good for something. He died there, on December 15, 1979. Just a ride there and a walk back. That fame shit sure drove a hard bargain.

THE MIDNIGHTERS

From the Sins of Annie to the Twist

It was towards the end of 1951 that Johnny Otis (born John Veliotes, he found it gainful to pass as black), the thirty-year-old Savoy recording star who also worked as a talent scout for King Records of Cincinnati, came upon a group called the Royals at a talent show at the Paradise Theatre in Detroit. Through Otis, the four-man group—Henry Booth, Sonny Woods, lead singer Charles Sutton, and guitarist Alonzo Tucker—were signed by King boss Syd Nathan, and in January 1952 the Royals began recording for King's sister R&B label, Federal.

The Royals' first record, "Every Beat of My Heart," written by Johnny Otis, was released in March 1952. This single did not do too well (although the song eventually became a hit by Gladys Knight and the Pips in 1961), nor did the four that followed; and in the early summer of 1953 lead singer Charles Sutton moved aside to make room for another Detroit son, Henry Bernard Ballard.

Born on November 18, 1936, Hank Ballard had known the Royals since their gospel-singing days, and he had assisted the group in writing their 1952 "Fifth Street Blues." His style was much less tamed, his voice rougher than Sutton's. "Get It," the first record that Ballard cut with the Royals, entered the R&B charts in July 1953, and rose to become a Number 8 hit. "Get It" was rather lewd and suggestive, as was much R&B in the mid-fifties; but it was nothing compared to what was soon to follow.

During the holiday season of 1953–54 Ballard wrote a song called "Sock It to Me, Mary." In the studio in January 1954 producer Ralph Bass told Ballard that the title was "too strong," and that it should be changed. King engineer Eddie Smith's pregnant wife,

Annie, came into the control room while Ballard was trying to amend his song, and, within a matter of minutes, "Sock It to Me, Mary" became "Work with Me, Annie."

> *Annie, please don't cheat,*
> *Gimme all my meat,*
> *Oo-oo-wee, so good to me;*
> *Work with me, Annie,*
> *Let's get it while the gettin' is good.*

Federal released "Work with Me, Annie" in February 1954. Though it was denounced as "smut" by *Variety, Downbeat,* and other arbiters of hep morality, the record sold well in local markets, especially Cincinnati, Detroit, and Philadelphia. In the second week of April it hit the national R&B charts. At that point, the Royals changed their name to the Midnighters—to avoid confusion with the "5" Royales, the successful Apollo group that had been signed by King.

"Work with Me, Annie" was the Number 1 R&B hit when, in the last week of May, Federal released the Midnighters' "Sexy Ways." Opening with the rude-blaring electric-guitar chords by Alonzo Tucker that would become the most commonly copied riff in rock 'n' roll, "Sexy Ways" elucidated the art of love according to Hank Ballard.

> *Wiggle, wiggle, wiggle, wiggle,*
> *I just love your sexy ways;*
> *Upside down, all around,*
> *Any old way, just pound, pound, pound.*

"Sexy Ways" appeared on the R&B charts at the end of June. Both it and "Work with Me, Annie" remained on the charts through the middle of August, when Federal released "Annie Had a Baby" (written not by Ballard, but by Federal's owner, Syd Nathan, under his pseudonym Lois Mann, and by producer Henry Glover). As August gave way to September, the Midnighters had three of the Top Ten R&B hits, with "Annie Had a Baby" in the Number 1 position.

There was a wave of "Annie" records throughout the rest of the year and well into the following year, beginning with Etta James's "The Wallflower (Dance with Me, Henry)" on Modern, and including the Midnights' "Annie Pulled a Humbug" (Music City), the

El-Dorados' "Annie's Answer" (Vee-Jay), Linda Hayes & the Platters' "My Name Ain't Annie" (King), Danny Taylor's "I'm the Father of Annie's Baby" (Bruce), and the Nu-Tones' "Annie Kicked the Bucket" (Hollywood Star). As for the Midnighters, they did not bother with the shameful girl after the fall of 1954, when they recorded "Annie's Aunt Fanny."

The Midnighters released nineteen more singles on Federal, through the end of 1958, but their last hit on the label was "It's Love, Baby" in the summer of 1955. A *Greatest Hits* album, including all their past and lascivious glories, was released by King in December 1957. In 1959, billed now as Hank Ballard & the Midnighters, the group's records began to bear the King imprint.

Their first King single was "Teardrops on Your Letter," a mundane weeper written by producer Henry Glover. The record hit the R&B charts in the second week of March 1959, but not too much attention was paid to the flip side, a fast dance song that Ballard had copyrighted in January under the title of "The Twist." One of those who did pay attention to it was Ernest Evans of Philadelphia, whose recording of it, under the name of Chubby Checker, was released by Cameo in the spring of 1960. King reissued the original "Twist" in July, as the craze was beginning to bloom, but the record rose no further than Number 28 on the pop charts.

Hank Ballard & the Midnighters continued to make records, and a few of these were hits: "Finger Poppin' Time" (1960), "Let's Go, Let's Go, Let's Go" (1960), "The Hoochi Coochi Coo" (1961), "The Continental Walk" (1961), "Nothin' but Good" (1961), and, finally and dismally, "Do You Know How to Twist" (1962). The group stopped recording in 1963. The next time that Hank Ballard was heard from was in the fall of 1968, when he asked Aretha Franklin, "How You Gonna Get Respect?", a King single that briefly appeared on the R&B charts in November of that year. In 1974 he recorded "Let's Go Streaking"—in the nude, he claimed.

Of scarlet-lettered Annie, and of her child, who shall not, even unto his tenth generation, enter the kingdom of God, alas, we have since heard even less.

The Midnighters, c. 1954. Hank Ballard stands at the center; guitarist Alonzo Tucker shows where Chuck Berry got it from.

JIMMIE LOGSDON

The Man Without a Subtitle

This is not a funny story, so try not to laugh. We begin in the small community of Panther, Kentucky, not far from the mighty Ohio River, which separates Kentucky from Indiana. The date is April 1, 1922, and Jimmie Logsdon is born. It is a common, unremarkable birth, unattended by wise men, indeed, unattended by all save the child's humble parents and himself. But a birth, nonetheless, it is. The father, a Methodist minister, offers his thanks to God.

Time passes slowly, as in a dream, and as it does we shift tenses, tiring of the historical-present. Time passed slowly, we tell ourselves; yes it did, as in a dream, a dream that lasted many years.

Reverend Logsdon's duties as a minister caused the Logsdon family to move frequently: from Panther to Bowling Green to Olive Hill to Corbin, and finally to Ludlow, which is directly across the Ohio from Cincinnati. Jimmie graduated from Ludlow High in the spring of 1940. In the fall of that year, he married his first wife, a girl named Evelyn.

In 1944 twenty-two-year-old Jimmie Logsdon decided to save America from the Nazis, and he enlisted in the Air Force. He was sent to an electronics school in Madison, Wisconsin, then was stationed in Texas where he was put to work as a lineman, repairing damaged B-17s. Two years later, in 1946, the Nazis having been put in their place, Logsdon was released from the Air Force. He returned to Kentucky and opened a radio shop in La Grange, about seventy miles south of Cincinnati. In addition to selling and repairing radios Logsdon sold records, which he bought from Jimmie Skinner, a Cincinnati distributor and two-bit country singer. Young Logsdon had until now not been too involved in music, but listening to the hillbilly and blues records that he sold at his store inspired him to buy a guitar. He found one for $11.95 at Abe Davis's Pawnshop in Louisville.

I told you that this wasn't funny. I forgot to tell you that it wasn't interesting, either.

In the spring of 1948 Jimmie Logsdon began singing and strumming his $11.95 guitar before the WLOU microphone in Louisville. In 1950 he was given his own daily fifteen-minute program. Hank Williams was the sensation of the hillbilly nation at the time, and Jimmie Logsdon idolized him, even though Hank was younger than he. Logsdon listened constantly to Hank's records, especially the primitive rockers such as "Rootie Tootie," and it got to the point where his own voice was often mistaken for Hank's by the folks out there in WLOU radioland.

In 1951 Logsdon hired a guitarist, Howard Whitehead, and a fiddler, Lonnie Pierce, to back him on club dates. Not long after forming this trio, Logsdon cut his first record. Financed by a Louisville businessman named Art Rhodes and recorded in Cincinnati with the help of Jimmie Skinner, "It's All Over but the Shouting," released on the Harvest label, was a song that Logsdon had written about fighting with broads. He played the record on his own WLOU radio program, thus distinguishing himself as the only disc-jockey possessing foresight in the matter of the promising career of Jimmie Logsdon.

He left WLOU in 1952 to become senior announcer for the competing station WKYW. In the fall of that year Logsdon was booked to open a show for Hank Williams at the Louisville Municipal Auditorium. Hank, who was, at the age of twenty-nine, living his final months, was greatly impressed by Logsdon; and when Hank returned to Nashville he told Paul Cohen, who ran Decca Records in that city, that Logsdon should be given a contract to record.

Logsdon began recording for Decca on October 8, 1952. His first release on the label was "I Wanna Be Mama'd"—which, these many years later, still stands as one of the finest of country music's many Oedipal love songs. His work for Decca, all of which was recorded at the Tulane Hotel in Nashville, was predominantly composed of country songs like those sung by his idol Hank the Great. (Hank died on January 1, not long after Logsdon began recording for Decca. A few weeks later, Logsdon wrote and cut a tribute called "Hank Williams Sings the Blues No More." On many of his subsequent recordings, Logsdon used Hank's old band, the Drifting Cowboys, to back him up.) But a good many of his Decca records were lurid rockabilly or boogie tunes, which perfectly suited his bluesy, dissipated voice. The best of these were "Let's Have a Happy Time" (co-written with Vic McAlpin, who had collaborated frequently with Hank Williams), "Midnight Boogie," and a version of the Crowley, Louisiana, swamp shuffle "Good Deal Lucille." But, try as he might with straight country or rockabilly, Jimmie Logsdon could not score a hit, and Decca dropped him in early 1955.

Later that year he cut two records for Randy Wood's Dot label, the best side of which, "Midnight Blues," received a good deal of airplay around Nashville but failed to break.

Jimmie Logsdon was on the skids. His career, which had never really been much to write home about, seemed to be dead. His wife was divorcing him. He, like his late idol, was fast becoming a pill-degenerate and a drunk. In 1956 he entered a hospital to overcome his weaknesses, and he stayed in that hospital for six long months.

He recorded again in 1957, singing into a portable tape machine in his fiddler's bedroom, while the fiddler played a maraca—actually a baby-bottle warmer filled with beans—behind him. The two songs he cut were released by Starday, a company not known for its high standards of technical excellence.

Later in 1957, under the name of Jimmie Lloyd, he cut two singles for Roulette. One of these sides, "I Got a Rocket in My Pocket"—a paean to the artist's dick—not only went on to become one of the most sought-after records in rockabilly history, but also inspired Iggy Pop to become the new Sinatra. Unfortunately for Jimmie Logsdon, it did little else.

He returned to Louisville in 1959, taking a job as a disc-jockey at WCKY, where he remained until 1964. In 1963 he cut a handful of records for King in nearby Cincinnati, but for the most part they were corny country-pop fare, such as "Mother's Flower Garden."

After 1964 Logsdon worked for several other radio stations, in Kentucky and in Alabama, recording occasionally for small, barely-there labels such as Jewel in Mt. Pleasant, Ohio, and Clark County in his home state.

He quit disc-jockeying in 1972 and, since 1973, has done no recording, but has earned his living working for the Commonwealth of Kentucky.

Here, coming fully round in both tense and geography, our little story ends. We have learned much—something, at least—and spent no time in idle laughter. Rocket in his pocket, indeed.

Jimmie Logsdon. Rocket in pocket not shown.

SCREAMIN' JAY HAWKINS

Horror
and the Foot-Shaped Ashtray

Screamin' Jay Hawkins stayed drunk through most of the psyche-
delic sixties. When I encountered him, in the early spring of 1973, he
had put his Black & White scotch aside and was on the wagon. He
drank coffee, a great deal of it, and orange juice. He smoked cigarettes, a great many of them. Sometimes he rolled his own Buglers,
but on this day he smoked Lucky Strikes.

He was living at the Hotel Bryant, in a shabby room nine floors
above Broadway in Times Square. With him were his wife, Jinny,
and an obnoxious four-month-old Siamese cat named Cookie. A
Jet calendar hung on one wall, variously weird hats from nails on
another. The television was on, but without sound. Hawkins sat on
the edge of the bed in a wool hat, Hawaiian-style sport-shirt, and
horn-rimmed eyeglasses, taping a Frank Sinatra album from his
stereo onto his reel-to-reel recorder. Beside him was a little ceramic
foot-shaped ashtray in which he snuffed his Lucky Strikes.

At his feet was a mess of tapes—recordings he had made over the
years for this company and that, but which, for this reason and that,
had never been released. One tape bore a label with the words
"Game of Love" on it. Thinking that it might be his version of the
greaseball classic of that name which Wayne Fontana and His
Mindbenders made in 1965, I asked Hawkins if he might let me hear
it. He looked at me as if I had said something that I should not have
said.

"Did you hear what song he wants to hear?" he said, turning to his
wife. She gave him a dirty look. He uttered small sounds of resigna-
tion and affixed the tape. Soon his slurred voice came through the
speakers, addressing some unseen audience: "We are gathered here

tonight, ladies and gentlemen, laying down some fine sounds that you have't heard and probably will never hear on the radio, simply because Decca is a stupid-ass record company and refuses to—"

Hawkins laughed. "I didn't mean for you to hear that." He manipulated the fast-forward mechanism until he located "The Game of Love." It turned out not to be a version of the Wayne Fontana song, but a Screamin' Jay Hawkins original, a ballad about a man torn between his wife and another woman. As the song progressed, Jinny waxed ostensibly more piqued.

"All right, Jinny, you win," Hawkins spat as the song faded out.

"Did you listen closely to that song? Did you?" Jinny flared at him in her Filipino accent.

"Will you come *on*," Hawkins groaned. "The lyrics keep repeating over and over and over and over that the wife finally won. So what's the problem? What's the argument? The tune is dedicated to the *wife,* you understand?"

"Yeah," Jinny yelled, "but at the end it says, 'I'm gonna love you forever!' Now, *what* does that imply, huh?"

"Just what it says! 'I'm gonna love you forever!' I'm talkin' to the *wife!*"

"Don't give me that! What you're saying is that the wife won but at the same time you're gonna love this other woman forever."

"Oh, for Godsakes, you misinterpret it!"

"No, no. Not me. Maybe *you* do!"

"Me! Come *on,* Jinny, who recorded the goddamn thing?"

"You! And the song says you're in love with this other . . ."

"Oh, come on, that's enough! I'm finished, I don't got no more to say."

"Well, then, you shouldn't have brought it up."

"God*damn!* Nick wanted to hear the tune! Blame Nick!"

"Well, you know, then, you, you don't have to . . ."

"Oh, man, come on. Let's not have an argument. It's only a goddamn song."

A strained stillness came, and Hawkins gazed vacantly into the little foot-shaped ashtray.

Jalacy J. Hawkins was born on July 18, 1929. He was placed in a Cleveland orphanage while in his infancy and adopted into a family of four children at the age of eighteen months. He fought in the Cleveland Golden Gloves as a teenager. He quit high school in 1945 and went to work as an entertainer in the Special Services Division of the U.S. Army-Air Force, performing at service clubs throughout

America, Germany, Japan, and Korea. In addition to singing and playing piano, he continued to pursue a career in boxing until 1949. In that year he defeated Billy McCann, the middleweight champion of Alaska, but the fight left Hawkins so badly beaten that he quit the business.

In 1952 he joined Tiny Grimes's band, both as a singer and as Grimes's chauffeur. Grimes had been one of Atlantic's first recording artists, signing with the label in December 1947, little more than a month after its start. It was with Tiny Grimes and His Rockin' Highlanders, at Grimes's last Atlantic session, in January 1953, that Jay Hawkins made his first recording, "Screamin' Blues." It was deemed by Atlantic to be unsuitable for release.

Not long after that session, Hawkins joined Johnny Sparrow and His Sparrows at the Powelton Café in Philadelphia. Early the next year he cut two singles, "Baptize Me in Wine" and "I Found My Way to Wine" (he had not yet graduated to Black & White), for the little Timely label. (Apollo bought out Timely in the summer of 1954 and eventually, in 1957, reissued these early Hawkins recordings.) In 1955 Hawkins recorded for Mercury and for its new subsidiary, Wing. The Mercury single, "(She Put the) Wamee (On Me)," presaged the outrageous and macabre vocal styling for which Hawkins would soon gain notoriety. At the end of the year, on a single for Grand called "I Is," he first used the nickname Screamin' Jay. It was also for Grand that Hawkins first recorded his song "I Put a Spell on You."

"I wrote the song," Hawkins told me, "because I was going out with some girl who decided that she was gonna put me down. I decided that I didn't want her to put me down. So I wrote a song to her, and the song was 'I Put a Spell on You.' It was just a sweet ballad the way I cut it for Grand."

In January 1956 Stan Pat, who was Hawkins's manager of sorts, signed him to Wing. Recordings followed, but the deal proved to be otherwise barren, and in the summer of that year Hawkins signed with Okeh Records, Columbia's R&B subsidiary. His first Okeh session was held in New York on September 12. It was on that day that he created the monster that haunted him ever after.

"We were gonna cut a new version of 'I Put a Spell on You,'" Hawkins recalled. "Arnold Matson, who was the head of Columbia at the time, felt that we had to do something different in regards to the song. So he brought in a case of Italian Swiss Colony Muscatel, and we all got our heads bent—me, Panama Francis, Al Lukas,

Screamin' Jay Hawkins, doing what he had to do.

Leroy Kirkland, Big Al Sears, Sam Taylor, Mickey 'Guitar' Baker. We all got blind drunk.

"Ten days later, the record came out. I listened to it and I heard all those drunken screams and groans and yells. I thought, oh, my God."

The record became an underground sensation. Screamin' Jay Hawkins's vocal hallucinations were perceived as being invocatory of all manner of horrible things, from anal rape to cannibalism. Self-appointed guardians of morality made their displeasure known to the record company. The record was re-mastered so that its closing groan-coda was censored to a fast fade-out. This measure failed to appease, and the record was in the end banned by most radio stations. The pubescent sleaze-seekers of America, however, continued to buy the record in great numbers. It became a hit without a chart position.

"I didn't know what I had done," Hawkins said. "This record comes out and I've created a monster. Man, it was *weird*. I was forced to live the life of a monster. I'd go to do my act at Rockland Palace and there'd be all these goddamn mothers walking the street with picket signs: 'WE DON'T WANT OUR DAUGHTERS TO LOOK AT SCREAMIN' JAY HAWKINS!' I mean, I'm some kinda bogeyman. I come outa coffins. Skulls, snakes, crawlin' hands, fire, and all that mess."

He had trouble with the caskets he used in his acts. For his first few shows, beginning with Alan Freed's 1956 New York Paramount show, he had rented coffins. This had cost him about fifty dollars a throw. Then the National Casket Association accused him of "making fun of the dead," and sent word to all funeral parlors not to rent any more coffins to one Mr. Jalacy Hawkins. He was thus forced to buy his own, which cost him $850.

"Those were some trying years. God, the things I remember. There was this guy by the name of Bob Horn who did 'American Bandstand' from the Philadelphia Arena, which was at Forty-sixth and Market in West Philadelphia. He got busted for a certain reason which isn't necessary to discuss at the present time, and that's when Dick Clark took over 'American Bandstand.' And when he did, he started off at the Steel Pier in Atlantic City, New Jersey. He called me to open his first show for him. He was so pleased with the opening that he asked me to stay over and do the second day also. His parting words to me were, 'If I can ever do anything for you, don't hesitate to call me.' And then when I made 'Shattered' and a few other records for Decca, I sent word to Dick Clark, asking him if he would please play my records on his show. The reply which I got back was: 'Who's Screamin' Jay Hawkins?' Man, there's some assholes in this business, some real assholes. People forget. Quickly.

"In 1957 I was on a show with the Cadillacs, Billy Williams, Billy & Lillie Ford, and Fats Domino. A young kid by the name of Paul Anka was on the show. He had just had a hit tune out called 'Diana.' I'm already tired, I just come off the road. Fats Domino was slated to close the show, but Fats canceled out for some reason which we don't have to go into here. My manager asked me to go on in Fats Domino's spot. So I insisted on the closing spot of the show, and I was politely told that Paul Anka was going to close the show. I said, 'To hell with Paul Anka.' So Paul Anka walks over to me and he says, 'I'll come to your funeral.' What a goddamn punk."

After a few years, Hawkins got sick of things. He felt that there was a vaguely organized conspiracy that kept his records from getting airplay after "I Put a Spell on You." His subsequent Okeh singles did not sell, nor did his remarkable 1958 Epic album, *At Home with Screamin' Jay Hawkins*. Records that he made for Decca, Chancellor, Enrica, and Roulette went unnoticed. In the summer of 1965 Nina Simone had a modest R&B hit with her Philips recording of "I Put a Spell on You." But two albums that Hawkins himself made for Philips, *What That Is* (1969) and *Screamin' Jay Hawkins* (1970), did not fare so well.

"I guess I've rubbed a lot of people the wrong way. But when you work your heart out for somebody and they pay you half your money in cash and the other half by a check and that check bounces, or payment on it is stopped, or you spend your bread travelin' to a gig and work hard and then some cat stands there with five or six musclemen and tells you that he ain't gonna pay you because he didn't make his money, you get to the point where you start to question things. . . .

"I used to go with a girl in Philadelphia. Some disc-jockey hit her. I punched his face. He never played any of my records again. . . .

"In those days, a nigger wasn't supposed to talk back, wasn't supposed to open his goddamn mouth, wasn't even supposed to say the word 'nigger.' Now things have changed because they found out that some niggers will kill ya. It's as simple as that. In those days, nobody fought back . . . I can't be concerned with other people, because I'm a nigger, and I speak from a nigger's viewpoint. . . .

"I got fed up. I went to Honolulu for ten years because I figured the world wasn't ready for me. In the meantime, all these people are recording my goddamn stuff. Nina Simone, Alan Price, the Animals, Creedence Clearwater Revival, the Who, Them, Manfred Mann, the Seekers, Arthur Brown. Melvin Van Peebles copied my whole act and put it on Broadway. . . .

"I mean, I've had some piss luck. All those people but me makin' money with my songs. I started Chuck Willis wearin' turbans. I started Little Richard wearin' capes. Look at Lord Sutch and Arthur Brown. Look at *Shaft*. Look at *Blacula*. [Hawkins was offered the title role in that 1972 movie by Jack Hammer, but he turned it down.] At one time or another, they've all taken a little something from me, and I get the impression that everybody's going places with what I was doing fifteen goddamn years ago. Everybody but me . . .

"Decca promised me the world if I'd only record for them. So what happened? Nothing. The record doesn't even get played once on the radio. Jesus, I recorded a country song for Philips ["Too Many Teardrops"]. I mean, that song was *something*. The steel-player was from the California Symphony Orchestra, and the rest of the band were jazz musicians. So what does the record company do? They only release it in *Hawaii!* Did you ever in your life hear of anything like that? I cut 'Itty Bitty Pretty One,' and what happens? A week later the Jackson 5 record it and have a hit with it, and meanwhile the company I cut it for [Hot Line] goes bankrupt and the record never gets distributed. It doesn't make sense to me."

It was fortunate for Hawkins that his music was at least more appreciated overseas than it was in his native land. He told me that his bimonthly royalty statements brought respectable residuals from England, Germany, Japan, Australia, Spain, Turkey, Finland, Mexico, and other countries. His Philips recording of "Constipation Blues" was actually a hit in Japan—and only Japan—in 1968. ("It was the first time I'd ever been constipated, so I decided to write a song about it. To this day, I don't know what brought it on. I thought it was pretty unusual, you know? I was in the hospital at the time, and I said to myself, 'A subject like this must be put to music.' I guess the pains of not bein' able to get it out were understood by the Japanese.")

As weary and resentful of the Screamin' Jay Hawkins image as he had become, Hawkins didn't succeed in ridding himself of its curse in the years after our meeting on opposite sides of the little foot-shaped ashtray. What recognition and rewards he has since received have been granted more to the monster than to him. The Rolling Stones asked him to open their spectacular Madison Square Garden show of 1981, but only with the understanding that Hawkins did not perform without his coffin or his other garish gimmicks of old.

There was a plaintive sincerity in Hawkins's voice when he told me, "If it were up to me I wouldn't be Screamin' Jay Hawkins. My screamin' was always just my way of being happy on stage. James Brown, he did an awful lot of screamin', but he didn't become Screamin' James Brown.

"I mean, I've got a voice. Why can't people just take me as a regular singer without makin' a bogeyman out of me? My musical background is people like Roy Milton, Wynonie Harris, Roy Brown, Cleanhead Vinson, Jay McShann, Louis Jordan, Varetta Dillard, Big Maybelle, Roy Hamilton, people like that. I come along and get a little weird, and all of a sudden I'm a monster or something. People won't listen to me as a singer. I'm some kind of monster. I don't wanna be a black Vincent Price. I'm sick of it, I hate it! I wanna do goddamn opera! I wanna *sing!* I wanna do *Figaro!* I wanna do 'Ave Maria!' 'The Lord's Prayer!' I wanna do real singing. I'm sick of being a monster."

WANDA JACKSON

Laced by Satan,
Unlaced by the Lord

Wanda Lavonne Jackson was, simply and without contest, the greatest menstruating rock 'n' roll singer whom the world has ever known. Born in Maud, Oklahoma, on October 20, 1937, the cherished daughter of Tom and Nellie Jackson, she was a prodigious child in more ways than one. At the age of nine, she had been encouraged to play the piano by her father, an indigent laborer who had himself, in days of greater leisure, passed his hands with some degree of unpolished skill across the keys of that instrument. Soon after, of her own will, she turned to the guitar. As her mother was quoted as saying (in an article in the May 1966 issue of *Hoedown*, one of the outstanding illiterate periodicals of an outstandingly illiterate day), "Wanda wasn't like other children after the guitar came into her life."

Not like other children, indeed. At the age of thirteen, a year after her family moved to Oklahoma City, where her father had landed a job as a used-car salesman, Wanda already had her own nylon stockings, brassieres, and daily radio show—the latter broadcast by KLPR, a station two blocks from Capitol Hill High School, where she attended classes with her legs crossed.

In late 1953 and early 1954, when she was sixteen, Wanda, in addition to her radio show, which had been expanded from fifteen minutes to a half-hour daily, sang locally with the Merle Lindsay Band. Then, in the spring of 1954, fortune tugged at her hem. Hank Thompson, whose Brazos Valley Boys were the most successful Western-swing band of the day, heard Wanda on KLPR and telephoned her with an invitation to tour with him and the Brazos Valley Boys.

Thompson brought Wanda together with his arranger and band-leader, Billy Gray. That spring Wanda made her first record, a duet with Gray (who, with Hank Thompson and others, had written it) called "You Can't Have My Love," released by Decca in June, a few days before Wanda finished her junior year at Capitol Hill. She toured the Northeast with Hank Thompson that summer, and recorded more songs for Decca.

Her Decca records—there were a total of seven of them, released from June 1954 through December 1956—were basically country love songs ("Lovin', Country Style," "The Right to Love," and so on), with occasional lapses into the cornbread abyss, such as the 1955 "Tears at the Grand Ole Opry" and the 1956 "Wasted," which she wrote with her father. None of these records did much for Wanda, aside from getting her cast as the lead in her high school's annual musical.

In September 1955, a few months after graduating from Capitol Hill, Wanda became a regular performer on "Ozark Jubilee," the weekly ABC-TV series originating from Springfield, Missouri. (Wanda appeared on the show, on and off, for several years, as its name changed to "Country Music Jubilee" in 1957, and then to "Jubilee U.S.A." in 1958. The show was canceled abruptly in 1960 when its host, country singer Red Foley, was busted for tax fraud.) In late 1955 and early 1956 she toured with Elvis Presley, who had recently been signed by RCA and was on the verge of becoming the biggest thing since Coca-Cola. In April 1956 Wanda signed a management deal with Jim Halsey, who also handled Hank Thompson. Halsey took her to Capitol Records, the company for which Hank Thompson had been recording since 1947; and that summer of 1956, in Los Angeles, eighteen-year-old Wanda Jackson began to sing the way the Devil had intended her to sing.

From her first Capitol record, "I Gotta Know," released in August 1956, to her version of the Robins' "Riot in Cell Block #9," released in February 1961, Wanda showed herself to be one of the most exceptional rock 'n' roll stylists of her or any other day. Her voice, a wild-fluttering thing of sexy subtleties and sudden harshnesses, feral feline purrings and raving banshee shriekings, was a vulgar wonder to hear. She was a girl who could growl. Furthermore, she was the only girl who could hold her own with the big guys of rock 'n' roll's golden era, as her 1955–56 tour with Elvis and her 1957 tour with Jerry Lee Lewis and Carl Perkins attested.

Many of the early Capitol recordings, and the best of them, were fast, loud songs about ambivalent carnality. "Hot Dog! That Made Him Mad" (1956) was a celebration of bitchdom. "Let's Have a Party" (1960) was a lewd-voiced invocation of prophylactic love. In "Mean Mean Man" (1960) the joys of being slapped around were praised through wet lips. Best of all, however, was "Fujiyama Mama," released in the first cold days of 1958. She sang Earl Burrows's audacious lyrics as if she meant every word of them:

> I been to Nagasaki, Hiroshima, too—
> The things I did to them, baby, I can do to you,
> 'Cause I'm a Fujiyama mama, and I'm just about to blow my top—
> Fujiyama-yama, Fujiyama—
> And when I start eruptin', ain't nobody gonna make me stop.

Not even twenty years old, she sounded like she could fry eggs on her G-spot. And that, more than anything, was the problem; for while Wanda's were among the most striking and finely wrought records of their time—and they were finely wrought on every level, produced as they were by the consummate West Coast studio craftsman of the fifties, Ken Nelson, and utilizing as they did the talents of guitarist Joe Naphis and unsung-hero pianist Merrill Moore—the public was simply not prepared to accept a young lady who looked and sang as Wanda Jackson did. It was too hot a package to sell over the counter. Teresa Brewer, Connie Francis, yes; Wanda Jackson, no. Of all the records she made for Capitol from 1956 to 1960, only one, "Let's Have a Party," appeared on the charts, and even then only as high as Number 37.

In 1961 Wanda began recording in Nashville, recrossing her legs and veering again towards tamer country stuff. "Right or Wrong," released in May of that year, hit Number 9 on the C&W charts, Number 29 on the pop charts. The cover photo of her *Right or Wrong* album, issued at the end of August (it was her fourth album, and the first to sell moderately well), provided the last glimpse of Wanda as *la bimbo fatale du rock 'n' roll,* showing her pouting, her extramusical blessings accentuated by a tightly laced corset.

But what the Devil laced, God unlaced. While she was fortunate enough to make a few dollars more with softer, more moralistic songs ("A Girl Don't Have to Drink to Have Fun," she vouched in 1967; two years more and it was a limping version of "If I Had a

Wanda Jackson with Billy Gray, flesh on flesh, hat on hat.

Hammer"), Wanda's fire was out. In October 1961 she married an IBM programmer named Wendell Goodman. A daughter, Gina Gail, came the next year; a son, Gregory Jackson, in 1964. From Fujiyama mama to hibachi hostess: such are the wages of survival in a democracy of mediocrity.

Wanda recorded for Capitol throughout the 1960s, into the early seventies. From 1965 to 1967, she had her own syndicated TV program, "Music Village." Her final Capitol album, *Country Keep-*

sakes, came out in January 1973. A year later she appeared briefly at the bottom of the country charts with "Come on Home to This Lonely Heart," a single on the Myrrh gospel label. In 1975 came a Myrrh album, *Now I Have Everything*, and a few more followed as the seventies faded away. Then, finally, the voice that had been too hot to handle twenty years before was heard no more. As it is writ: menopause hath no mercy in the land. Or something like that.

JOHNNY ACE

Number One with a Bullet

The boy called Johnny Ace was brought here by death. He was not like those who came before him; he did not know the Devil from the old days. He was the first fallen angel, the first lost mother's son of rock 'n' roll, eaten up and spat out by fame before he'd had a chance to read Virgil's words on the back of the dollar bill.

John Marshall Alexander, Jr., came into the world on June 9, 1929, in Memphis. He was one of six sons and three daughters born to the Reverend and Mrs. John Alexander. Like most preachers' boys, Johnny played the piano. He went to La Rose Grammar School, then to Booker T. Washington High School. He enlisted in the Navy at the end of World War Two. After basic training, he was stationed in Orange, Virginia. The closest body of water was Lake Anna. He got married, and he had two children. The boy was named Glenn, the girl was named Sandra. It could have all evanesced into middle-class pleasance; but it didn't.

By the end of 1949 Johnny had become involved with the Beale Street Blues Boys, an important Memphis group led by tenor saxophonist Adolph Duncan. The lead singer of the Beale Streeters was nineteen-year-old Robert Calvin Bland, who later became famous as Bobby "Blue" Bland; the guitarist was Riley "B.B." King.

The Beale Streeters were the premier band of Memphis throughout 1950 and 1951. Then, at the end of 1951, Bobby Bland received his draft notice; in early 1952 B.B. King, who was recording for RPM, set off on his own.

In January 1952, just before he entered the service, Bland cut four sides for Modern at Sam Phillips's studio. Johnny accompanied him on piano. He also continued to play on the Saturday afternoon

"Beale Street Blues Boys" program on radio station WDIA. New musicians had been brought in, and the reshuffled Beale Streeters were now billed as "Bee Bee King's Original Band." It was on one of those WDIA shows that Johnny surrendered to the instigation of Earl Forrest and began to sing.

It was at this time that disc-jockey James Mattis started Duke Records with the idea of capitalizing on the local talent not already signed to RPM or the other companies to whom Sam Phillips was selling his recordings. Johnny signed with Duke in the spring of 1952. It was understood from the beginning that Johnny's actual surname would not be used, so that his father, the Reverend, might be saved from any shame.

Johnny Ace's first record was released in early June. Like most of the records that followed—there were only ten—it coupled a slow, melancholy song ("My Song") with a hard, bluesy rocker ("Follow the Rule"). Wondrously, this record—by a boy no one had ever heard of, on a little southern label no one knew—became a hit. "My Song" entered the national R&B charts during the last week of July, and it rose until it hit Number 1. It remained on the charts for five months.

"Cross My Heart," Johnny's second single, was released in December. It too became a hit. By then Don Robey, the black Jew who had been running Peacock Records in Houston since 1949, had moved in on James Mattis. Soon Mattis was bought out, and Duke was a part of Robey's Houston operation. In March 1953 Johnny went on tour with Willie Mae Thornton, whose Peacock recording of "Hound Dog" was beginning to gather momentum.

Johnny's third record, "The Clock," coupled with the instrumental "Aces Wild," was released in June 1953. Like the record that had been released the previous June, it hit Number 1 on the R&B charts. "Saving My Love for You," his fourth record, came out in November. It was another hit.

The whole thing was uncanny, really. All he had done, this preacher's son whose first twenty years on earth had been a dull vacillation between being and nothingness, typified by his joining the Navy and going no farther than a five-dollar bus ticket would have gotten him; all he had done was opened his mouth and sung. Fame and fortune had been instantly his, not for a moment, but for every moment since. No rise to lasting fame had ever been so sudden, nor would any other ever be. It *was* uncanny. His records were fine, but they were not so fine as all this. He was not even an

Johnny Ace, not long before he got his gun, 1954.

accomplished performer. The month before "Saving My Love for You" was released, he had appeared at the Apollo Theatre in New York. Reviewing his show, *Variety* found him "too stiff and wooden." It was concluded that he possessed a smooth baritone voice, "but unfortunately his song salesmanship isn't commensurate with the quality of his voice." Then why? He had summoned a greater congregation, wrung more gold from its purse, than any

Protestant God's furtive-copulating sermoner ever could; and there really was no reason why.

A fifth single, "Please Forgive Me," came in May 1954. It was a hit, but not of the magnitude of those that had come before it. It spent only two weeks on the R&B charts, and rose only to Number 10. His sixth record, "Never Let Me Go," was the first of Johnny Ace's records not to make the charts. It was released in September 1954. By then, another Memphis boy, Elvis Presley, who had listened to the Beale Streeters during his high school years, was on his way to becoming the new rage.

Johnny's lucky seventh single, "Pledging My Love," recorded with the Johnny Otis Orchestra, was scheduled to be released in the first week of the new year, 1955. The song had been written for Johnny by Fats Washington and Don Robey. (It was, in any event, they who took the credit for the song.) The flip side, however, had been written by Johnny himself. It was a tough, brassy rocker called "No Money," and it was arguably the best piece of work that Johnny had ever done. "I'm in this world alone!" he ended the song, as Johnny Board's Orchestra swelled to a climax behind him.

By the time that the record was released, Johnny was no longer in this world, alone or otherwise. Though he had more than most twenty-five-year-old boys, or their fathers, might dare to dream of having, he did not have it all.

It happened backstage at the Houston City Auditorium on Christmas Eve, 1954, little more than an hour after he had signed the papers for a shining new 1955 Oldsmobile. It was late, and Christmas was almost there. He held a .32 revolver to his right temple, pulled the trigger, and blew what little brains he had to kingdom-come. His eyes filled with blood, his scrawny limbs convulsed, and, in the words of Big Mama Thornton, "that kinky hair of his shot straight out." He was pronounced dead on Christmas morning.

The accepted story is that Johnny was playing Russian roulette. There is another story, but lawyers will not let it be printed here, since it implicates living people who have lawyers of their own.

"Pledging My Love" was released on schedule. *Billboard* was correct in choosing it as "This Week's Best Buy." Popular culture has always loved the self-killed. The record hit the R&B charts immediately, and it rose to Number 1. In February it crossed to the pop charts, and it entered the Top Twenty. Singers, songwriters, and record companies rushed to seek gold in the grave-dirt. Varetta

Dillard's record, "Johnny Has Gone," was first, released by Savoy in mid-January. Hollywood Records was almost as fast with its two-sided "tribute" single, "Why, Johnny, Why" by Johnny Moore's Blazers, featuring singer Linda Hayes, and "Johnny Ace's Last Letter" by Frankie Irwin. Johnny Fuller's version of "Johnny Ace's Last Letter" came next, on the Aladdin label. The Rovers' "Salute to Johnny Ace" was put out by Music City. From Don Robey's headquarters in Houston came the Peacock single, "In Memory," by the Johnny Otis Orchestra with Marie Adams. Perhaps the most grotesquely pitiful of all was the single released by King Records on February 10: "Johnny Has Gone" c/w "Johnny's Still Singing" by the Five Wings. The former explains how Johnny was called to heaven because the angels had heard an advance copy of "Pledging My Love" and enjoyed it so much that they decided on recruiting Johnny for a command performance. The latter assured listeners that "Johnny's still singing somewhere up above." Promotional copies of the single went to disc-jockeys with a note informing them that "The Five Wings are from New York City and take up singing after regular working hours. . . . They were selected as the group to sing these specially written songs. . . . Each side of this record is fitting memorial to Ace." One could only hope that the Five Wings were not foolish enough to give up their day-jobs.

The April 1955 issue of *Rhythm and Blues,* published in February, eulogized that "On December 24th, 1954, Johnny Ace received his call from the Great Beyond. Tho' he has departed, his music will remain with us down through all the ages as a reminder of a wonderful singer and a wonderful man. Our Johnny is gone, but he shall never, never be forgotten." Side bet.

"Anymore," a recording on which Johnny had played vibes instead of piano, was issued in June. The *coup de grâce* was delivered by Don Robey in July of 1956, when Duke released a final posthumous single, "Still Love You So." This record, Duke 154, was advertised together with Duke 155, a single by a character called Buddy Ace. "Complete your collection with this *LAST* record on the LATE GREAT *JOHNNY ACE*," the ad copy implored; "Start your collection with the *FIRST* record release on this up and coming artist."

What exactly occurred that long-ago Christmas Eve in Houston will never be known. Presuming that the incident had nothing to do with business—and I think it had nothing to do with business—leaves us to wonder why Johnny pulled the trigger. Surely there must have been a less ruinous way to deal with the problem of last-minute Christmas shopping. No, I believe it had to be something deeper than that. One thing alone is certain: he sure wasn't thinking of the porter. In the end, what one really wonders about is who got the Olds. They don't make them like that anymore.

ESAU SMITH

The Hairy and the Smooth

I first heard about him in the winter of 1982, from a half-assed south Jersey wise guy who used to come by a bar I occasionally worked at in Newark. The wise guy liked me because I had gotten tickets for his kids to see the Rolling Stones at Madison Square Garden. Since then, if it was a Thursday or a Friday (those were the days I usually worked there), and if he was on his way to or from the airport, and if he had time to kill, he would drop in, have two J&Bs, and leave a five-dollar tip. Though the tickets had cost me nothing but the price of a telephone call and the minor abasement of having to exchange hollow pleasantries with a record company publicist, they ended up bringing me in more than two hundred dollars in five-dollar tips. Needless to say, he was my favorite customer.

He knew that I wrote ("Nicky the Book-Writer" was the droll sobriquet that he had bestowed on me) and that I had written a lot about rock 'n' roll. This, and those tickets, was why he told me what he did.

I did not believe a word of what he said, though I felt that he believed it, or, rather, that he did not disbelieve it. The more he told me, the more I grinned.

"Yeah, huh?" he concluded. "Well, not for nothing, but the guy's all right."

"Not in the head, it sounds," I said.

It was left at that for more than a year. I did not think again of what I had heard from my five-dollar wise guy acquaintance about the character called Smitty who worked at his—it was partly his, anyway; I later found out that it had almost as many partners as customers—after-hours joint in Los Angeles. It was so patently incredible that it failed to titillate that gullible craving for contradictory evidence to the dull, known facts of life which we euphemistically call inquisitiveness. I had more important things to think about, such as why I was working twelve-hour shifts in a bar instead of leaving five-dollar tips to some other *citrullo* who was working twelve-hour shifts in a bar. Like the man said, life is funny. Soon it got funnier.

In the spring of 1983 I was sent to China by the mistakenly resurrected *Vanity Fair* magazine. On my way home, I stopped for a few days in Los Angeles. Sitting in a bar on Olympic Boulevard one morning, I realized that I was only a few blocks from the after-hours joint that, back in Newark, I had so often been invited to visit. Maybe the five-dollar tipper himself would be there, I thought.

It was like every other after-hours joint I had ever been in, right down to the indoor-outdoor carpeting and the regulation ash-blonde dyke barmaid. There were three guys at the bar and four at the blackjack table. I took one look at the dealer. In a sudden, jarring instant, I knew that he was Smitty, and I knew—rather, I wanted to know—that his story was true. I put down five twenties and told him that I wanted ten-dollar chips.

"You can split pairs," he said. "Push goes to the house."

A couple of hours later we were sitting in Philippe's, eating lamb sandwiches and drinking beer. He told me that I had missed what's-his-face from Jersey by three days.

"He's some kind of guy, ain't he?" he grinned. "The joint is just a candy store. Him, a few other guys. I get a piece of the table, a small piece. He's got a broad out here or some shit. He hardly even looks at the joint's receipts when he comes by. He's good people, though, I'll tell you that. He's done good by me."

I agreed, told him about the Rolling Stones tickets and the fives. "That's him."

As we eased, with our beer and our small talk, into the intimacy, however wary, of devious-cruising, chance-crossed kindred, I asked him straightforward if what our mutual acquaintance had told me about him was true.

He started slightly, looking as if to say, "He told you that?" Then he smiled sidewise. "You gonna write about it?"

"If somebody pays me."

"I like your attitude," he said. "But I wasn't made with a finger. You know what's-his-name. To me, that's as good a credential as you could have. That you're a writer, that doesn't mean anything to me. Don't get me wrong, I respect anybody who's self-employed. Hell, I like to read; I just don't have much time for it. You know who I like? I like Eric Ambler. You ever meet him?" I confessed that I had not. "He's probably dead by now," Smitty said. He drank some beer and looked away for a moment. Then he raised his left hand and turned it. "Anyway," he said, "if it is true, what does it matter?" I shrugged, and he smiled. We ordered two more lamb sandwiches and two more beers.

"Look at it this way," he said. "Some guy in yellow pants—I'm using this as an analogy; see, I read—he walks around shifting his belt like there's a gun in it, telling everybody that Jimmy Hoffa's buried under the track at the Meadowlands. Next thing you know, there's a thousand guys in yellow pants telling ten thousand guys in blue pants that Jimmy Hoffa's buried in the Meadowlands. It ain't long before the whole world—green pants, pink pants, the whole shooting match—thinks that Jimmy Hoffa's buried in the Meadowlands. Meanwhile, maybe he's working in a hardware store selling the shovels that nobody's buying to dig him up with. Do you follow me?"

My imagination dyed his graying clove-brown hair black, shaved off his moustache, restored to fullness the vestigial Southern accent that softly colored his speech.

"What I mean is, everybody believes that Jesse Garon Presley died at birth, but nobody's ever bothered to look up the death certificate."

I didn't nod, I didn't say anything, I just kept looking at him.

"As is usually the case, the truth is rather dull. There wasn't any dead child. There was just one mouth too many to be fed by some poor old sucker who couldn't saddle a Guernsey cow if he had four niggers holdin' it still for him. As far back as I can remember, I lived with my Aunt Reenie, in Belden, about ten miles from where I was born. I lucked out pretty good. Aunt Reenie was a good lady. She was my mother's cousin, a few years older than her. She's dead now close to twenty years.

"We were together a lot when we were little kids, especially in the summertime. I remember spending a lot of days playing near Chickasaw Village, which was about halfway between Tupelo and Belden. Me, Elvis, my mother, and Aunt Reenie. We got along. There didn't seem to be anything odd about the situation at all. If anything, I think I felt like I was better off. I ate better than Elvis, I knew that much.

"We were a lot alike. He was a little taller than me even then. He was a little slower, maybe, a little quieter. I used to clench my hand like this, like I was holding something in it. 'Come here,' I'd tell him, 'look what I got.' When he put his face real close to my hand— *wap!*—I'd smack him. What I never got over," he laughed in a bemused way, "was that he kept falling for it, over and over again." He paused. "Real interesting, huh?" To me it was, but I didn't say so. "It was Aunt Reenie who got us started in on the guitars, little old toy things she sent away for to Sears. We must've been ten then. It was Christmas, I know that much. We thought we were regular little Gene Autrys.

"It seems like I skipped as soon as I was old enough to raise a hard-on. I couldn't have been more than fourteen. Mom and Elvis and my father had moved up to Memphis right about then. I could have gone with them. I really think they wanted me to go with them. But . . ." He moved his shoulders.

"I was a crazy kid. I walked right out there onto Highway 15 like I owned it. It wasn't like I was running away, really. Aunt Reenie knew I was going. I didn't say I was going, and she didn't say she knew I was going; but it was understood. She had a Bible—she had two or three of them, but there was this one little old beat-up one that looked like it might've been autographed by Jesus Christ —that she kept a ten-dollar bill in. She took to leaving it on the wicker chair by the door, instead of on the mantel. This was her way of letting me know that she knew. I took them both, the Bible and the ten.

"I ended up in Pascagoula. That's sort of the Pismo Beach of Mississippi. For a week I just sat out on the pier, eatin' vanilla cookies and smokin' cigarettes. At night I slept under it. Man, I thought I was it. The folding money started turning into silver, and I learned my first great lesson: a man can buy only so many vanilla cookies and Camels with a ten-dollar bill. I got a job as a delivery boy for a butcher. He was an old Irish guy named Davey Blue. I gave him a line of shit about how I was an orphan a long way from home. I think I took it from *Boys Town*. Aunt Reenie took me to see that one Thanksgiving or something when it came around, I guess so that I could see how well off I was. Anyway, old Davey Blue had a heart of gold—hands like rusted, musselled-up anchors, but a heart of gold. He paid me two dollars a day, and he got me a little room in a boarding-house—I guess that's what you'd call it— that cost five dollars a week. It was a great set-up for a crazy kid that didn't want to do anything but eat cookies and smoke cigarettes on the end of a pier. I wrote a letter to Aunt Reenie, telling her that I was fine and for her not to worry. I didn't put a return address on it, though.

"I don't think I worked for Davey for more than a year. I lied about my age and got a job on the platforms. I guess, what with the Korean draft and all, they weren't being too choosey. So there I was, gone from ten to fifty dollars a week. And I was stashing most of it away, too, since my tastes still hadn't gotten too far beyond cigarettes and vanilla cookies—except for a certain girl that I ended up marrying, which I don't really want to go into here, except to say that she was the reason for my next move. I skipped on her and moved to Hattiesburg. That was in 1953, and I was a wise old man of eighteen.

"When I first hit Hattiesburg, I went to work on the platforms there, for Red Ball. That was one good thing about platform jobs in those days: if you had one in Miami, you could get one in Seattle. It was in Hattiesburg that I took up where I'd left off on the guitar, which, to tell the truth, wasn't all that far along, maybe the third page of *Alfred's Easy Guitar Lessons*. The foreman at the job had him a hole-in-the-wall bottle club out near the Okatoma turn-off, and we used to play there on weekend nights, me and this other kid who must have been stuck on page three of whatever the piano equivalent of *Alfred's* is. We'd do a lot of country stuff. Eddy Arnold, Lefty Frizzell, Hank Williams were real big then. People wanted to hear that stuff. We didn't only do country. Hell, we butchered just about every sort of music known to man, and a few that ain't. We had fun, and we made a few extra bucks.

"That's when I made my first record." He laughed and shook his head in good-natured delectation of what seemed to him to be a cherished, secret folly. "And what a record it was." He here affected the voice of a deep-southern radio pitchman: "'Bosom Divine' by Jesse Presley with Jo-Jo Fineaux and His Hattiesburg Hepcats." He laughed again; I with him. "Jo-Jo Fieneaux was the kid that played piano with me at the club, and the Hattiesburg Hepcats were sons of the guy who put the record out. He owned a furniture store there in town. I think that record sold a good dozen copies, unless that old bastard with the furniture store made his own sons pay for theirs. I still got a few at the house. I'll bring one by the joint for you if you want.

"Like I said, I was making money. The trouble was, I was also learning how to spend it. I fell in with this guy that was on the arm at the club there. He did some small-time shylocking around town, and he had a cut of the numbers action, which was probably about two rolls of nickels a day. I fell in with him, taking numbers and shylocking for him down on the platforms. All the numbers action there—I guess it's still the same today—runs out of New Orleans, not out of Jackson like most people think. So, through this one guy I meet this other guy, blah-blah-blah, one thing leads to another, and I move to New Orleans. I took single action all around St. Louis Cathedral there. I worked straight salary. I could maybe have made more working percentage, but this way I didn't risk sharing any losses. A hundred dollars a week bought a lot of vanilla cookies thirty years ago, I'll tell you that much. I was like a pig in shit. I was still crazy, though. I remember I was drunk one night, and this broad at the bar—I didn't even know her—she was complaining that she had to go to New York to visit her sister and it was freezing in New York and she didn't have a coat, blah-blah-blah. I went out and bought her one, just like that." He paused. "Usually when I tell that story, I make it a mink, but it was just one of those ski-jacket things.

"It was right around then that I found out that Elvis was turning into tomorrow's news. I heard his record 'Milkcow Blues Boogie' on the radio. It was the third one he'd made. Jesus, I was excited. I hadn't talked to any of them, not even Aunt Reenie, in five years. But I really wanted to get in touch now, you know? I remember putting all those nickels in that pay phone, calling Aunt Reenie. She sounded a lot older, like those five years had been fifty, and she sounded like she was hearing from a ghost. 'Your daddy's been tellin' folks that'—and she couldn't finish. The old bastard had written me off! Elvis was starting to make it. People were asking questions, doing interviews and such. Somebody—it couldn't have been the old man; his wiles had quit somewhere round that first plus-sign in the second grade—somebody must have come up with this wonderful solution to the problem of the twin that wasn't around. Jesus, I felt like . . ." He sighed, and his exhalation was like an erasure of years.

"I gave Aunt Reenie two phone numbers, my number at the apartment and the number at the bar where I hung out. I told her to give them to Elvis or my mother, or to my old man if he wanted them. 'You still got that Bible?' she asked me. I told her that I did. 'Good boy,' she said, 'good boy.'

"Right after that, I got pinched taking the single action. I ended up doing three months for those guys down there. So I had no way of knowing if Elvis, or anybody, had called me back. The bartender at that place I hung out at was worthless, about as good with messages as he was with mixed drinks. I just didn't know. To this day . . ." He laid his fist without force upon the table. "And a few years later, at my mother's funeral, the way the old man tried to—ah, fuck it; the beer's talking now.

"Anyway, nobody called me once I was back out, that much I know. I figured, hell, what is this? I still had the foolish pride of a boy who'd been hit but not knocked down. I dropped my real name, came up with that 'Esau Smith.' I had finally gotten to reading that Bible, and that's where I got the 'Esau' from. Look in Genesis and you'll see what I mean, or what I meant then. This character down there who ran a juke-box label had been after me to cut a record. I said I would under the condition that he put my new name on it. He finally agreed. That's how that second and final work of art came into being. I don't even know if I have any of those to give you. After that, I just sort of let the singing lie. I will tell you one thing, though. I always enjoyed Elvis's records, and I was always proud of him.

"One thing I knew for sure," his voice livened, "was that I wasn't cut out for doing more than a day's time. I talked to my friends. They put me down in some basement dive spinning a Big Six. Eventually I moved up to dealing. I was good at it. I was sharp and I was straight. They took me out of the basement and started me working at the fancy joint on Carrollton. I kept my nose clean and did well. I always dealt an honest game. Hell, in this racket you don't have to cheat. That push-goes-to-the-house shit breaks 'em all in the end.

"I stayed there until 1964, then I came out here. By then I was plain old Johnny Smith. I miss New Orleans once in a while. It's some kind of town, that's for sure. But it's quieter here. I have a wife, two kids. I ain't getting any younger." He took a last, slow swig, and he looked at his watch. "Then again, at least I'm still here."

I went back to see him the following morning. The same guys were sitting at the bar and at the blackjack table. An additional, younger patron had bestowed his presence upon the scene. He leaned over the bar, asking the barmaid if she liked raw oysters.

Smitty—or whatever it is that I should call him—bought me a

drink. He alluded in no way to our conversation of the previous day. Nor, his eyes and manner insinuated, should I. Sure enough, he had brought the records for me. "Now, remember," he said lightly as he gave them to me, "if you listen to these things, it's just some silly-ass kid fucking around."

I smiled and thanked him.

"You gonna write me up?" he finally asked, in a clip.

"I don't know," I told him.

"Yeah, well, whatever."

A few days later, when I was back home, I put one of the records, a 78 with a still-glossy blue label, on the turntable. It lacked that certain salability without which few things in this world succeed. But it was, notwithstanding the Hattiesburg Hepcats, one of the finest things that I had ever heard, and it made me smile and it made me laugh.

> *I dreamt last night of a bosom divine,*
> *A bosom so pristine, so pure,*
> *And from it bubbled whiskey like milk;*
> *I sucked till my poor jowls were sore.*

If I never see him again, I'll never cease to wonder about him. Just as he, most likely, will never cease to wonder if that phone rang thirty years ago. The man, as usual, was right. Life is funny.

WHAT THAT WAS

A Chronology of the
Coming of Rock 'n' Roll

1945

January	"Tell Me You'll Wait for Me" by Johnny Moore's Three Blazers (Atlas 107) is released.
February	Ezra Pound, indicted for treason, is incarcerated in the criminal ward of St. Elizabeths Hospital, Washington, D.C.
March	Joe, Jules, and Saul Bihari form Modern Records in Los Angeles. The company's first release is Hadda Brooks's "Swingin' the Boogie" (Modern 101).
	Louis Jordan's "Caldonia Boogie" (Decca 8670) is released.
April	Ed and Leo Mesner, owners of the Philharmonic Music Shop in Los Angeles, inaugurate their Philo Records company with the release of Illinois Jacquet's "Flying Home" (Philo 101).
June	"Sweet Marijuana Brown" by the Barney Bigard Sextet (Black & White 13) is released.
	"Guitar Boogie" by the Rambler Trio (Super Disc 1004) is released.
July	Four-Star Records is founded in Los Angeles by Richard A. Nelson.

August	America drops atomic bombs on Hiroshima and Nagasaki.
September	Wynonie Harris's first solo record, "Around the Clock" (Philo 103), is released.
	Louis Prima's "Felicia No Capecia" (Majestic 7154) is released.
December	"Who Put the Benzedrine in Mrs. Murphy's Ovaltine" by Harry "The Hipster" Gibson (Musicraft 346) is released.

1946

January	"Milton's Boogie" by Roy Milton and His Solid Senders (Juke Box 503) is released.
February	Due to legal complications, Philo Records becomes Aladdin Records.
March	"Hillbilly Boogie" by the Delmore Brothers (King 527) is released.
	Big Joe Turner's "Rebecca" (Decca 11001) is released.
April	Jim Bulleit's new Nashville company, Bullet, releases its first singles: "Nashville Jumps" by Cecil Gant (Bullet 250), "Zeb's Mountain Boogie" by Owen Bradley (Bullet 600), and "They Have Gone Away" by the Baxter Quartet (Bullet 100).
	"The House of Blue Lights" by Ella Mae Morse (Capitol 251) is released.
May	The Ravens' first record, "Honey" (Hub 3030), is released.
June	On the 19th, NBC telecasts the Joe Louis-Billy Conn fight. By the end of the month, Aladdin releases a ringside recording of the "Louis-Conn Knockout Round" (Aladdin 150).
July	On the 2nd, blacks vote for the first time in Mississippi Democratic primaries.

October	Moon Mulligan's "New Milk Cow Blues" (King 578) is released.
November	Louis Jordan's "Let the Good Times Roll" (Decca 2374) is released.

1947

January	Sterling Records of New York, a subsidiary of Juke Box, introduces its new country line with Hank Williams's first record, "Calling You" (Sterling 201). "For singing real country songs Hank Williams is a favorite wherever he is heard," says an advertisement in the January 18 *Billboard*.
March	"That's All Right" by Arthur "Big Boy" Crudup (Victor 20-2205) is released.
April	"I Sold My Heart to the Junk Man" by Etta Jones and the J. C. Heard Band (Victor 20-2231) is released.
	St. Louis Jimmy's "Goin' Down Slow" (Bullet 270) is released.
	Abbott and Costello's two-part recording of "Who's on First?" (Enterprise 501) is released.
	On the 11th, Jackie Robinson of the Brooklyn Dodgers becomes the first black to play on a major-league baseball team.
June	Hank Williams's first MGM record, "Move It on Over" (MGM 10033), is released.
	The Trenier Twins' first record, "Buzz, Buzz, Buzz" (Mercury 8045), is released.
	On the 13th, the Supreme Court in Atlanta revokes the national charter of the Ku Klux Klan.
July	Flying-saucer hysteria overtakes America. "During the past fortnight," notes the July 8 London *Times*, "reports that dish-like objects, nicknamed 'flying saucers,' have been seen traveling through the air at great speed . . . have come from the United States

and Canada." Both *Time* and *Newsweek* report on the phenomenon in their issues of the 14th. By the end of the month, from Little Rock, Arkansas, comes "Flying Saucers" by a country duo called Buddy and Claude (President 10).

September   Roy Brown's "Good Rockin' Tonight" (DeLuxe 1093) is released.

October   On the 10th, the first bodies of the American dead of World War Two arrive in the United States.

During the third week of the month, Hank Williams's "Move It on Over" becomes his first record to hit the country charts.

November   On the 4th, Tennessee Williams's *A Streetcar Named Desire* opens in New York.

December   Blues singer Andrew Tibbs's "Bilbo Is Dead" (Aristocrat 1101) is released, lamenting the loss of Mississippi Democratic Senator-elect Theodore G. Bilbo, who died on August 31. (Congress had opposed Bilbo's seating on the grounds that he had won his election through a campaign based on "white supremacy.")

1948

January   Morris Ballen purchases the Gotham label of Philadelphia.

February   "Television" by the Zeke Manners Band (Victor 20-2730) is released, commenting on that new appliance's effect on the quality of life.

Wynonie Harris's "Good Rockin' Tonight" (King 4210) is released.

March   Nat King Cole's "Nature Boy" (Capitol 15054) is released.

April   Lionel Hampton's restyling of the 1931 Duke Ellington piece "Rockin' in Rhythm" (Decca 24415) is released. *Billboard* notes its "wild sax solos" and its "heavy handed rhythm."

May

Brownie McGhee's R&B tribute to Jackie Robinson of the Brooklyn Dodgers and Larry Dobey of the Cleveland Indians, "Robbie-Dobie Boogie" (Savoy 5550), is released. "It Jumps, It's Made, It Rocks, It Rolls," proclaims the Savoy advertisement in the May 22 issue of *Billboard.*

June

During the second week of the month, Wynonie Harris's "Good Rockin' Tonight" hits Number 1 on the R&B charts.

On the 21st, at its dealers' convention in Atlantic City, Columbia introduces its new $33^1/_3$-rpm microgroove discs. The company's initial LP catalogue, made public the following week, consists mostly of classical works, with *The Voice of Frank Sinatra* (CL 6001) as a notable exception.

July

Wild Bill Moore's "We're Gonna Rock" (Savoy 666) is released. In its review on the 17th, *Billboard* declares that "Paul Williams' baritone sax is featured, but not to advantage as he honks, shrieks and makes unmusical noises."

Joe Lutcher's "Rockin' Boogie" (Specialty 303) is released.

Bill Haley receives his first notice from the press. His record "Four Leaf Clover Blues" (Cowboy 1201) is described by *Billboard* as "dull, draggy . . . uninspired."

The Orioles' first record, "It's Too Soon to Know" (It's a Natural 5000), is released.

August

Capitol becomes the first record company to use magnetic tape.

On the 16th, Babe Ruth dies at Memorial Hospital in New York.

October

Amos Milburn's "Chicken Shack Boogie" (Aladdin 3014) is released.

"Shout 'n' Rock" by the Billy Williams Orchestra (Atlantic 852) is released.

November   Decca announces the formation of its Coral subsidiary.

Memphis Slim's "Rockin' the House" (Miracle 103) is released.

December   As Christmas week begins, Amos Milburn's "Chicken Shack Boogie" hits Number 1 on the R&B charts.

1949

January   Hank Williams's "Lovesick Blues" (MGM 10352) is released. In its review the following month, *Billboard* praises "Hank's razz-mah-tazz approach."

Hattie Noel's "Rockin' Jenny Jones" (MGM 10355) is released.

Johnny Otis's "Barrel House Boogie" (Excelsior 536), a follow-up to his "Good Boogdi Googi" (Excelsior 518), is released. *Billboard* declares it to be "One of the loudest records ever made."

Roy Brown's "Rockin' at Midnight" (DeLuxe 3212) is released.

February   The Hucklebuck dance craze flourishes. Paul Williams's original recording of "The Hucklebuck" (Savoy 683), rising to Number 1 on the R&B charts, is soon covered by Tommy Dorsey (RCA-Victor 3427) and Frank Sinatra (Columbia 38466), among others.

March   RCA-Victor introduces 45-rpm records.

As Hank Williams's "Lovesick Blues" ascends the country charts, Rex Griffin's 1937 Decca version of the song is reissued (Coral 64007).

May   Wild Bill Moore's "Rock and Roll" (Modern 20-674) is released.

Hank Williams's "Lovesick Blues" hits Number 1 on the country charts during the last week of the month, inspiring an R&B cover version by Eddie Crosby (Decca 46168).

June — Bill Nettles's "Hadacol Boogie" (Mercury 6190), the first of many songs celebrating the wonders of Dudley J. LeBlanc's patent elixer, is released.

Beginning with its June 15 issue, *Billboard* forsakes the terms "hillbilly" and "race" for "country and western" and "rhythm and blues."

July — Jimmy Preston's "Rock the Joint" (Gotham 188) is released.

August — Wynonie Harris's "All She Wants to Do Is Rock" (King 4304) is released.

The first issue of *Country Song Roundup* is published by the Charlton company of Derby, Connecticut.

September — The RKO movie *I Married a Communist* is released.

October — Ruth Brown's slow "Rocking Blues" (Atlantic 887) is released.

December — Fats Domino's first record, "The Fat Man" (Imperial 5058), is released.

Tiny Grimes's "Rock the House" (Atlantic 894) is released.

1950

January — Randy Wood's Dot Records of Gallatin, Tennessee, releases its first record, "Boogie Beat Rag" by the Tennessee Drifters (Dot 1001).

Macy Lela Henry of Houston inaugurates her Macy's Records company with Lester Williams's "Wintertime Blues" (Macy's 5000).

Johnny Lee Wills's "Rag Mop" (Bullet 696), the most-covered song of the year, is released. In ensuing weeks, versions follow by the Ames Brothers (Coral

60140), Ralph Flanagan (RCA-Victor 3212), Lionel Hampton (Decca 24855), Chuck Merrill (Bullet 322), and the one and only Doc Sausage (Regal 3251).

Roy Brown's two-part "Butcher Pete" (DeLuxe 1504) is released. "Not for airplay," cautions *Billboard*.

Connie Jordan's "I'm Gonna Rock" (Coral 65022) is released. *Billboard* opines that it "doesn't have the real gone spirit."

On the last day of the month, President Truman authorizes the production of the H-bomb.

February	Pee Wee Crayton's "Rockin' the Blues" (Modern 20-732) is released.
March	"Rock with It" by Johnny Moore's Three Blazers (RCA-Victor 50-0007) is released.

"Birmingham Bounce" by Hardrock Gunter and the Pebbles (Bama 104) is released. It is promptly covered by R&B singers Amos Milburn (Aladdin 3058) and Chuck Merrill (MGM 10695), and by country singers Pee Wee King (RCA-Victor 21-0332) and Red Foley (Decca 46234).

Intro Records is formed as the C&W subsidiary of Aladdin.

May Nat King Cole's "Mona Lisa" (Capitol 1010) is released.

Hank Williams's wife, Audrey, begins her ill-fated solo recording career with a Hadacol song, "Who Put the Pop in Grandma?" (Decca 6223).

Charles Olson, living in Washington, D.C., writes the first of the *Maximus* poems, "I, Maximus of Gloucester, to You."

Doc Sausage's "Sausage Rock" (Regal 3256) is released.

June Dudley J. LeBlanc's Hadacol Caravan, featuring Hank Williams, Chico Marx, and others, sets off on its 3,000-mile tour of the South.

Willard and Lillian McMurry start the Trumpet label in Jackson, Mississippi.

On the 27th, Truman orders the Air Force and Navy into Korea.

July Harry Choates, right behind Truman, warns "Korea, Here We Come" (Macy's 141).

New York radio personality Symphony Sid begins broadcasting his Saturday midnight-to-dawn WJZ program from Birdland.

Pee Wee Barnum's "Rockin' Rhythm" (Imperial 5097) is released.

September Modern Records forms the RPM label.

Piano Red's "Rockin' with Red" (RCA-Victor 50-0099) is released.

As anti-communism surges, Hank Williams, doing business as Luke the Drifter, reprimands Stalin with "No, No, Joe" (MGM 10806). His feelings are echoed by Arthur "Guitar Boogie" Smith's "Mr. Stalin, You're Eating Too High on the Hog" (MGM 10829).

November Arkie Shibley's "Hot Rod Race" (Gilt Edge 5015) is released.

Nat King Cole's "Frosty the Snowman" (Capitol 1203) is released.

Johnny Otis's "Rocking Blues" (Savoy 766) is released.

December The Dominoes' first record, "Do Something for Me" (Federal 12001), is released.

"Payola to disk jockeys is at an all-time peak," declares *Billboard* in its issue of the 23rd.

William Faulkner accepts the Nobel Prize for Literature.

January	Piney Brown's "How about Rocking with Me" (Apollo 423) is released.
	The first great rock 'n' roll album, *Party after Hours* (Aladdin 33-703), is released. The 10-inch LP includes recordings by Amos Milburn, Wynonie Harris, and others.
February	The Clovers sign with Atlantic.
	On the 4th, Cecil Gant dies at Hubbard Hospital in Nashville.
	Specialty Records begins issuing 45-rpm singles.
	Aladdin signs the Five Keys of Newport, Virginia.
	On the 28th, the preliminary report of Senator Estes Kefauver's investigation into organized crime is delivered. The outstanding moment of the hearings comes when Senator Charles Toby asks Virginia Hill, "Young lady, what makes you the favorite of the underworld?" and Virginia Hill answers, "Senator, I'm the best goddamned cocksucker in the world."
March	"Rockin'" by the Robins (Modern 20-807) is released.
	"Let's Rock a While" by Amos Milburn (Aladdin 3080) is released.
	"Rockin' after Hours" by Chuck Norris (Aladdin 3081) is released.
April	Joe Turner signs a three-year contract with Atlantic Records.
	"Rocket '88'" by Jackie Brenston and His Delta Cats (Chess 1458) is released.
	Capitol introduces its "optional-center" 45-rpm singles.

	Little Son Jackson's "Rockin' and Rollin'" (Imperial 5113) is released.
May	The Dominoes' "Sixty-Minute Man" (Federal 12022) hits the R&B charts.
	Bob Lamm's "That's When Your Heartaches Begin" (Dot 1050) is released.
	Columbia revives the Okeh label. Among the first acts signed to Okeh are the Treniers.
June	On the 28th, "Amos 'n' Andy" (CBS) is first telecast.
July	Peppermint Harris's "I Got Loaded" (Aladdin 3097) is released.
	Harmonica Frank's "Swamp Root" (Chess 1473) is released.
	On the 27th, the Korean War ends.
August	The Dominoes' "Sixty-Minute Man" crosses over to the pop charts.
	Alan Freed begins broadcasting his "Moondog Rock and Roll Party" over WJW in Cleveland, Ohio.
	Ernie Young of Nashville starts the Nashboro label.
October	Hank Williams signs a five-year movie deal with MGM.
	On the 26th, Rocky Marciano beats Joe Louis in eight rounds at Madison Square Garden in New York.
December	Little Richard's first record, "Taxi Blues" (RCA-Victor 47-4392), is released.

1952

January	H-Bomb Ferguson's "Good Lovin'" (Savoy 830) is released.

Dana Andrews is featured in the ZIV radio drama, "I Was a Communist for the F.B.I."

The TV Dinner is introduced by C. A. Swanson & Son of Omaha, Nebraska. Its entree is turkey, and it sells for $1.09.

March   The Royals' first record, "Every Beat of My Heart" (Federal 12064), is released.

April   Bill Haley's version of "Rock the Joint" (Essex 303) is released.

May   Sheriff Tex Davis adds a "Prayer Time" to his nightly radio show on WLOW in Norfolk, Virginia.

June   "Rock, Rock, Rock" by Willis "Gator Tail" Jackson (Atlantic 967) is released.

As Eisenhower and Stevenson campaign against each other, Louis Jordan's "Jordan for President" (Decca 28225) is released.

July   Louis Prima's version of "One Mint Julep" (Columbia 39823) is released.

The Onyx Publishing Company, a subsidiary of the Charlton organization of Derby, Connecticut, begins the publication of *Rhythm and Blues* magazine.

Hank Williams leaves the cast of the WSM "Grand Ole Opry."

August   The Treniers' "Rockin' on Sunday Night" (Okeh 6904) is released.

September   "Really Real" by Viola Watkins & Otis Blackwell (Jubilee 5095) is released.

On the 23rd, Rocky Marciano wins the world heavyweight title with a 13th-round knockout against Jersey Joe Walcott in Philadelphia.

Excello Records is formed as a subsidiary of Nashboro.

October	"Rock Me All Night Long" by the Ravens (Mercury 8291) is released.
	Ray Charles's first Atlantic record, "Roll with My Baby" (Atlantic 976), is released.
	Okeh Records signs Big Maybelle Smith.
	RCA-Victor introduces Orthophonic Sound and EP albums.
	Luke McDaniels's "Whoa, Boy!" (Trumpet 184) is released.
	"We're Gonna Rock This Joint" by the Jackson Brothers Orchestra (RCA-Victor 20-5004) is released.
	On the 20th, Hank Williams marries Miss Billie Jones of Bossier City, Louisiana, on the stage of the New Orleans Municipal Auditorium. Ticket prices range from $1 to $2.80, and more than 14,000 people attend.
November	Sam Phillips's Sun Records of Memphis releases its first single, "Blues in My Condition" by Jackie Boy and Little Walter (Sun 174).
	The first hydrogen device is exploded at Eniwetok Atoll in the Pacific.
	Hank Williams's "I'll Never Get Out of This World Alive" (MGM 11366) is released.
	Amos Milburn's "Rock, Rock, Rock" (Aladdin 3159) is released.
December	Lester Bihari of RPM starts the Meteor label in Memphis.
	Rockin' Records is formed in Los Angeles.
	Coral Records revives the Brunswick label.

January   In the first hours of the new year, near Oak Hill, West Virginia, twenty-nine-year-old Hank Williams dies in the back seat of a car en route to Canton, Ohio. His funeral service, held in Montgomery, Alabama, on the 4th, is the largest in the history of that city. "They came from everywhere," reports the Montgomery *Advertiser* the next day, "dressed in their Sunday best, babies in their arms, hobbling on crutches and canes, Negroes, Jews, Catholics, Protestants, small children, and wrinkled faced old men and women. Some brought their lunch. . . ."

"The Death of Hank Williams" by Jack Cardell (King 1172), issued at mid-month, is the first of the Hank Williams "tribute" records. It is soon followed by "Hank Williams Will Live Forever" by Johnnie and Jack (RCA-Victor 47-5164), "Tribute to Hank Williams" by Joe Rumore with J. T. Adams and the Men of Texas (Republic 100), "In Memory of Hank Williams" by Arthur Smith (MGM 11433), "The Life of Hank Williams" by Hawkshaw Hawkins (King 1174), "The Death of Hank Williams" by Jimmie Logsdon (Decca 28584), "That Heaven Bound Train" by Johnny Ryon (Coral 60148), and "The Last Letter" by Jimmy Swan (MGM 11450).

By the end of the month, a legal battle over Hank Williams's estate breaks out among Audrey Williams, Billie Jones Williams, and the late singer's mother, Mrs. W. W. Stone of Montgomery.

"Real Rock Drive" by Bill Haley and Haley's Comets (Essex 310) is released.

"You're a Heartbreaker" by Jimmie Heap (Capitol 2294) is released.

February   "Hound Dog" by Willie Mae Thornton (Peacock 1612) is released.

March   On the 5th, Joseph Stalin dies. This event is celebrated by Buddy Hawk's "The Death of Joe Stalin

(Good Riddance)" (Atlantic 7074) and Ray Anderson's "Stalin Kicked the Bucket" (Kentucky 573).

Frank Sinatra signs with Capitol.

Rufus Thomas's "Bear Cat" (Sun 181), a comical response to Willie Mae Thornton's "Hound Dog," is released. *Billboard* declares it to be "the fastest answer song yet to hit the market."

Abbott and Costello Go to Mars is released by Universal.

April	"Crazy, Man, Crazy" by Bill Haley and Haley's Comets (Essex 321) is released.

On the 25th, a Superior Court judge in Hollywood appoints Mrs. Mary Stein and Mrs. Adelyn Stoller, the mothers of the twenty-year-old authors of "Hound Dog"—Jerry Leiber and Mike Stoller—to be their sons' legal guardians.

May   "THE ONE AND ONLY! AUDREY (Mrs. Hank) WILLIAMS * THE GIRL FOR WHOM THE LATE, GREAT HANK WILLIAMS WROTE HIS FAMOUS SONGS!" is, according to an advertisement in the May 2 *Billboard*, "Now available as a single or with her own all-star show for auditoriums, parks, fairs, theatres, T.V."

Bill Haley's "Crazy, Man, Crazy" hits the pop charts during the second week of the month.

Clyde McPhatter quits as the lead singer of the Dominoes, forms the Drifters, and signs with Atlantic.

June   Between middleweight titles, Sugar Ray Robinson makes his recording debut with "Knock Him Down, Whiskey" (King 4641).

Lucky Joe Almond's "Rock Me" (Trumpet 199) is released.

August   The Charms' first record, "Heaven Only Knows" (Rockin' 516), is released.

The Spaniels' first record, "Baby, It's You" (Chance 1141), is released.

The Flairs sign with Flair Records.

Country singer Eddy Arnold and Col. Tom Parker, his manager since 1945, end their association. Parker's new protégé is Tommy Sands, recently signed to RCA-Victor as a country singer.

September   Clyde McPhatter and the Drifters' first record, "Money Honey" (Atlantic 1006), is released.

Webb Pierce's "There Stands the Glass" (Decca 28834) is released.

"Kinsey's Book" by Talkin' Charlie Aldrich (Intro 6083) is released, commenting on the effects of the recently published *Sexual Behaviour in the Human Female.*

October   The formation of Epic Records ("with Radial Sound") is announced.

Capitol introduces its "Special Hi-Fi" line of classical albums.

The Moonglows, the Cleveland group managed by Alan Freed, are signed to Chance Records.

Otis Blackwell's "Daddy Rollin' Stone" (Jay-Dee 784) is released.

Johnny Otis's "Rock Me Baby" (Peacock 1625) is released.

Bobby Blue Bland's "No Blow, No Show" (Duke 115) is released.

Sam Butera's "Easy Rocking" (RCA-Victor 20-5469) is released.

Dean Martin's "That's Amore" (Capitol 2589) is released.

Betty Hutton's "Hot Dog! That Made Him Mad" (Capitol 2608) is released.

Illinois Jacquet's "Sittin' and Rockin'" (Clef 89084) is released.

November	Louis Jordan announces that he will sign with Aladdin when his Decca contract expires on New Year's Day.

Louis Prima's first Jubilee record, "Man, Dig That Crazy Chick" (Jubilee 6054), is released.

"Mystery Train" by Little Junior's Blue Flames (Sun 192) is released.

"Raid on the After Hour Joint" by Jimmie Coe and His Gay Cats of Rhythm (States 129) is released.

December	As 3-D movies such as *It Came from Outer Space* and *House of Wax* captivate our noble democracy, "My Baby's 3-D" by Billy Ward and the Dominoes (Federal 12162) is released.

1954

January	On the 4th, a few days before his nineteenth birthday, Elvis Presley pays four dollars to make an acetate-disc record at Sam Phillips's Memphis Recording Service.

On the 21st, the first atomic-powered submarine, the *Nautilus*, is launched at Groton, Connecticut.

February	"X" Records is formed by RCA.

Hickory Records is founded in Nashville.

"Work with Me, Annie" by the Royals (Federal 12169) is released.

"Gee" by the Crows (Rama 5) is released.

"I'm Your Hoochie Koochie Man" by Muddy Waters (Chess 1560) is released.

April	On the 5th, Major Donald Kehoe of the U.S. Marine Corps appears on "The Betty White Show" (NBC) and

accuses the Air Force of a flying-saucer cover-up. "Within the next few months," he predicts, "the whole flying-saucer story will break open, with an announcement probably from the White House."

Joe Turner's "Shake, Rattle and Roll" (Atlantic 1026) is released.

The Spark label of Los Angeles, owned in part by Jerry Leiber and Mike Stoller, releases its first single, "Farewell" by Willie and Ruth (Spark 101).

Atlantic Records introduces the Cat label.

On the 22nd, Senator Joseph McCarthy begins his televised hearings into purported Communist influences in the U.S. Army.

Savoy Records signs Nappy Brown, formerly the lead singer with the Selah Jubilee Singers.

"Sh-Boom" by the Chords (Cat 104) is released.

May

On the 1st, at the Newark Armory, Alan Freed holds his first East Coast dance concert. The show's acts—the Clovers, Muddy Waters, Charles Brown, Sam Butera, Arnett Cobb, and others—cost Freed less than $3,500, but draw a crowd of more than 10,000 people, who pay two dollars each to get in.

"(We're Gonna) Rock Around the Clock" by Bill Haley and His Comets (Decca 29124) is released.

On the 7th, Clyde McPhatter is drafted into the Army.

Saul Bihari's Modern and RPM labels, Joe Bihari's Flair, and Jules Bihari's Crown consolidate their facilities into a new recording, manufacturing, and office complex in Culver City.

RCA-Victor introduces its CT-100 Compatible Color TV, which sells for $1,000.

On the 17th, the U.S. Supreme Court rules unanimously that racial segregation in public schools is unconstitutional.

Howlin' Wolf's "Rockin' Daddy" (Chess 1566) is released.

Art Carney's "Song of the Sewer" (Columbia 40242) is released.

On the 29th, *Billboard* writer Bob Rolontz observes in an editorial, "The youth movement that swept pop records only a few years ago appears to have dissipated itself during 1953 and especially during 1954."

George Jones's "Play It Cool, Man, Play It Cool" (Starday 146) is released.

Dallas Frazier's "Space Command" (Capitol 2813) is released.

"Riot in Cell Block No. 9" by the Robins (Spark 103) is released, while Don Siegel's *Riot in Cell Block 11*, the movie that inspired it, is still showing in neighborhood theatres.

"Sexy Ways" by the Midnighters (Federal 12185) is released.

June   Bill Haley's version of "Shake, Rattle and Roll" (Decca 29204) is released.

July   Mercury becomes the first company to send out 45-rpm D.J. singles, rather than 78s, to radio stations and reviewers.

Harmonica Frank's "Rockin' Chair Daddy" (Sun 205) is released.

On the 17th and 18th, the Newport Festival of American Jazz is held.

Lucky Joe Almond's "Gonna Roll and Rock" (Trumpet 221) is released.

"Rock, Roll, Ball and Wail" by Big Dave and His Orchestra (Capitol 2884) is released.

Elvis Presley's first record, "That's All Right" (Sun 209), is released at the end of the month.

August	"Annie Had a Baby" by the Midnighters (Federal 12195) is released.
	Alan Freed begins broadcasting nightly over WINS in New York.
	The New York *Daily Mirror* claims that the Mafia is taking over the American Society of Composers, Authors, and Publishers.
	Joe Turner and Ruth Brown are filmed for Willie Bryant's "Showtime at the Apollo" TV program.
	Ed Mesner opens an Aladdin Records office in New York. Jesse Stone is hired to run the company's Lamp subsidiary.
	"Earth Angel" by the Penguins (DooTone 348) is released.
	"Blue Moon of Kentucky," the flip side of Elvis Presley's first record, appears on the Memphis C&W chart for the week ending August 18.
September	"Hearts of Stone" by the Charms (DeLuxe 6062) is released.
October	Muddy Waters's "I'm Ready" (Chess 1579) is released.
	On the night of the 16th, Elvis Presley performs on the KWKH "Louisiana Hayride" in Shreveport.
November	Arthur Gunter's "Baby, Let's Play House" (Excello 2047) is released.
	"Open Up the Doghouse (Two Cats Are Comin' In)" by Dean Martin and Nat King Cole (Capitol 2985) is released.
	Jack Clement's "I Can't Say Nothin' at All" (Sheraton 1002) is released.
	"Ko Ko Mo" by Gene and Eunice (Combo 64) is released.

Rosemary Clooney's "Mambo Italiano" (Columbia 40361) is banned by ABC, which claims that the record does not meet "standards of good taste."

December Marty Robbins's version of "That's All Right" (Columbia 21351) is released.

Neshui Ertegun joins his brother, Ahmet, at Atlantic Records.

Malcolm Yelvington's "Drinkin' Wine Spo-Dee-O-Dee" (Sun 211) is released.

On Christmas Eve, twenty-five-year-old Johnny Ace blows his brains out.

1955

January Johnny Ace's "Pledging My Love" (Duke 136) is released, and is recommended by *Billboard* as "This Week's Best Buy." Varetta Dillard's "tribute" record, "Johnny Has Gone" (Savoy 1153), is first, followed by Johnny Moore's Blazers' "Why, Johnny, Why" c/w Frankie Irwin's "Johnny Ace's Last Letter" (Hollywood 1031), the Five Wings' "Johnny Has Gone" (King 4778), the Rovers' "Salute to Johnny Ace" (Music City 780), Johnny Fuller's "Johnny Ace's Last Letter" (Aladdin 3278), and "In Memory" by Marie Adams and the Johnny Otis Orchestra (Peacock 1649).

February Anisteen Allen's "Fujiyama Mama" (Capitol 3048) is released.

Stormy Herman's "Trouble Blues" (DooTone 358) is released.

March Bo Diddley's first record, "Bo Diddley" (Checker 814), is released.

Charlie Feathers's "Peepin' Eyes" (Flip 503) is released.

Blackboard Jungle is released. Bosley Crowther of the *New York Times* questions whether the movie is "a desirable stimulant to spread before the young." Clare Booth Luce, ambassador to France, demands that it be withdrawn as an entry at the Venice Film Festival. The Shelby County Board of Censors bans it from being shown in Memphis. Bill Haley's "Rock Around the Clock," the film's theme song, is reissued by Decca.

April   Elvis Presley's version of "Baby, Let's Play House" (Sun 217) is released.

July   "Maybelline" by Chuck Berry (Chess 1604) is released.

August   Atco Records is formed as a subsidiary of Atlantic.

               George Jones's "Why, Baby, Why" (Starday 202) is released.

               "Whole Lotta Shakin' Goin' On" by Big Maybelle (Okeh 7060) is released.

September   Elvis Presley's last Sun record, "Mystery Train" (Sun 223), is released.

October   On the 30th, Ezra Pound turns seventy in the nuthouse.

November   On the 26th, Elvis Presley, now under the general management of Col. Tom Parker, signs a three-year-plus-options contract in New York with RCA-Victor. Sam Phillips is paid close to $40,000 to relinquish his contract with Elvis (which has another year to run) along with all of Presley's Sun recordings. "Mystery Train" is reissued (RCA-Victor 6357), and Presley's first RCA session is scheduled for January 5 in Nashville.

December   Fuck it, Doc Sausage figures.

ARCHAEOLOGIA ROCKOLA

Archaeologia Rockola

The discographies that follow have been arranged according to release dates. This has not been an easy task. The less respectable tributaries of popular music were for the most part ignored when these records were made. They were not, as they are today, thought to be an important part of that thing called culture. For better or for worse, rock 'n' roll was not something to be taken seriously. No one chronicled it, no one wrote about it, no one thought of preserving it. To date these records, trade weeklies and record company catalogues of the period, along with existing discographies—and of course the records themselves—had to be exhaustively examined. Lost were uncounted days that could have been spent at the track. But I think this sort of discography is more enlightening, and certainly more digestible, than that composed of recording dates and matrix numbers, blank spaces and question marks. It is only when a record—or a book, a movie, a poem, a new brand of deodorant, whatever—is put on the cultural block that it takes on meaning for anyone beyond its maker. Knowing when it was put on the block helps to place it in historical context.

Most of these discographies cover their subjects' recording careers from their beginnings to the end of 1956—if they lasted that long. (Nineteen fifty-six has been chosen as the cut-off year because rock 'n' roll had by then—depending on how one looks at it—either subsumed or been subsumed by the mainstream.) Four exceptions have been made: Nat King Cole and Louis Prima, for reasons given in the introductory notes to their discographies, and Jay Hawkins and Wanda Jackson, who came along later than the rest, and whose discographies have been accordingly extended here by a year. All pertinent albums released up to and including 1958 have been listed. In a seizure of common sense, I have omitted a very few records which are not known beyond doubt to exist. (There is purported to be a 1949 Bill Haley record on the Center label, for instance; but I do not know anyone who has ever seen a copy of it.)

Many of these records are rare. Much of this music, however, is reissued periodically by companies great and small (but mostly small) in America, England, Europe, and Japan. These reissue albums tend to become available and to go out of print with equal suddenness. To find out what is available at any given time, the best source in the world is probably Down Home Music, Inc. (10341 San Pablo Avenue, El Cerrito, California 94530), which publishes catalogues regularly and does business the right way.

JOHNNY ACE

DUKE 102 (May 1952)
 My Song
 Follow the Rule
DUKE 107 (December 1952)
 Cross My Heart
 Angel
DUKE 112 (June 1953)
 The Clock
 Aces Wild
DUKE 118 (November 1953)
 Saving My Love for You
 Yes Baby
DUKE 128 (May 1954)
 Please Forgive Me
 You've Been Gone So Long
DUKE 132 (September 1954)
 Never Let Me Go
 Burley Cutie
DUKE 136 (January 1955)
 Pledging My Love
 No Money
DUKE 144 (June 1955)
 How Can You Be So Mean
 Anymore
DUKE 148 (December 1955)
 So Lonely
 I'm Crazy Baby
DUKE 154 (July 1956)
 Still Love You So
 Don't You Know

ALBUMS

DUKE 70   (1955)
Memorial Album (10-inch LP)
DUKE 71   (1956)
Memorial Album (12-inch LP)

Duke also issued two Ace 45-rpm EPs, Nos. 80 and 81, in 1955.

JACKIE BRENSTON

This listing includes only those records on which Jackie Brenston sang. For details of those recordings on which Brenston played saxophone, see the "Ike Turner Discography, Part 1: You're Driving Me Insane, 1951–1959" in *Blues Unlimited* No. 140 (London, 1981).

Jackie Brenston and His Delta Cats
CHESS 1458   (April 1951)
   Rocket "88"
   Come Back Where You Belong
CHESS 1469   (June 1951)
   My Real Gone Rocket
   Tuckered Out
CHESS 1472   (July 1951)
   Independent Woman
   Juiced

Jackie Brenston and Edna McCraney
CHESS 1496   (January 1952)
   Hi Ho Baby
   Leo the Louse

Jackie Brenston and His Delta Cats
CHESS 1532   (June 1953)
   Starvation
   Blues Got Me Again

Jackie Brenston with Ike Turner's Kings of Rhythm
FEDERAL 12283   (October 1956)
   What Can It Be
   Gonna Wait for My Chance
FEDERAL 12291   (December 1956)
   The Mistreater
   Much Later

ROY BROWN

In 1948–49 Brown's first eight DeLuxe records were reissued, the initial digits of their catalogue numbers changed to 3 to conform with the label's new numerical system. Those reissues are not included here.

Roy Brown
GOLD STAR 636 (1946)
  Deep Sea Diver
  Bye Baby Bye
DeLUXE 1093 (September 1947)
  Good Rocking Tonight
  Lolly Pop Mama
DeLUXE 1098 (October 1947)
  Special Lesson No. 1
  Woman's a Wonderful Thing
DeLUXE 1107 (November 1947)
  Roy Brown's Boogie
  Please Don't Go
DeLUXE 1128 (December 1947)
  Mighty Mighty Man
  Miss Fanny Brown

Roy Brown and His Mighty-Mighty Men
DeLUXE 1154 (March 1948)
  'Long 'Bout Midnight
  Whose Hat Is That?
DeLUXE 1166 (June 1948)
  All My Love Belongs to You
  [reverse: not by Brown]
DeLUXE 1189 (September 1948)
  Miss Fanny Brown Returns
  Roy Brown's Boogie
DeLUXE 1198 (November 1948)
  'Fore Day in the Morning
  Rainy Weather Blues
DeLUXE 3212 (January 1949)
  Rockin' at Midnight
  Judgment Day Blues
DeLUXE 3226 (June 1949)
  Please Don't Go (Come Back, Baby)
  Riding High
DeLUXE 3300 (September 1949)
  Boogie at Midnight
  The Blues Got Me Again

DeLUXE 3301   (January 1950)
  Butcher Pete, Part 1
  Butcher Pete, Part 2
DeLUXE 3302   (February 1950)
  End of My Journey
  I Feel That Young Man's Rhythm
DeLUXE 3304   (April 1950)
  Hard Luck Blues
  New Rebecca
DeLUXE 3306   (June 1950)
  Love Don't Love Nobody
  Dreaming Blues
DeLUXE 3308   (August 1950)
  Cadillac Baby
  'Long About Sundown
DeLUXE 3311   (December 1950)
  Teenage Jamboree
  Double Crossin' Woman
DeLUXE 3312   (March 1951)
  Good Man Blues
  Sweet Peach
DeLUXE 3313   (April 1951)
  Beautician Blues
  Wrong Woman Blues
DeLUXE 3318   (June 1951)
  Train Time Blues
  Big Town
DeLUXE 3319   (September 1951)
  Good Rockin' Man
  Bar Room Blues
DeLUXE 3323   (February 1952)
  I've Got the Last Laugh Now
  Brown Angel

Roy Brown
KING 4602   (January 1953)
  Travelin' Man
  Hurry Hurry Back Baby
KING 4609   (February 1953)
  Grandpa Stole My Baby
  Money Can't Buy Love
KING 4627   (March 1953)
  Mr. Hound Dog's in Town
  Gamblin' Man
KING 4637   (May 1953)
  Old Age Boogie, Part 1
  Old Age Boogie, Part 2

KING 4654   (September 1953)
  Laughing but Crying
  Crazy Crazy Woman
KING 4669   (November 1953)
  A Fool in Love
  Caldonia's Wedding Day
KING 4684   (December 1953)
  Midnight Lover Man
  Letter from Home
KING 4689   (January 1954)
  Lonesome Lover
  Everything's All Right
KING 4704   (March 1954)
  Trouble at Midnight
  Bootleggin' Baby
KING 4715   (May 1954)
  This Is My Last Goodbye
  Up Jumped the Devil
KING 4722   (June 1954)
  Don't Let It Rain
  No Love at All
KING 4731   (August 1954)
  Ain't It a Shame
  My Gal from Kokomo
KING 4743   (October 1954)
  Worried Life Blues
  Black Diamond
KING 4761   (December 1954)
  Fanny Brown Got Married
  Queen of Diamonds
KING 4816   (July 1955)
  Letter to My Baby
  Shake 'Em Up Baby
KING 4834   (October 1955)
  My Little Angel Child
  She's Gone Too Long

ALBUMS

KING 536   (1956)
Rock 'n' Roll Dance Party (one cut by Brown)
KING 607   (1958)
Battle of the Blues (seven cuts by Brown)
KING 627   (1958)
Battle of the Blues, Vol. 2 (six cuts by Brown)

King also released two Roy Brown–Wynonie Harris *Battle of the Blues* 45-rpm EPs, Nos. 250 and 254, in 1958.

THE CLOVERS

RAINBOW 122   (December 1950)
   Yes Sir, That's My Baby
   When You Come Back to Me
ATLANTIC 934   (April 1951)
   Don't You Know I Love You
   Skylark
ATLANTIC 944   (August 1951)
   Fool, Fool, Fool
   Needless
ATLANTIC 963   (February 1952)
   One Mint Julep
   Middle of the Night
ATLANTIC 969   (May 1952)
   Ting-a-Ling
   Wonder Where My Baby's Gone
ATLANTIC 977   (September 1952)
   I Played the Fool
   Hey, Miss Fannie
ATLANTIC 989   (February 1953)
   Crawlin'
   Yes, It's You
ATLANTIC 1000   (June 1953)
   Good Lovin'
   Here Goes a Fool
ATLANTIC 1010   (October 1953)
   Comin' On
   The Feeling Is So Good
ATLANTIC 1022   (February 1954)
   Lovey Dovey
   Little Mama
ATLANTIC 1035   (June 1954)
   Your Cash Ain't Nothin' but Trash
   I've Got My Eyes on You
ATLANTIC 1046   (October 1954)
   I Confess
   All Rightie, Oh Sweetie
ATLANTIC 1052   (December 1954)
   Blue Velvet
   If You Love Me
ATLANTIC 1060   (May 1955)
   Love Bug
   In the Morning Time
ATLANTIC 1073   (August 1955)
   Nip Sip
   If I Could Be Loved by You

ATLANTIC 1083   (January 1956)
  Devil or Angel
  Hey, Baby Doll
ATLANTIC 1094   (May 1956)
  Love, Love, Love
  Your Tender Lips
ATLANTIC 1107   (August 1956)
  From the Bottom of My Heart
  Bring Me Love
ATLANTIC 1118   (November 1956)
  Baby, Baby, Oh My Darling
  A Lonely Fool

ALBUMS

ATLANTIC 1248   (December 1956)
  The Clovers
ATLANTIC 8001   (1957)
  The Greatest Rock & Roll (one cut by the Clovers)
ATLANTIC 8009   (1957)
  The Clovers
ATLANTIC 8010 (1957)
  Rock & Roll Forever (two cuts by the Clovers)

Atlantic also issued two Clovers 45-rpm EPs, No. 504 (1953) and No. 537 (1954). Both were called *The Clovers Sing*.

NAT KING COLE

Those recordings Cole made in 1936, 1939, and 1940, before he began to sing, are not included here. And while he continued to record prolifically after 1948, this listing ends with "Nature Boy," his immense hit of that year; for by then Cole's records had little relevancy to rock 'n' roll.

The King Cole Trio
DECCA 8520   (March 1941)
  Sweet Lorraine
  This Side Up
DECCA 8535   (April 1941)
  Honeysuckle Rose
  Gone with the Draft
DECCA 8541   (May 1941)
  Babe
  Early Morning Blues

DECCA 8556   (June 1941)
  Scotchin' with the Soda
  Slow Down
DECCA 8571   (September 1941)
  This Will Make You Laugh
  Hit the Ramp
DECCA 8592   (December 1941)
  I Like to Riff
  Stop, the Red Light's On

The King Cole Quartet
AMMOR 108   (January 1942)
  I Like to Riff
  On the Sunny Side of the Street
AMMOR 109   (January 1942)
  Black Spider
  By the River Sainte Marie

The King Cole Trio
DECCA 8604   (March 1942)
  Call the Police
  Are You Fer It?
DECCA 8630   (July 1942)
  That Ain' Right
  Hit That Jive, Jack

The King Cole Quintet
DISC 2010   (1942)
  Heads
  It Had to Be You
DISC 2011   (1942)
  Pro-sky
  I Can't Give You Anything but Love

The King Cole Trio
EXCELSIOR 102   (November 1942)
  Vom Vim Veedle
  All for You
CAPITOL 139   (October 1943)   [reissue of Excelsior 102]
  All for You
  Vom Vim Veedle
PREMIER 100   (April 1944)
  F.S.T.
  My Lips Remember Your Kisses
CAPITOL 154   (April 1944)
  Straighten Up and Fly Right
  I Can't See for Lookin'

PREMIER 103   (June 1944)
  Got a Penny
  Let's Pretend
CAPITOL 169   (September 1944)
  Gee, Baby, Ain't I Good to You
  I Realize Now
ATLAS 100   (September 1944)   [reissue of Premier 100]
  F.S.T.
  My Lips Remember Your Kisses
ATLAS 102   (October 1944)   [reissue of Premier 103]
  Got a Penny
  Let's Pretend
EXCELSIOR 105   (December 1944)
  I'm Lost
  Pitchin' Up a Boogie
EXCELSIOR 106   (December 1944)
  Beautiful Moons Ago
  Let's Spring One
ATLAS 106   (May 1945)   [reissue of Premier 103]
  Got a Penny
  Let's Pretend
CAPITOL 192   (May 1945)
  If You Can't Smile and Say Yes
  Bring Another Drink
CAPITOL 208   (July 1945)
  I'm a Shy Guy
  I Tho't You Ought to Know
CAPITOL 224   (November 1945)
  Come to Baby, Do
  The Frim Fram Sauce
CAPITOL 239   (February 1946)
  Sweet Georgia Brown
  It Is Better to Be by Yourself
SAVOY 600   (April 1946)   [reissue of Ammor 108]
  I Like to Riff
  On the Sunny Side of the Street
CAPITOL 256   (April 1946)
  (Get Your Kicks on) Route 66
  Everyone Is Sayin' Hello Again
CAPITOL 274   (June 1946)
  You Call It Madness (But I Call It Love)
  Oh, But I Do
CAPITOL 304   (September 1946)
  (I Love You) For Sentimental Reasons
  The Best Man
CAPITOL 311   (October 1946)
  The Christmas Song
  In the Cool of the Evening

CAPITOL 328 (November 1946)
  But She's My Buddy's Chick
  That's the Beginning of the End
CAPITOL 356 (January 1947)
  I Want to Thank You Folks
  You Should Have Told Me
CAPITOL 393 (April 1947)
  You Didn't Learn That in School
  Meet Me at No Special Place
CAPITOL 418 (May 1947)
  Come In Out of the Rain
  Can You Look Me in the Eyes?
DECCA 25109 (June 1947)
  That Ain't Right   [reissue of Decca 8630]
  Scotchin' with the Soda   [reissue of Decca 8556]
CAPITOL 437 (July 1947)
  That's What
  Naughty Angeline

Johnny Mercer and the King Cole Trio
CAPITOL 15000 (October 1947)
  Harmony
  Save the Bones for Henry Jones ('Cause Henry Don't Eat No Meat)

The King Cole Trio
CAPITOL 15011 (October 1947)
  Those Things Money Can't Buy
  Now He Tells Me
CAPITOL 15019 (November 1947)
  I Feel So Smoochie
  What'll I Do

Johnny Mercer and the King Cole Trio
CAPITOL 15026 (December 1947)
  My Baby Likes to Be-Bop
  You Can't Make Money Dreaming

The King Cole Trio
CAPITOL 15036 (February 1948)
  I've Only Myself to Blame
  The Geek
CAPITOL 15054 (March 1948)
  Nature Boy
  Lost April

ALBUMS

CAPITOL A-8   (September 1944)
  The King Cole Trio
CAPITOL BD-29   (June 1946)
  The King Cole Trio, Vol. 2
ALADDIN A-1   (July 1946)
  King Cole-Lester Young-Red Callander Trio
CAPITOL CE-18   (1947)
  Then Came Swing (Cole plays piano on two sides)
CAPITOL CE-19   (1947)
  This Modern Age (one side by Cole)
CAPITOL CC-59   (December 1947)
  The King Cole Trio, Vol. 3
CAPITOL DC-89   (July 1948)
  King Cole for Kids
CAPITOL CC-139   (June 1949)
  The King Cole Trio, Vol. 4

Capitol eventually reissued these albums in LP form, along with many 45-rpm EPs drawn from them, beginning in 1949.

THE DOMINOES

The Dominoes
FEDERAL 12001   (December 1950)
  Do Something for Me
  Chicken Blues
FEDERAL 12010   (January 1951)
  Harbor Lights
  No! Says My Heart

Little Esther with the Dominoes
FEDERAL 12016   (February 1951)
  Other Lips, Other Arms
  The Deacon Moves In

The Dominoes
Federal 12022   (April 1951)
  Sixty-Minute Man
  I Can't Escape from You

Little Esther with the Dominoes
FEDERAL 12036   (November 1951)
  Heart to Heart
  [reverse: Esther without the Dominoes]

The Dominoes
FEDERAL 12039   (November 1951)
  Weeping Willow Blues
  I Am with You
FEDERAL 12059   (February 1952)
  That's What You're Doing to Me
  When the Swallows Come Back to Capistrano
FEDERAL 12068   (April 1952)
  Have Mercy Baby
  Deep Sea Blues
FEDERAL 12072   (May 1952)
  That's What You're Doing to Me   [reissue of Federal 12059]
  Love, Love, Love

Billy Ward and His Dominoes
FEDERAL 12105   (October 1952)
  No Room
  I'd Be Satisfied
FEDERAL 12106   (November 1952)
  Yours Forever
  I'm Lonely
FEDERAL 12114   (December 1952)
  Pedal Pushin' Papa
  The Bells
FEDERAL 12129   (April 1953)
  These Foolish Things Remind Me of You
  Don't Leave Me This Way
FEDERAL 12139   (July 1953)
  You Can't Keep a Good Man Down
  Where Now, Little Heart?
KING 1280   (October 1953)
  Rags to Riches
  Don't Thank Me
KING 1281   (November 1953)
  Christmas in Heaven
  Ringing in a Brand New Year
FEDERAL 12162   (December 1953)
  My Baby's 3-D
  Till the Real Thing Comes Along
FEDERAL 12178   (March 1954)
  Tootsie Roll
  The Outskirts of Town
KING 1342   (March 1954)
  A Little Lie
  Tenderly
FEDERAL 12184   (May 1954)
  Handwriting on the Wall
  One Moment with You

KING 1364   (May 1954)
  Three Coins in the Fountain
  Lonesome Road
KING 1368   (June 1954)
  Little Things Mean a Lot
  I Really Don't Want to Know
FEDERAL 12193   (August 1954)
  Above Jacob's Ladder
  Little Black Train
JUBILEE 5163   (September 1954)
  Come to Me, Baby
  Gimme, Gimme, Gimme
FEDERAL 12209   (January 1955)
  Can't Do Sixty No More
  If I Never Get to Heaven
FEDERAL 12218   (April 1955)
  Cave Man
  Love Me Now or Let Me Go
KING 1492   (July 1955)
  Learnin' the Blues
  May I Never Love Again
JUBILEE 5213   (August 1955)
  Sweethearts on Parade
  Take Me Back to Heaven
KING 1502   (September 1955)
  Over the Rainbow
  Give Me You
FEDERAL 12263   (April 1956)
  Bobby Sox Baby
  How Long, How Long Blues
DECCA 29933   (May 1956)
  St. Therese of the Roses
  Home Is Where You Hang Your Heart
DECCA 30043   (September 1956)
  Will You Remember
  Come On, Snake, Let's Crawl
DECCA 30149   (December 1956)
  Evermore
  Half a Love

ALBUMS

DECCA 8621   (November 1957)
  Billy Ward and the Dominoes
LIBERTY 3056   (1957)
  Sea of Glass
LIBERTY 3083   (1958)
  Yours Forever

KING 548   (1958)
  Billy Ward and His Dominoes with Clyde McPhatter
KING 559   (1958)
  Clyde McPhatter with Billy Ward and His Dominoes

Federal issued three 45-rpm EPs by the group: *Billy Ward and His Dominoes* (Nos. 212 and 262) and *Billy Ward and His Dominoes Sing the All Time Hit Standards* (No. 269). Decca also issued an EP entitled *Billy Ward and His Dominoes* (No. 2549).

CECIL GANT

It should be noted that all of Gant's Four-Star records were originally recorded for Gilt-Edge in 1944–45 (the same man, Richard A. Nelson, ran both those Los Angeles labels), and that all his Dot releases were purchased from Bullet.

Pvt. Cecil Gant
GILT-EDGE 501   (September 1944)
  I Wonder
  Cecil's Boogie
GILT-EDGE 502   (February 1945)
  Wake Up, Cecil, Wake Up
  Boogie Blues
GILT-EDGE 503   (March 1945)
  Put Another Chair at the Table
  Cecil's Boogie No. 2
GILT-EDGE 504   (April 1945)
  I'll Remember You
  Cecil's Mop Mop
GILT-EDGE 505   (April 1945)
  The Grass Is Getting Greener Every Day
  Syncopated Boogie
GILT-EDGE 506   (May 1945)
  I'm Tired
  Are You Ready?
GILT-EDGE 507   (May 1945)
  You're Going to Cry
  Cecil Knows Better Now
GILT-EDGE 508   (June 1945)
  Lost Baby Blues
  Sooner or Later
GILT-EDGE 509   (June 1945)
  I Believe I Will
  Fit as a Fiddle
GILT-EDGE 510   (June 1945)
  Blues in L.A.
  When I Wanted You

GILT-EDGE 511   (June 1945)
  In a Little Spanish Town
  Hey Boogie
GILT-EDGE 512   (July 1945)
  Rhumba Boogie Woogie
  Little Baby, You're Running Wild
GILT-EDGE 513   (July 1945)
  Way Down
  Nothing Bothers Me
GILT-EDGE 514   (August 1945)
  What's on Your Worried Mind?
  I Gotta Girl
GILT-EDGE 515   (August 1945)
  Make Believable Girl
  Stuff You Gotta Watch
GILT-EDGE 516   (September 1945)
  Jam Jam Blues
  I Feel It
GILT-EDGE 517   (September 1945)
  Lightning Blues
  Solitude
GILT-EDGE 518   (September 1945)
  If I Had a Wish
  It's a Great Life
GILT-EDGE 519   (September 1945)
  Midnight on Central Avenue
  How Can I Sleep
BRONZE 117   (October 1945)
  I Wonder   [reissue of Gilt-Edge 501]
  My Last Goodbye
BRONZE 119   (October 1945)
  It's All Over Now
  Soft and Mellow
BRONZE 120   (October 1945)
  Cecil's Boogie   [reissue of Gilt-Edge 501]
  Goodbye
GILT-EDGE 525   (November 1945)
  Am I to Blame?
  Stella
GILT-EDGE 526   (November 1945)
  My Little Baby
  In the Evening When the Sun Goes Down
GILT-EDGE 534   (November 1945)
  Rainy Weather for Me
  Hit That Jive, Jack
GILT-EDGE 538   (January 1946)
  Jump, Jump, Jump
  Special Delivery

Cecil Gant

BULLET 250 (April 1946)
  Nashville Jumps
  Loose as a Goose
BULLET 255 (June 1946)
  Train Time Blues
  Sloppy Joe's
BULLET 256 (July 1946)
  Boogie Woogie Baby
  If It's True
BULLET 257 (September 1946)
  I'm All Alone Now
  Anna Mae
BULLET 258 (December 1946)
  Ninth Street Jive
  It's the Girl
BULLET 264 (February 1947)
  Boozie Boogie
  Every Minute of the Hour
BULLET 265 (April 1947)
  Go to Sleep, Little Baby
  My, My, My
BOP FEATURES 106 (August 1947)
  It's All Over, Darling [reissue of Bronze 119]
  I'm Traveling Alone
FOUR-STAR 1159 (September 1947) [reissue of Gilt-Edge 500]
  I Wonder
  Cecil Boogie
FOUR-STAR 1176 (September 1947) [reissue of Gilt-Edge 538]
  Jump, Jump, Jump
  Special Delivery
FOUR-STAR 1205 (November 1947) [reissue of Gilt-Edge 502]
  Wake Up, Cecil, Wake Up
  Boogie Blues
FOUR-STAR 1221 (December 1947)
  Killer Diller Boogie
  Rainy Weather for Me [reissue of Gilt-Edge 534]
FOUR-STAR 1243 (March 1948)
  Am I to Blame? [reissue of Gilt-Edge 525]
  Soft and Mellow [reissue of Bronze 119]
BULLET 272 (June 1948)
  I Wonder
  I Believe I'll Go Back Home
KING 4231 (June 1948)
  Why?
  Hogan's Alley

BULLET 280   (July 1948)
  Another Day, Another Dollar
  Three Little Girls
BULLET 289   (September 1948)
  I'm a Good Man, but a Poor Man
  Cecil's Jam Session
FOUR-STAR 1284   (November 1948)
  I'm Traveling Alone   [reissue of Bop Features 106]
  God Bless My Daddy
BULLET 299   (April 1949)
  I Ain't Gonna Cry Anymore
  Screwy Boogie
FOUR-STAR 1452   (March 1950)
  Coming Round the Mountain
  [reverse: by Ivory Joe Hunter]
IMPERIAL 5066   (March 1950)
  You'll Be Sorry
  When You Left Me, Baby
FOUR-STAR 1482   (June 1950)
  You're Going to Cry   [reissue of Gilt-Edge 507]
  I've Heard That Jive Before

Gunter Lee Carr
DECCA 48167   (June 1950)
  Goodnight Irene
  My House Fell Down
DECCA 48170   (July 1950)
  We're Gonna Rock
  Yesterday

Cecil Gant
DECCA 48171   (July 1950)
  Someday You'll Be Sorry
  Someday You'll Be Sorry   [recitation]
DOWN BEAT 209   (May 1949)
  Deal Yourself Another Hand
  All Because of You
BULLET 300   (June 1949)
  I Hate to Say Goodbye
  My Little Baby
FOUR-STAR 1339   (July 1949)
  Fare Thee, My Baby
  I'll Remember You
BULLET 313   (September 1949)
  Rose Room
  I'm Singing the Blues Today
FOUR-STAR 1377   (November 1949)
  Vibology
  Long Distance Call

BULLET 320   (December 1949)
  What's the Matter?
  You Can't Do Me Right
RECORD SHOP SPECIAL 1   (December 1949)   [reissue of Bullet 255]
  Train Time Blues
  Sloppy Joe's
FOUR-STAR 1526   (September 1950)
  My Baby Changed
  Can't Get You Off My Mind
DECCA 48185   (November 1950)
  It's Christmas Time Again
  Hello, Santa Claus
DOT 1016   (November 1950)
  Cryin' to Myself
  Nobody Loves You
DECCA 48190   (December 1950)
  Train Time Blues No. 2
  It Ain't Gonna Be Like That
DECCA 48200   (January 1951)
  Rock Little Baby
  Shot Gun Boogie
DOT 1030   (March 1951)
  Waiting for My Train
  Cindy Lou
IMPERIAL 5112   (April 1951)
  Blues by Cecil
  Come Home
DOT 1053   (May 1951)
  I'm Still in Love with You
  Alma
DECCA 48212   (May 1951)
  My Little Baby
  Don't You Worry
DOT 1069   (July 1951)
  Goodbye Blues
  Raining Blues
DECCA 48231   (August 1951)
  Owl Stew
  Playin' Myself the Blues
SWING TIME 209   (August 1951)   [reissue of Down Beat 209]
  Deal Yourself Another Hand
  All Because of You
FOUR-STAR 1561   (August 1951)
  Rocking the Boogie
  I Will Go on Lovin' You
FOUR-STAR 1584   (September 1951)
  Where I Belong
  Time Will Tell

DECCA 48249   (October 1951)
   God Bless My Daddy
   The Grass Is Gettin' Greener
DOT 1112   (February 1952)
   All by Myself
   It Hurts Me Too
SWING TIME 302   (June 1952)
   You're Going to Cry
   Baby, I'm Losing You
DOT 1121   (July 1952)   [reissue of Bullet 255]
   Train Time Blues
   Sloppy Joe's
FOUR-STAR 1606   (August 1952)
   I'm Losing You
   Peace and Love

ALBUM

SOUND 601
   The Incomparable Cecil Gant

Four-Star issued two Cecil Gant 45-rpm EPs, Nos. 24 and 25.

HARDROCK GUNTER

Hardrock Gunter and the Pebbles
BAMA 104   (March 1950)
   Birmingham Bounce
   How Can I Believe You Love Me
BAMA 201   (June 1950)
   Gonna Dance All Night
   Why Don't You Show Me That You Care

Hardrock Gunter
BULLET 725   (December 1950)
   The Little Things You Do
   My Bucket's Been Fixed
BAMA 202   (January 1951)
   Lonesome Blues
   Dad Gave My Hog Away
BULLET 727   (March 1951)
   Maybe, Baby, You'll Be True to Me
   Rifle Belts and Bayonets

DECCA 46300 (March 1951)
  Boogie Woogie on a Saturday Night
  Honky Tonk Blues
DECCA 46350 (July 1951)
  I've Done Gone Hog Wild
  I Believe That Mountain Music Is Here to Stay

Hardrock Gunter and Roberta Lee
DECCA 46363 (September 1951)
  Sixty-Minute Man
  Tennessee Blues

Hardrock Gunter
DECCA 46367 (September 1951)
  Dixieland Boogie
  If I Could Only Live My Dreams
DECCA 46383 (November 1951)
  Hesitation Boogie
  Don't You Agree
DECCA 46401 (January 1952)
  Silver and Gold
  The Senator from Tennessee
DECCA 28191 (May 1952)
  I'm Looking for Another You
  Honky Tonk Baby
MGM 11520 (May 1953)
  Like the Lovers Do
  Naptown, Indiana
DECCA 28932 (November 1953)
  You Played on My Piano
  Perfect Woman
SUN 201 (May 1954)
  Gonna Dance All Night
  Fallen Angel
KING 1416 (January 1955)
  First Last and Always Game of Love
  I Won't Tell Who's to Blame
KING 4858 (November 1955)
  Turn the Other Cheek
  Before My Time
SUN 248 (June 1956)
  Fiddle Bop
  Jukebox Help Me Find My Angel

Bill Haley and the Four Aces of Western Swing
COWBOY 1201   (July 1948)
   Four Leaf Clover Blues
   Too Many Parties and Too Many Pals
COWBOY 1202   (February 1949)
   Candy Kisses
   Tennessee Border

Bill Haley and the Saddle-Men
KEYSTONE 5101   (January 1950)
   Deal Me a Hand
   Ten Gallon Stetson (With a Hole in the Crown)
KEYSTONE 5102   (March 1950)
   I'm Not to Blame
   Susan Van Dusan

Bill Haley and R. Browne
COWBOY 1201   (October 1950)
   My Palomino and I
   My Sweet Little Girl from Nevada

Bill Haley and the Saddle-Men
ATLANTIC 727   (November 1950)
   Why Do I Cry Over You
   I'm Gonna Dry Every Tear with a Kiss
HOLIDAY 105   (July 1951)
   Rocket "88"
   Tearstains on My Heart
HOLIDAY 108   (August 1951)
   Green Tree Boogie
   Down Deep in My Heart

Bill and Loretta with the Saddlemen
HOLIDAY 110   (November 1951)
   Pretty Baby
   I'm Crying

Bill Haley and the Saddlemen
HOLIDAY 111   (November 1951)
   I Don't Want to Be Alone This Christmas
   Years Ago This Christmas
HOLIDAY 113   (January 1952)
   Juke Box Cannon Ball
   Sundown Boogie

ESSEX 303   (March 1952)
   Rock the Joint
   Icy Heart
ESSEX 305   (June 1952)
   Rocking Chair on the Moon
   Dance with a Dolly (With a Hole in Her Stocking)

Bill Haley and Haley's Comets
ESSEX 310   (January 1953)
   Real Rock Drive
   Stop Beatin' Round the Mulberry Bush
ESSEX 321   (April 1953)
   Crazy, Man, Crazy
   Whatcha Gonna Do
ESSEX 327
   Pat-a-Cake
   Fractured
ESSEX 332
   Live It Up
   Farewell, So Long, Goodbye
ESSEX 340
   I'll Be True
   Ten Little Indians
ESSEX 348
   Straight Jacket
   Chattanooga Choo-Choo

Bill Haley and His Comets
DECCA 29124   (April 1954)
   (We're Gonna) Rock Around the Clock
   Thirteen Women (And Only One Man in Town)
DECCA 29204   (June 1954)
   Shake, Rattle and Roll
   ABC Boogie
DECCA 29317   (October 1954)
   Dim Dim the Lights (I Want Some Atmosphere)
   Happy Baby
DECCA 29418   (January 1955)
   Mambo Rock
   Birth of the Boogie
DECCA 29552   (June 1955)
   Razzle-Dazzle
   Two Hound Dogs
ESSEX 399   (June 1955)
   Rock the Joint   [reissue of Essex 303]
   Farewell, So Long, Goodbye   [reissue of Essex 332]
DECCA 29713   (October 1955)
   Rock-a-Beatin' Boogie
   Burn That Candle

DECCA 29791   (December 1955)
  See You Later, Alligator
  The Paper Boy
DECCA 29870   (March 1956)
  The Saints Rock 'n' Roll
  R-O-C-K
DECCA 29948   (May 1956)
  Hot Dog, Buddy Buddy
  Rockin' through the Rye
DECCA 30028   (July 1956)
  Teenager's Mother (Are You Right?)
  Rip It Up
DECCA 30085   (September 1956)
  Rudy's Rock
  Blue Comet Blues
DECCA 30148   (November 1956)
  Don't Knock the Rock
  Choo Choo Ch'Boogie

ALBUMS

ESSEX 202   (1955)
  Rock with Bill Haley and the Comets
DECCA 5260   (1955)
  Shake, Rattle and Roll (10-inch LP)
DECCA 8225   (December 1955)
  Rock Around the Clock
DECCA 8315   (1956)
  He Digs Rock 'n' Roll (four cuts by Haley)
DECCA 8345   (June 1956)
  Rock 'n' Roll Stage Show
DECCA 8569   (1958)
  Rockin' the Oldies

In addition to these albums, both Essex and Decca issued various 45-rpm EPs: *Bill Haley's Dance Party* (Essex 102), *Rock with Bill Haley and the Comets* (Essex 117 and 118), *Shake, Rattle and Roll* (Decca 2168), *Dim, Dim the Lights* (Decca 2209), *Rock 'n' Roll* (Decca 2322), *He Digs Rock 'n' Roll* (Decca 2398), *Rock 'n' Roll Stage Show* (Decca 2416, 2417, and 2418), and *Rockin' the Oldies* (Decca 2532, 2533, and 2534).

Roy Hall and His Cohutta Mountain Boys
FORTUNE 126   (1949)
   Okee Doaks
   Dirty Boogie
FORTUNE 133   (December 1949)
   Never Marry a Tennessee Girl
   We Never Get Too Big to Cry
FORTUNE 139   (March 1950)
   Five Years in Prison [vocal by Frankie Brumbalough]
   My Freckle Face Gal [vocal by Bud White]

Roy Hall
BULLET 704   (April 1950)
   Mule Boogie
   Old Folks Jamboree
BULLET 712   (August 1950)
   Ain't You Afraid?
   Turn My Picture to the Wall
TENNESSEE 813   (1952)
   Back Up and Push
   Golden Slippers
TENNESSEE 835   (1952)
   John Henry
   Put On Your Old Gray Bonnet
DECCA 29697   (September 1955)
   Whole Lotta Shakin' Goin' On
   All by Myself
DECCA 29786   (December 1955)
   See You Later, Alligator
   Don't Stop Now
FORTUNE 521   (December 1955)
   Don't Ask Me No Questions
   Corrine Corrina
DECCA 29880   (January 1956)
   Blue Suede Shoes
   Luscious
DECCA 30060   (May 1956)
   Three Alley Cats
   Diggin' the Boogie

WYNONIE HARRIS

Lucky Millinder and His Orchestra
DECCA 18609   (July 1944)
  Hurry, Hurry
  [reverse: without Harris]
DECCA 18674 (April 1945)
  Who Threw the Whiskey in the Well?
  [reverse: without Harris]

Wynonie "(Mr. Blues)" Harris and Johnny Otis' All Stars
PHILO 103   (September 1945)
  Around the Clock, Part 1
  Around the Clock, Part 2
PHILO 104   (September 1945)
  Cock-A-Doodle-Doo
  Yonder Comes My Baby

Wynonie "Blues" Harris
APOLLO 360 (October 1945)
  Young Man's Blues
  Straighten Him Out
APOLLO 361   (October 1945)
  That's the Stuff You Gotta Watch
  Baby, Look at You
APOLLO 362   (October 1945)
  Wynonie's Blues
  Somebody Changed the Lock on My Door
APOLLO 363   (November 1945)
  She's Gone with the Wind
  Here Comes the Blues
APOLLO 372   (April 1946)
  Playful Baby
  Papa Tree Top

Wynonie (Mr. Blues) Harris
BULLET 251   (April 1946)
  Dig This Boogie
  Lightnin' Struck the Poor House
BULLET 252   (May 1946)
  My Baby's Barrel House
  Drinkin' by Myself

Wynonie Harris with the Hamp-Tone All Stars
HAMP-TONE 100   (May 1946)
  Hey Ba-Ba-Re-Bop, Part 1
  Hey Ba-Ba-Re-Bop, Part 2

HAMP-TONE 103   (May 1946)
  Good Morning Corinne
  In the Evenin' Blues

Wynonie "Blues" Harris
APOLLO 378   (November 1946)
  Time to Change Your Town
  Everybody's Boogie
APOLLO 381   (December 1946)
  Young and Wild
  Take Me Out of the Rain

Wynonie "Mr. Blues" Harris and His All Stars
ALADDIN 171   (January 1947)
  Mr. Blues Jumped the Rabbit
  Whiskey & Jelly Roll Blues
ALADDIN 172   (January 1947)
  Rugged Road
  Come Back Baby

Wynonie "Blues" Harris
APOLLO 387   (March 1947)
  I Gotta Lyin' Woman
  Rebecca's Blues

Wynonie "Mr. Blues" Harris and His All-Stars
ALADDIN 196   (September 1947)
  Ghost of a Chance
  Big City Blues
ALADDIN 208   (February 1948)
  Hard Ridin' Mama
  You Got to Get Yourself a Job, Girl

Wynonie Harris
KING 4202   (February 1948)
  Wynonie's Boogie
  Rose Get Your Clothes
KING 4210   (February 1948)
  Good Rockin' Tonight
  Good Morning Mr. Blues
KING 4217   (March 1948)
  Your Money Don't Mean a Thing
  Love Is Like Rain
KING 4226   (May 1948)
  Lollipop Mama
  Blow Your Brains Out
KING 4252   (September 1948)
  Bite Again, Bite Again
  Blowin' to California

KING 4276   (January 1949)
  I Feel That Old Age Coming On
  Grandma Plays the Numbers
MONOGRAM 123   (June 1949)
  Wynonie's Blues   [reissue of Apollo 362]
  Playful Baby   [reissue of Apollo 372]
KING 4292   (June 1949)
  Drinkin' Wine, Spo-Dee-O-Dee
  She Just Won't Sell No More
KING 4304   (August 1949)
  All She Wants to Do Is Rock
  I Want My Fanny Brown
KING 4330   (December 1949)
  Baby, Shame on You
  Sittin' on It All the Time
KING 4342   (February 1950)
  I Can't Take It No More
  I Like My Baby's Pudding
KING 4378   (June 1950)
  Stormy Night Blues
  Good Morning Judge
KING 4389   (August 1950)
  Rock Mr. Blues
  Be Mine My Love
KING 4402   (September 1950)
  Mr. Blues Is Coming to Town
  I Want to Love You Baby
KING 4415   (October 1950)
  Triflin' Woman
  Put It Back

Wynonie Harris and the Lucky Millinder Orchestra
KING 4418   (October 1950)
  Oh, Babe!
  [reverse: without Harris]
KING 4419   (October 1950)
  Teardrops from My Eyes
  [reverse: without Harris]

Wynonie Harris
KING 4445   (April 1950)
  A Love Untrue
  I Believe I'll Fall in Love
KING 4448   (April 1950)
  Tremblin'
  Just Like Two Drops of Water
KING 4461   (June 1950)
  Bloodshot Eyes
  Confessin' the Blues

KING 4468   (August 1951)
  Man, Have I Got Troubles
  I'll Never Give Up

Wynonie Harris with the Todd Rhodes Orchestra
KING 4485   (November 1951)
  Lovin' Machine
  Luscious Woman

Wynonie Harris
KING 4507   (February 1952)
  My Playful Baby's Gone
  Here Comes the Night

Wynonie Harris with the Todd Rhodes Orchestra
KING 4526   (March 1952)
  Married Women—Stay Married
  Keep on Churnin'

Wynonie Harris
KING 4555   (July 1952)
  Night Train
  Do It Again, Please
KING 4565   (October 1952)
  Drinking Blues
  Adam Come and Get Your Rib
KING 4592   (December 1952)
  Rot Gut
  Greyhound
KING 4593   (December 1952)
  Bad News Baby
  Bring It Back
KING 4620   (March 1953)
  Wasn't That Good
  Mama, Your Daughter Done Lied to Me
KING 4635   (May 1953)
  The Deacon Don't Like It
  Song of the Bayou

Wynonie Harris and Joe Turner
ALADDIN 3184   (June 1953)
  Battle of the Blues, Part 1
  Battle of the Blues, Part 2

Wynonie Harris
KING 4668   (October 1953)
  Please, Louise
  Nearer My Love to Thee

KING 4685 (January 1954)
  Quiet Whiskey
  Down Boy Down
KING 4716 (May 1954)
  Keep A Talkin'
  Shake That Thing
KING 4724 (July 1954)
  I Get a Thrill
  Don't Take My Whiskey Away from Me
KING 4763 (November 1954)
  All She Wants to Do Is Mambo
  Christina
KING 4774 (February 1955)
  Good Mambo Tonight
  Git to Gittin' Baby
KING 4789 (April 1955)
  Mr. Dollar
  Fishtail Blues
KING 4814 (June 1955)
  Drinkin' Sherry Wine
  Git with the Grits
KING 4826 (August 1955)
  Wine, Wine, Sweet Wine
  Man's Best Friend
KING 4839 (October 1955)
  Shotgun Wedding
  I Don't Know Where to Go
KING 4852 (November 1955)
  Bloodshot Eyes [reissue of King 4461]
  Good Morning Judge [reissue of King 4378]

Wynonie Harris with Orchestra
ATCO 6081 (October 1956)
  Tell a Whale of a Tale
  Destination Love

ALBUMS

ALADDIN 703 (January 1951)
  Party After Hours (10-inch LP; two cuts by Harris)
ALADDIN 813 (1956)
  Party After Hours (12-inch LP)
KING 536 (1956)
  Rock 'n' Roll Dance Party (one cut by Harris)
KING 607 (1958)
  Battle of the Blues (seven cuts by Harris)
KING 627 (1958)
  Battle of the Blues, Vol. 2 (seven cuts by Harris)

King also released two Roy Brown–Wynonie Harris *Battle of the Blues* 45-rpm EPs, Nos. 250 and 254, in 1958, and one called *Wynonie Harris*, No. 260.

JAY HAWKINS

Jalacy Hawkins with the Tiny Grimes Band
GOTHAM 295   (1953)
    Why Do You Waste My Time?
    Carnation Hop Boogie

Jalacy Hawkins
TIMELY 1004   (March 1954)
    Baptize Me in Wine
    Not Anymore
TIMELY 1005   (March 1954)
    I Found My Way to Wine
    Please Try to Understand

Jay Hawkins
MERCURY 70549   (February 1955)
    (She Put the) Wamee (On Me)
    This Is All
WING 90005   (May 1955)
    Well, I Tried
    You're All of Life to Me

Screamin' Jay Hawkins
GRAND 135   (January 1956)
    I Is
    Take Me Back

Jay Hawkins
WING 90055   (January 1956)
    Talk About Me
    Even Though

Screamin' Jay Hawkins
OKEH 7072   (October 1956)
    I Put a Spell on You
    Little Demon
OKEH 7084   (December 1956)
    You Made Me Love You
    Darling Please Forgive Me
OKEH 7087   (1957)
    Frenzy
    Person to Person

OKEH 7101   (1957)
   Alligator Wine
   There's Something Wrong with You
APOLLO 506   (1957)
   Not Anymore   [reissue of Timely 1004]
   Please Try to Understand   [reissue of Timely 1005]
APOLLO 528   (1957)
   Baptize Me in Wine   [reissue of Timely 1004]
   Not Anymore   [alternate take]

ALBUM

EPIC LN-3448   (April 1958)
   At Home with Screamin' Jay Hawkins

WANDA JACKSON

DECCA 29140   (June 1954)
   You Can't Have My Love   [with Billy Gray]
   Lovin', Country Style
DECCA 29253   (August 1954)
   The Right to Love
   If You Knew What I Knew
DECCA 29267   (September 1954)
   If You Don't Somebody Else Will   [with Billy Gray]
   You'd Be the First One to Know
DECCA 29514   (April 1955)
   Tears at the Grand Ole Opry
   Nobody's Darlin' but Mine
DECCA 29677   (October 1955)
   It's the Same World
   Don't Do the Things He'd Do
DECCA 29803   (January 1956)
   Wasted
   I Cried Again
CAPITOL 3485   (July 1956)
   I Gotta Know
   Half as Good a Girl
CAPITOL 3575   (October 1956)
   Hot Dog! That Made Him Mad
   Silver Threads and Golden Needles
DECCA 30153   (November 1956)
   You Won't Forget (About Me)
   The Heart You Could Have Had

CAPITOL 3637 (January 1957)
  Cryin' through the Night
  Baby Loves Him
CAPITOL 3683 (March 1957)
  Don'a Wan'a
  Let Me Explain
CAPITOL 3764 (July 1957)
  Cool Love
  Did You Miss Me?
CAPITOL 3843 (December 1957)
  Fujiyama Mama
  No Wedding Bells for Joe

ALBUM

CAPITOL T-1041 (July 1958)
  Wanda Jackson

LOUIS JORDAN

For the various recordings, 1929–1938, on which Louis Jordan played alto saxophone, see the index of Brian Rust's *Jazz Records 1897–1942.*

Chick Webb and His Orchestra
DECCA 1115 (1937)
  Gee, But You're Swell
  Love Marches On [vocal by trio]
DECCA 1213 (1937)
  It's Swell of You
  Wake Up and Live [vocal by trio]
DECCA 1273 (1937)
  Rusty Hinge
  Cryin' Mood [vocal by Ella Fitzgerald]

Louis Jordan's Elks Rendezvous Band
DECCA 7556 (1939)
  Honey in the Bee Ball
  Barnacle Bill the Sailor

Louis Jordan and His Tympany Five
DECCA 7590 (1939)
  Doug the Jitterbug
  Flat Face

DECCA 7609 (1939)
  At the Swing Cats' Ball
  Keep A-Knockin'
DECCA 7623 (1939)
  Sam Jones Done Snagged His Britches
  Swingin' in the Cocoanut Trees
DECCA 7675 (1939)
  Honeysuckle Rose
  But I'll Be Back
DECCA 7693 (1940)
  You Ain't Nowhere
  'Fore Day Blues
DECCA 7705 (1940)
  You Run Your Mouth and I'll Run My Business
  Hard Lovin' Blues [vocal by Yack Taylor]
DECCA 7719 (1940)
  You're My Meat
  Jake, What a Snake
DECCA 7723 (1940)
  I'm Alabama Bound
  June Tenth Jamboree
DECCA 7729 (1940)
  You Got to Go When Your Wagon Comes   [vocal by Daisy Winchester]
  After School Swing Session
DECCA 7745 (1940)
  Somebody Done Hoodooed the Hoodoo Man
  Lovie Joe [vocal by Mabel Robinson]
DECCA 7777 (1940)
  Never Let Your Left Hand Know What Your Right Hand's Doin'
  Penthouse in the Basement
DECCA 3253 (1940)
  Don't Come Cryin' on My Shoulder
  Bounce the Ball (Do Da Dittle Um Day)
DECCA 3360 (1940)
  Oh Boy, I'm in the Groove
  Waitin' for the Robert E. Lee
DECCA 8500 (1940)
  Do You Call That a Buddy?
  Pompton Turnpike
DECCA 8501 (1940)
  A Chicken Ain't Nothin' but a Bird
  I Know (I Know What You Wanna Do)
DECCA 8525 (1941)
  T-Bone Blues
  Pinetop's Boogie Woogie
DECCA 8537 (1941)
  The Two Little Squirrels (Nuts to You)
  Pan-Pan

DECCA 8560 (1941)
  Saxa-Woogie
  Brotherly Love
DECCA 8581 (1941)
  Boogie Woogie Came to Town
  St. Vitus Dance
DECCA 8593 (January 1942)
  I'm Gonna Move to the Outskirts of Town
  Knock Me a Kiss
DECCA 8605 (1942)
  How 'Bout That?
  The Green Grass Grows All Around
DECCA 8627 (June 1942)
  Small Town Boy
  Mama Mama Blues
DECCA 8638 (August 1942)
  I'm Gonna Leave You on the Outskirts of Town
  It's a Low-Down Dirty Shame
DECCA 8645 (September 1942)
  What's the Use of Getting Sober (When You're Gonna Get Drunk Again)?
  The Chicks I Pick Are Slender and Tender and Tall
DECCA 8653 (November 1943)
  Five Guys Named Moe
  That'll Just 'bout Knock Me Out
DECCA 8654 (December 1943)
  Ration Blues
  Deacon Jones
DECCA 8659 (January 1944)
  G.I. Jive
  Is You Is or Is You Ain't

Bing Crosby with Louis Jordan and His Band
DECCA 2347 (October 1944)
  (Yip Yip Hootie) My Baby Said Yes
  Your Socks Don't Match

Louis Jordan and His Tympany Five
DECCA 8668 (March 1945)
  Mop! Mop!
  You Can't Get That No More
DECCA 8670 (May 1945)
  Caldonia Boogie
  Somebody Done Changed the Lock on My Door
DECCA 18734 (October 1945)
  Buzz Me
  Don't Worry 'bout That Mule
DECCA 18762 (January 1946)
  Reconversion Blues
  Salt Pork, West Virginia

DECCA 18818   (March 1946)
  Beware
  Don't Let the Sun Catch You Cryin'

Ella Fitzgerald with Louis Jordan and His Tympany Five
DECCA 23546   (June 1946)
  Stone Cold Dead in the Market (He Had It Comin')
  Peetootie Pie

Louis Jordan and His Tympany Five
DECCA 23610   (July 1946)
  Choo Choo Ch'Boogie
  That Chick's Too Young to Fry
DECCA 23669   (September 1946)
  Ain't That Just Like a Woman
  If It's Love You Want, Baby
DECCA 23741   (November 1946)
  Ain't Nobody Here but Us Chickens
  Let the Good Times Roll
DECCA 23810   (January 1947)
  I Like 'Em Fat Like That
  Texas and Pacific
DECCA 23841   (February 1947)
  Open the Door, Richard
  It's So Easy
DECCA 23901   (May 1947)
  Jack, You're Dead
  I Know What You're Puttin' Down
DECCA 23931   (June 1947)   [reissue of Decca 18818]
  Beware
  Don't Let the Sun Catch You Cryin'
DECCA 23932   (June 1947)   [reissue of Decca 8670]
  Caldonia Boogie
  Somebody Done Changed the Lock on My Door
DECCA 24104   (July 1947)
  Boogie Woogie Blue Plate
  Sure Had a Wonderful Time
DECCA 24155   (September 1947)
  Look Out
  Early in the Mornin'
DECCA 24300   (January 1948)
  Reet Petite and Gone
  Inflation Blues
DECCA 24448   (May 1948)
  Run Joe
  All for the Love of Lil
DECCA 24483   (June 1948)
  Don't Burn the Candle at Both Ends   [with Martha Davis]
  We Can't Agree

DECCA 25394 (July 1948)
  Saxa-Woogie [reissue of Decca 8560]
  Pinetop's Boogie Woogie [reissue of Decca 8525]
DECCA 24502 (September 1948)
  Daddy-O [with Martha Davis]
  You're on the Right Track, Baby [with Martha Davis]
DECCA 24527 (March 1949)
  Have You Got Gumption?
  Roamin' Blues
DECCA 24633 (May 1949)
  Every Man to His Own Profession
  Cole Slaw
DECCA 24673 (July 1949)
  Beans and Corn Bread
  Chicky-Mo Craney Cow
DECCA 24725 (September 1949)
  Saturday Night Fish Fry, Part 1
  Saturday Night Fish Fry, Part 2
DECCA 24815 (December 1949)
  I Know What I've Got
  School Days
DECCA 24877 (January 1950)
  Hungry Man
  Push Ka Pee Shee Pie
DECCA 24981 (February 1950)
  Heed My Warning
  Baby's Gonna Go Bye-Bye
DECCA 25473 (March 1950)
  Honeysuckle Rose [reissue of Decca 7675]
  T-Bone Blues [reissue of Decca 8525]
DECCA 27058 (April 1950)
  Onions
  Psycho-Loco
DECCA 27114 (July 1950)
  Blue Light Boogie, Part 1
  Blue Light Boogie, Part 2
DECCA 27129 (August 1950)
  I Want a Roof over My Head (And Bread on the Table)
  Show Me How (To Milk the Cow)
DECCA 27203 (October 1950)
  Tambouritza Boogie
  Trouble then Satisfaction
DECCA 27324 (December 1950)
  Chartreuse
  Lemonade
DECCA 27428 (February 1951)
  Teardrops from My Eyes
  It's a Great, Great Pleasure

DECCA 27547   (March 1951)
  Weak Minded Blues
  Is My Pop in There?
DECCA 27620   (June 1951)
  I Can't Give You Anything but Love
  You Will Always Have a Friend
DECCA 27648   (July 1951)
  If You're So Smart
  How Blue Can You Get?

Louis Jordan and His Orchestra
DECCA 27694   (September 1951)
  Three Handed Woman
  Please Don't Leave Me
DECCA 27784   (October 1951)
  Trust in Me
  Cock-a-Doodle-Doo
DECCA 27806   (November 1951)
  May Every Day Be Christmas
  Bone Dry
DECCA 27898   (December 1951)
  Lay Something on the Bar (Besides Your Elbows)
  No Sale
DECCA 27969   (January 1952)
  Work, Baby, Work
  Louisville Lodge Meeting
DECCA 28088   (March 1952)
  Never Trust a Woman
  Slow Down

Louis Jordan and His Tympany Five
DECCA 28211   (May 1952)
  Junco Partner
  Azure-Te
DECCA 28225   (June 1952)
  Jordan for President
  Oil Well, Texas

Louis Jordan and His Orchestra
DECCA 28335   (July 1952)
  All of Me
  There Goes My Heart

Louis Jordan and His Tympany Five
DECCA 28444   (October 1952)
  Friendship
  You're Much Too Fat

DECCA 28543   (December 1952)
  You Didn't Want Me, Baby
  A Man's Best Friend Is a Bed

Louis Jordan with Nelson Riddle's Orchestra
DECCA 28664   (March 1953)
  It's Better to Wait for Love
  Just Like a Butterfly (That's Caught in the Rain)

Louis Jordan and His Tympany Five
DECCA 28756   (June 1953)
  House Party
  Hog Wash
DECCA 28820   (August 1953)
  There Must Be a Way
  Time Marches On
DECCA 28883   (October 1953)
  I Want You to Be My Baby
  You Know It Too
DECCA 28983   (December 1953)
  The Soona Baby
  Fat Sam from Birmingham
DECCA 29018   (January 1954)
  Lollipop
  Nobody Knows You When You're Down and Out
ALLADIN 3223   (January 1954)
  Dad Gum Ya Hide, Boy
  Whiskey, Do Your Stuff
ALADDIN 3227   (February 1954)
  I'll Die Happy
  Ooo-Wee
ALADDIN 3243   (April 1954)
  Hurry Home
  A Dollar Down
ALADDIN 3246   (May 1954)
  I Seen Whatcha Done
  Messy Bessy
DECCA 29166   (July 1954)
  Only Yesterday
  I Didn't Know What Time It Was
ALADDIN 3249   (July 1954)
  Louis' Blues
  If I Had Any Sense
DECCA 29263   (August 1954)
  Wake Up, Jacob
  If It's True
ALADDIN 3264   (October 1954)
  Put Some Money in the Pot, Boy, 'Cause the Juice Is Running Low
  Yeah, Yeah, Yeah, Baby

ALADDIN 3270   (November 1954)
   Fat Back and Corn Liquor
   The Dripper
DECCA 29424   (January 1955)
   Perdido
   Locked-Up
ALADDIN 3279   (February 1955)
   Gal, You Need a Whippin'
   Time Is Passin'
DECCA 29655   (September 1955)
   Come and Get It
   I Want You to Be My Baby   [reissue of Decca 28883]
ALADDIN 3295   (October 1955)
   It's Hard to Be Good
   Gotta Go
VIK 0148   (December 1955)
   Baby, Let's Do It
   Bananas
VIK 0182   (January 1956)
   Chicken Back
   Where Can I Go?
VIK 0192   (February 1956)
   Rock 'n' Roll Call
   Baby, You're Just Too Much
DECCA 29860   (March 1956)
   I Gotta Move
   Everything That's Made of Wood
MERCURY 70993   (November 1956)
   Big Bess
   Cat Scratchin'

ALBUMS

DECCA A-246   (February 1942)
   Alto Saxology ("Waitin' for the Robert E. Lee")
DECCA A-459   (August 1946)
   Louis Jordan and His Tympany Five
DECCA A-645   (March 1948)
   Louis Jordan and His Tympany Five, Vol. II
MERCURY 20242   (February 1957)
   Somebody Up There Digs Me
MERCURY 20331   (January 1958)
   Man, We're Wailin'
SCORE 4007   (April 1958)
   Go Blow Your Horn

A 45-rpm EP album, *Louis Jordan and His Tympany Five* (Decca ED-2029), was issued in May 1953.

JIMMIE LOGSDON

DECCA 28502   (November 1952)
  That's When I'll Love You Best
  I Wanna Be Mama'd
DECCA 28584   (January 1953)
  The Death of Hank Williams
  Hank Williams Sings the Blues No More
DECCA 28726   (June 1953)
  As Long as We're Together
  The Love You Gave Me
DECCA 28864   (September 1953)
  Where the Old Red River Flows
  Let's Have a Happy Time
DECCA 28913   (October 1953)
  Pa-Paya Mama
  In the Mission of St. Augustine
DECCA 29075   (March 1954)
  Good Deal Lucille
  Midnight Boogie
DECCA 29122   (May 1954)
  My Sweet French Baby
  These Lonesome Blues
DECCA 29337   (December 1954)
  I'm Goin' Back to Tennessee
  You Ain't Nothin' but the Blues
DOT 1274   (November 1955)
  Cold, Cold Rain
  Midnight Blues

SKEETS McDONALD

Skeets Donald
LONDON 16046   (November 1950)
  Please, Daddy, Don't Go to War
  So I Cried Myself to Sleep

Johnny White and His Rhythm Riders
FORTUNE 145   (December 1950)
  The Tattooed Lady
  Mean and Evil Blues

Skeets McDonald
CAPITOL 1518   (May 1951)
  Scoot, Git and Begone
  Blues Is Bad News

CAPITOL 1570 (June 1951)
  Bless Your Little Ol' Heart
  Today I'm Movin' Out
CAPITOL 1771 (August 1951)
  I'm Hurtin'
  Ridin' with the Blues

Skeets McDonald, Benny Walker, Johnny White's Band
FORTUNE 165 (September 1951)
  Birthday Cake Boogie
  [reverse: by Bob Sykes]

Skeets McDonald
CAPITOL 1890 (November 1951)
  Fuss and Fight
  Baby Brown Eyes
CAPITOL 1967 (January 1952)
  Be My Life's Companion
  Tell Me Why
CAPITOL 1993 (February 1952)
  Wheel of Fortune
  The Love That Hurt Me So
CAPITOL 2073 (May 1952)
  Curtain of Tears
  Please Come Back
CAPITOL 2216 (September 1952)
  Don't Let the Stars Get in Your Eyes
  Big Family Trouble
CAPITOL 2326 (January 1953)
  Let Me Know
  I'm Sorry to Say I'm Sorry
CAPITOL 2434 (April 1953)
  I Can't Last Long
  I've Got to Win Your Love Again
CAPITOL 2523 (June 1953)
  It's Your Life
  Baby, I'm Countin'
CAPITOL 2607 (September 1953)
  Looking at the Moon and Wishing on a Star
  I Need Your Love
CAPITOL 2696 (December 1953)
  Look Who's Cryin' Now
  Walking on Teardrops
CAPITOL 2774 (April 1954)
  I Love You, Mama Mia
  Remember You're Mine
CAPITOL 2885 (August 1954)
  Your Love Is Like a Faucet
  But I Do

CAPITOL 2976 (October 1954)
  Smoke Comes Out of My Chimney Just the Same
  Each Time a New Love Dies
CAPITOL 3038 (January 1955)
  I Can't Stand It Any Longer
  Number One in Your Heart
CAPITOL 3117 (April 1955)
  You're Too Late
  A Losing Hand
CAPITOL 3215 (August 1955)
  Strollin'
  You Turned Me Down
CAPITOL 3312 (December 1955)
  I Got a New Field to Plow
  Baby, I'm Lost without You
CAPITOL 3378 (February 1956)
  It'll Take Me a Long, Long Time
  Fallen Angel
CAPITOL 3461 (June 1956)
  You Oughta See Grandma Rock
  Heart-Breakin' Mama
CAPITOL 3525 (August 1956)
  You Gotta Be My Baby
  Somebody
CAPITOL 3600 (November 1956)
  You Better Not Go
  Don't Push Me Too Far

ALBUM

CAPITOL T-1040 (June 1958)
  Goin' Steady with the Blues

A 45-rpm EP, *Country and Hillbilly Songs by Skeets McDonald* (Capitol EP-451), was issued in August 1953.

STICK McGHEE

Stick McGhee and His Buddies
HARLEM 1018 (1947)
  Drinkin' Wine Spo-Dee-O-Dee
  Blues Mixture
ATLANTIC 873 (March 1949)
  Drinkin' Wine Spo-Dee-O-Dee
  Blues Mixture

DECCA 48104   (May 1949)
  Drinkin' Wine Spo-Dee-O-Dee   [reissue of Harlem 1018]
  Baby, Baby Blues
ATLANTIC 881   (June 1949)
  I'll Always Remember
  Lonesome Road Blues
ATLANTIC 898   (January 1950)
  Drank Up All the Wine Last Night
  Southern Menu

Van Walls Orchestra
ATLANTIC 904   (March 1950)
  Ain't Gonna Scold You
  Tee-Nah-Nah

Stick McGhee and His Buddies
ATLANTIC 909   (May 1950)
  My Baby's Comin' Back
  Venus Blues

Stick McGhee and His Spo-Dee-O-Dee Buddies
ATLANTIC 910   (July 1950)
  Let's Do It (Stick's Confusion)
  She's Gone

Stick McGhee and His Buddies
ATLANTIC 926   (January 1951)
  Housewarming Boogie (Warm This House)
  Blue and Brokenhearted
ATLANTIC 926   (February 1951)
  Housewarming Boogie (Warm This House) [same as above]
  Tennessee Waltz Blues

Sticks McGhee
LONDON 970 (February 1951)
  Oh, What a Face
  You Gotta Have Something on the Ball

Stick McGhee and His Buddies
ATLANTIC 937   (April 1951)
  One Monkey Don't Stop the Show
  Blues Barrelhouse
ATLANTIC 955   (January 1952)
  Wee Wee Hours, Part 1
  Wee Wee Hours, Part 2

Brownie McGhee
SAVOY 835   (January 1952)
  So Much Trouble
  Diamond Ring

Sticks McGhee
ESSEX 709   (1952)
  My Little Rose
  No More Reveille

Stick McGhee and His Buddies
ATLANTIC 991 (March 1953)
  New Found Love
  Meet You in the Morning

Sticks McGhee
KING 4610   (March 1953)
  Head Happy with Wine
  Little Things We Used to Do
KING 4628   (May 1953)
  Blues in My Heart
  Whiskey, Women and Loaded Dice
KING 4672   (November 1953)
  Dealin' from the Bottom
  Jungle Juice
KING 4700   (March 1954)
  I'm Doin' All This Time (And You Put Me Down)
  The Wiggle Waggle Woo

Stick McGhee and the Ramblers
SAVOY 1148   (January 1955)
  Things Have Changed
  Help Me Baby

Stick McGhee
KING 4783   (March 1955)
  Double Crossin' Liquor
  Six to Eight
KING 4800   (May 1955)
  Get Your Mind Out of the Gutter
  Sad, Bad, Glad

ALBUM

AUDIO-LAB 120   (1958)
  Highway of Blues (seven cuts by McGhee)

THE MIDNIGHTERS

The Royals
FEDERAL 12064   (March 1952)
  Every Beat of My Heart
  All Night Long

FEDERAL 12077   (June 1952)
  Starting from Tonight
  I Know I Love You So
FEDERAL 12088   (July 1952)
  Moonrise
  Fifth Street Blues
FEDERAL 12113   (November 1952)
  Are You Forgetting?
  What Did I Do?
FEDERAL 12121   (April 1953)
  The Shrine of St. Cecilia
  I Feel So Blue
FEDERAL 12133   (May 1953)
  Get It
  No It Ain't
FEDERAL 12150   (October 1953)
  Hey Miss Fine
  I Feel That-a-Way
FEDERAL 12160   (December 1953)
  That's It
  Someone Like You
FEDERAL 12169   (February 1954)
  Work with Me Annie
  Until I Die

The Midnighters
FEDERAL 12169   (March 1954)
  Work with Me Annie
  Until I Die
FEDERAL 12177   (March 1954)
  Give It Up
  That Woman
FEDERAL 12185   (May 1954)
  Sexy Ways
  Don't Say Your Last Goodbye
FEDERAL 12195   (August 1954)
  Annie Had a Baby
  She's the One
FEDERAL 12200   (October 1954)
  Annie's Aunt Fanny
  Crazy Loving
FEDERAL 12202   (December 1954)
  Tell Them
  Stingy Little Thing
FEDERAL 12205   (January 1955)
  Moonrise [reissue of Federal 12088]
  She's the One

FEDERAL 12210   (February 1955)
  Ashamed of Myself
  Ring A-Ling A-Ling
FEDERAL 12220   (April 1955)
  Why Are We Apart?
  Switchie Witchie Titchie
FEDERAL 12224   (May 1955)
  Henry's Got Flat Feet
  Whatsoever You Do
FEDERAL 12227   (June 1955)
  It's Love Baby
  Looka Here
FEDERAL 12230   (July 1955)   [reissue of Federal 12177]
  Give It Up
  That Woman
FEDERAL 1240   (August 1955)
  Rock and Roll Wedding
  That House on the Hill
FEDERAL 12243   (September 1955)
  Don't Change Your Pretty Ways
  We'll Never Meet Again
FEDERAL 12251   (January 1956)
  Partners for Life
  Sweet Mama, Do Right
FEDERAL 12260   (February 1956)
  Rock, Granny, Roll
  Open Up the Back Door
FEDERAL 12270   (April 1956)
  Tore Up over You
  Early One Morning
FEDERAL 12285   (October 1956)
  I'll Be Home Someday
  Come On and Get It
FEDERAL 12288   (December 1956)
  Let Me Hold Your Hand
  Ooh Bah Baby

ALBUMS

FEDERAL 541   (December 1957)
  Their Greatest Hits
FEDERAL 581   (August 1958)
  Greatest Hits, Vol. 2

A 45-rpm EP, *The Midnighters Sing Their Greatest Hits* (FEP-333), was
issued by Federal in 1958. A Midnighters cut was also included in the Federal
EP *Rock and Roll Hit Parade* (FEP-387).

Amos Milburn
ALADDIN 159   (July 1946)
  After Midnight
  Amos' Blues
ALADDIN 160   (August 1946)
  My Baby's Boogin'
  Darling How Long
ALADDIN 161   (September 1946)
  Down the Road Apiece
  Don't Beg Me
ALADDIN 173   (January 1947)
  Amos' Boogie
  Everything I Do Is Wrong
ALADDIN 174   (January 1947)
  Operation Blues
  Cinch Blues
ALADDIN 191   (August 1947)
  Money Hustlin' Woman
  Real Gone!
ALADDIN 201   (October 1947)
  My Love Is Limited
  Blues at Sundown
ALADDIN 202   (October 1947)
  Sad and Blue
  That's My Chick
ALADDIN 206   (January 1948)
  Train Time Blues
  Bye Bye Boogie
ALADDIN 211   (March 1948)
  Pool Playing Blues
  I Still Love You
ALADDIN 3014   (September 1948)
  Chicken Shack Boogie
  It Took a Long, Long Time
ALADDIN 3018   (October 1948)
  Bewildered
  A&M Blues
ALADDIN 3023   (March 1949)
  Jitterbug Parade
  Hold Me Baby
ALADDIN 3026   (May 1949)
  Pot Luck Boogie
  In the Middle of the Night

ALADDIN 3032   (August 1949)
   Roomin' House Boogie
   Empty Arms Blues

Amos Milburn and His Aladdin Chicken-Shackers
ALADDIN 3037   (October 1949)
   Let's Make Christmas Merry, Baby
   Bow-Wow!
ALADDIN 3038   (November 1949)
   Real Pretty Mama Blues
   Drifting Blues
ALADDIN 3043   (January 1950)
   I'm Just a Fool in Love
   How Long Has This Train Been Gone
ALADDIN 3049   (February 1950)
   Johnson Rag
   Walking Blues
ALADDIN 3056   (April 1950)
   Square Dance Boogie
   Anybody's Blues
ALADDIN 3058   (April 1950)
   Birmingham Bounce
   I Love Her

Amos Milburn
ALADDIN 3059   (May 1950)
   Hard Luck Blues
   Two Years of Torture

Amos Milburn and His Aladdin Chicken-Shackers
ALADDIN 3064   (August 1950)
   Sax Shack Boogie
   Remember
ALADDIN 3068   (October 1950)
   Bad, Bad Whiskey
   I'm Going to Tell My Mama
ALADDIN 3080   (March 1951)
   Tears, Tears, Tears
   Let's Rock a While
ALADDIN 3093   (July 1951)
   Just One More Drink
   Ain't Nothing Shaking
ALADDIN 3105   (October 1951)
   She's Gone Again
   Boogie-Woogie
ALADDIN 3124   (January 1952)
   Trouble in Mind
   Thinking and Drinking

ALADDIN 3125 (March 1952)
  Put Something in My Hand
  Flying Home
ALADDIN 3133 (May 1952)
  Roll, Mr. Jelly
  I Won't Be a Fool Any More
ALADDIN 3146 (August 1952)
  Button Your Lip
  Everything I Do Is Wrong
ALADDIN 3150 (September 1952)
  Greyhound
  Kiss Me Again
ALADDIN 3159 (November 1952)
  Rock, Rock, Rock
  Boo Hoo
ALADDIN 3164 (January 1953)
  Let Me Go Home, Whiskey
  Three Times a Fool
ALADDIN 3168 (May 1953)
  Long, Long Day
  Please, Mr. Johnson
ALADDIN 3197 (August 1953)
  One Scotch, One Bourbon, One Beer
  What Can I Do?
ALADDIN 3218 (November 1953)
  Good, Good Whiskey
  Let's Have a Party
ALADDIN 3226 (February 1954)
  Rocky Mountain
  How Could You Hurt Me So
ALADDIN 3240 (April 1954)
  Milk and Water
  I'm Still a Fool for You
ALADDIN 3248 (June 1954)
  Baby, Baby All the Time
  Glory of Love
ALADDIN 3253 (September 1954)
  Vicious, Vicious Vodka
  I Done Done It
ALADDIN 3269 (November 1954)
  One, Two, Three, Everybodsy
  That's It
ALADDIN 3281 (February 1955)
  Why Don't You Do Right
  I Love You Anyway
ALADDIN 3293 (August 1955)
  All Is Well
  My Happiness Depends on You

ALADDIN 3306 (November 1955)
  House Party
  I Guess I'll Go
ALADDIN 3320 (May 1956)
  French Fried Potatoes and Ketchup
  I Need Someone
ALADDIN 3332 (August 1956)
  Juice, Juice, Juice
  Chicken Shack Boogie

The Amos Milburn Band
ALADDIN 3340 (October 1956)
  Every Day of the Week
  Girl of My Dreams

ALBUMS

ALADDIN 703 (January 1951)
  Party After Hours (10-inch LP; three cuts by Milburn)
ALADDIN 704 (1951)
  Rockin' the Boogie (10-inch LP)
ALADDIN 710 (July 1956)
  Rock 'n' Roll with Rhythm & Blues (12-inch LP; two cuts by Milburn)
ALADDIN 810 (1956)
  Rockin' the Boogie (12-inch LP)
ALADDIN 813 (1956)
  Party After Hours (12-inch LP; five cuts by Milburn)
SCORE 4002 (1957)
  I Dig Rock & Roll (two cuts by Milburn)
SCORE 4012 (1958)
  Let's Have a Party

MERRILL MOORE

CAPITOL 2226 (September 1952)
  Corrine, Corrina
  Bed Bug Boogie
CAPITOL 2386 (February 1953)
  Red Light
  Bartender's Blues
CAPITOL 2574 (August 1953)
  The House of Blue Lights
  Bell Bottom Boogie
CAPITOL 2691 (December 1953)
  Snatchin' and Grabbin'
  Sweet Jennie Lee

CAPITOL 2796   (April 1954)
  Nola
  Fly Right Boogie
CAPITOL 2924   (September 1954)
  Doggie House Boogie
  Ten, Ten A.M.
CAPITOL 3034   (January 1955)
  Rock Rockola
  Cow Cow Boogie
CAPITOL 3140   (May 1955)
  Yes, Indeed
  One Way Door
CAPITOL 32226   (September 1955)
  Hard Top Race
  Five Foot Two, Eyes of Blue
CAPITOL 3311   (December 1955)
  Cooing to the Wrong Pigeon
  Down the Road Apiece
CAPITOL 3397   (March 1956)
  Rock Island Line
  King Porter Stomp
CAPITOL 3563   (September 1956)
  Gotta Gimme What'cha Got
  She's Gone

ELLA MAE MORSE

The Freddie Slack Orchestra
CAPITOL 102   (July 1942)
  Cow-Cow Boogie
  [reverse: Slack without Morse]
CAPITOL 115   (October 1942)
  Mister Five by Five
  The Thrill Is Gone
CAPITOL 133   (September 1943)
  Old Rob Roy
  Get on Board, Little Children

Ella Mae Morse
CAPITOL 143   (December 1943)
  Shoo-Shoo, Baby
  No Love, No Nothin'
CAPITOL 151   (April 1944)
  Milkman, Keep Those Bottles Quiet
  Tess' Torch Song
CAPITOL 163   (August 1944)
  Invitation to the Party
  Patty-Cake Man

CAPITOL 176   (December 1944)
  Why Shouldn't I?
  Hello, Suzanne
CAPITOL 193   (May 1945)
  Captain Kidd
  You Betcha
CAPITOL 226   (November 1945)
  Rip Van Winkle
  Buzz Me
CAPITOL 251   (April 1946)
  The House of Blue Lights
  Hey, Mr. Postman
CAPITOL 278   (June 1946)
  Pig Foot Pete
  Your Conscience Tells You So
CAPITOL 301   (September 1946)
  That's My Home
  The Merry Ha! Ha!
CAPITOL 370   (February 1947)
  Hoodle Addle
  Pine Top Schwartz
CAPITOL 424   (May 1947)
  Get Off It and Go
  Old Shank's Mare
CAPITOL 487   (December 1947)
  On the Sunny Side of the Street
  Early in the Morning
CAPITOL 15097   (May 1948)
  A Little Farther Down the Road a Piece
  Bombo B. Bailey
CAPITOL 15188   (September 1948)
  Cow-Cow Boogie   [reissue of Capitol 102]
  The House of Blue Lights   [reissue of Capitol 251]
CAPITOL 1903   (December 1951)
  Tennessee Saturday Night
  Sensational
CAPITOL 1922   (January 1952)
  The Blacksmith Blues
  Love Me or Leave Me
CAPITOL 2072   (April 1952)
  Oakie Boogie
  Love Ya Like Mad
CAPITOL 1286   (July 1952)
  A-Sleepin' at the Foot of the Bed
  Male Call

Tennessee Ernie Ford and Ella Mae Morse
CAPITOL 2215 (August 1952)
  I'm Hog-Tied Over You
  False-Hearted Girl

Ella Mae Morse
CAPITOL 2276 (September 1952)
  Greyhound
  Jump Back, Honey
CAPITOL 2346 (January 1953)
  The Guy Who Invented Kissin'
  Good
CAPITOL 2441 (March 1953)
  Big Mamou
  Is It Any Wonder
CAPITOL 2539 (July 1953)
  40 Cups of Coffee
  Oh! You Crazy Moon
CAPITOL 2658 (November 1953)
  Taint What You Do It's the Way that Cha Do It
  It Ain't Necessarily So
CAPITOL 2800 (April 1954)
  Goodnight, Sweetheart, Goodnight
  Happy Habit
CAPITOL 2882 (July 1954)
  Money Honey
  I Love You, Yes I Do
CAPITOL 2959 (October 1954)
  (We've Reached) The Point of No Return
  Give a Little Time
CAPITOL 2992 (November 1954)
  Bring My Baby Back to Me
  Lovey Dovey
CAPITOL 3105 (April 1955)
  Smack Dab in the Middle
  Yes, Yes I Do
CAPITOL 3147 (June 1955)
  Heart Full of Hope
  Livin', Livin', Livin'
CAPITOL 3199 (July 1955)
  Razzle Dazzle
  Seventeen
CAPITOL 3263 (October 1955)
  Sing-ing-ing-ing
  When Boy Kiss Girl (It's Love)
CAPITOL 3387 (February 1956)
  Rock and Roll Wedding
  Down in Mexico

CAPITOL 3458   (June 1956)
   I'm Gonna Walk
   Coffee Date

ALBUMS

CAPITOL H-513   (July 1954)
   Barrelhouse, Boogie, and the Blues (10-inch LP)
CAPITOL T-513   (April 1955)
   Barrelhouse, Boogie, and the Blues (12-inch LP)
CAPITOL T-898   (November 1957)
   Morse Code

Capitol also issued a *Barrelhouse, Boogie, and the Blues* 45-rpm EP set in July 1954 (EAP-1-513 and EAP-2-513).

LOUIS PRIMA

Louis Prima made records—hundreds of them, for more than a dozen companies—the way many people smoke cigarettes, one after another, as if he could not control himself. The greater part of this surfeit of recordings is unexceptional and of practically no interest to any but the most severely perverse of ears. Thus, this listing does not pretend to completeness. If there is anyone who has been so driven as to exhaustively chronicle Louis Prima's recording career, I should like to meet him, if not quite to shake his hand.

HIT 7106   (September 1945)
   Oh Marie
   Angelina
MAJESTIC 7154   (September 1945)
   Felicia No Capicia
   The White Cliffs of Dover
MAJESTIC 1116   (February 1947)
   Just a Gigolo
   Baciagaloop (Makes Love on da Stoop)
MAJESTIC 1131   (March 1947)
   Sing, Sing, Sing
   Chinatown, My Chinatown
MAJESTIC 1133   (April 1947)
   Mahzel
   Chi-Baba, Chi-Baba
MAJESTIC 1157   (June 1947)
   Maria Mia
   Do a Little Business on the Side

RCA-VICTOR 20-2400 (October 1947)
 Civilization
 Forsaking All Others
RCA-VICTOR 20-2711 (January 1948)
 Tutti Tutti Pizzicato
 The Bee Song
RCA-VICTOR 20-2763 (April 1948)
 I Feel So Smoochie
 Betty Blue
VICTOR 20-3034 (August 1948)
 All of Me
 Sweet Nothings
RCA-VICTOR 20-3329 (November 1948)
 California Is Wonderful (If You're a Grapefruit)
 Mean to Me
RCA-VICTOR 20-3376 (January 1949)
 Anticipation without Realization
 Everybody's Friend but Nobody's Sweetheart [with Cathy Allen]
RCA-VICTOR 20-3410 (March 1949)
 All Right, Louie, Drop the Gun
 It's a Cruel, Cruel World
RCA-VICTOR 47-2960 (June 1949)
 For Mari-Yootch (I Walka da Pooch)
 Five Foot Two, Eyes of Blue
MERCURY 5338 (November 1949)
 Yes, We Have No Bananas
 Charley, My Boy [with Keely Smith]
MERCURY 5451 (June 1950)
 Here, Pretty Kitty [with Keely Smith]
 Buona Sera
COLUMBIA 39735 (May 1952)
 The Bigger the Figure
 Boney Bones
COLUMBIA 39823 (July 1952)
 One Mint Julep
 Chili Sauce
COLUMBIA 39969 (March 1953)
 Oh, Marie
 Luigi
COLUMBIA 40015 (June 1953)
 It's as Good as New
 Paul Revere
JUBILEE 6054 (November 1953)
 Man, Dig That Crazy Chick
 Non Cha Shame
DECCA 29128 (May 1954)
 The Happy Wanderer
 Until Sunrise

DECCA 29162 (June 1954)
  Dummy Song
  Paper Doll
CAPITOL 3566 (October 1956)
  5 Months, 2 Weeks, 2 Days
  Banana Split for My Baby
CAPITOL 3615 (December 1956)
  Whistle Stop
  Be Mine (Little Babe)

ALBUMS

MAJESTIC M-3 (April 1946)
  Louis Prima
MERCURY 25142 (April 1953)
  Louis Prima Plays (10-inch LP)
CAPITOL 755 (September 1956)
  The Wildest
CAPITOL 836 (April 1957)
  Call of the Wildest
CAPITOL 908 (November 1957)
  The Wildest Show at Tahoe
CAPITOL 1010 (July 1958)
  Las Vegas Prima Style

ESAU SMITH

Jesse Garon Presley, the pseudonymous Esau Smith, is not to be confused with the Esau Smith who recorded several mundane country records for the Snope-Tone label in 1952.

Jesse Presley with Jo-Jo Fineaux and His Hattiesburg Hepcats
FURNITURE FROLIC 107 (June 1954)
  Bosom Divine
  God's Bar-B-Q

Esau Smith
JOE'S RECORDS 220 (July 1955)
  My Gal Shaves
  Combinate That Number, Jack

Jesse Stone and His Band
RCA-VICTOR 20-2554   (November 1947)
  Hey Sister Lucy
  An Ace in the Hole
RCA-VICTOR 20-2788   (June 1948)
  Who Killed 'Er?
  Mr. Jelly Finger
RCA-VICTOR 20-2988   (August 1948)
  Don't Let It Get Away
  The Donkey and the Elephant
RCA-VICTOR 20-3127   (December 1948)
  Who's Zat?
  Bling-a-Ling-a-Ling
RCA-VICTOR 20-3282   (January 1949)
  Get It While You Can
  Keep Your Big Mouth Shut
RCA-VICTOR 50-0026   (June 1949)
  Cole Slaw
  Do It Now

Jesse Stone
ATLANTIC 1028   (March 1954)
  Oh, That'll Be Joyful
  Runaway

The Charlie Calhoun Orchestra
MGM 11989   (April 1955)
  Smack Dab in the Middle
  (I Don't Know Why) The Car Won't Go

Jesse Stone and His Houserockers
ATCO 6051   (August 1955)
  Night Life
  The Rocket

Charles Calhoun
GROOVE 0149   (April 1956)
  Jamboree
  My Pigeon's Gone

Chuck Calhoun
ATLANTIC 1120   (December 1956)
  Hey Tiger
  Barrel House

ALBUMS

ATLANTIC 8013   (November 1957)
  Dance the Rock & Roll   (two cuts by Stone)
ATCO 103   (November 1958)
  Rock & Roll   (one cut by Stone)

THE TRENIERS

The first three records listed, by Lunceford, Bigard, and Mingus, feature Claude Trenier as vocalist. The 1949 Coral record, featuring Claude and Cliff Trenier, had been cut for Decca in early 1945 but was unissued by that label.

Jimmie Lunceford and His Orchestra
DECCA 18655   (February 1945)
  I'm Gonna See My Baby
  That Someone Must Be You

The Barney Bigard Quintet
LAMPLIGHTER 102   (1946)
  Young Man's Blues, Part 1
  Young Man's Blues, Part 2

Charlie Mingus and His Orchestra
EXCELSIOR 163   (1946)
  Weird Nightmare
  [reverse: without Treniers]

The Trenier Twins
MERCURY 8045   (June 1947)
  Buzz Buzz Buzz
  Sure Had a Wonderful Time Last Night
MERCURY 8058   (October 1947)
  I Miss You So
  Hey Sister Lucy
MERCURY 8071   (January 1948)
  No Baby No
  Oh Looka There—Ain't She Pretty
MERCURY 8078   (March 1948)
  Ain't She Mean
  It's a Quiet Town in Crossbone County
MERCURY 8089   (June 1948)
  My Convertible Cadillac
  Sometimes I'm Happy
MERCURY 8089   (November 1948)
  My Convertible Cadillac [same as above]
  Near to Me

Jimmie Lunceford and His Orchestra
RAL 60041 (January 1949)
  Buzz Buzz Buzz
  [reverse: without Treniers]

The Trenier Twins
LONDON 17007 (February 1950)
  Everybody Get Together
  Why Did You Get So High, Shorty

The Treniers
OKEH 6804 (June 1951)
  Go! Go! Go!
  Plenty of Money
OKEH 6826 (September 1951)
  Hey Little Girl
  Old Woman Blues
OKEH 6853 (January 1952)
  It Rocks, It Rolls, It Swings
  Taxi Blues
OKEH 6876 (April 1952)
  Hadacol, That's All
  Long Distance Blues
OKEH 6904 (September 1952)
  Rockin' on Sunday Night
  Cheatin' on Me
OKEH 6932 (November 1952)
  Hi-Yo, Silver
  Poon-Tang!
OKEH 6937 (December 1952)
  The Moondog
  Poon-Tang! [same as above]

Milt Trenier and His Solid Six
RCA-Victor 47-5275 (March 1953)
  Squeeze Me
  Rock Bottom

The Treniers
OKEH 6960 (April 1953)
  Rockin' Is Our Business
  Sugar Doo
OKEH 6984 (July 1953)
  I Do Nothin' but Grieve
  This Is It

Milt Trenier and His Solid Six
RCA-VICTOR 47-5487 (October 1953)
  You're Killin' Me
  Flip Our Wigs

The Treniers
OKEH 7012   (February 1954)
   You Know Yeah, Tiger
   Bud Dance
OKEH 7023   (March 1954)
   Rock-a-Beatin' Boogie
   Trapped

Milt Trenier
GROOVE 0008   (March 1954)
   Straighten Up, Baby
   Why?
GROOVE 0028   (June 1954)
   Day Old Bread
   Give a Little Time

The Treniers
OKEH 7035   (July 1954)
   Bald Head
   Come On, Let's Face It
OKEH 7050   (January 1955)
   Get Out the Car
   Who Put the "Ongh" in the Mambo
OKEH 7057   (June 1955)
   Devil's Mambo
   Do Do Do
EPIC 9066   (August 1954)
   Say Hey [with Willie Mays]
   Out of the Bushes
EPIC 9127   (October 1955)
   Doin' 'Em Up
   Go! Go! Go!
EPIC 9144   (January 1956)
   Rock 'n' Roll Call
   Day Old Bread and Canned Beans
EPIC 9162   (April 1956)
   Good Rockin' Tonight
   Boodie Green
VIK 0214   (June 1956)
   Sorrentino
   Lover Come Back to Me
VIK 0227   (September 1956)
   Cool It Baby
   Rock 'n' Roll Permanent

ALBUM

EPIC LN-3125   (May 1955)
   The Treniers on TV

JOE TURNER

Joe Turner and Pete Johnson
VOCALION 4607 (January 1939)
  Roll 'Em, Pete
  Goin' Away Blues

Pete Johnson and His Boogie Woogie Boys
VOCALION 4997 (1939)
  Cherry Red
  Baby, Look at You
VOCALION 5186 (1939)
  Lovin' Mama Blues
  Cafe Society Rag

The Varsity Seven
VARSITY 8173 (1940)
  Shake It and Break It
  How Long, How Long Blues

Joe Sullivan and His Café Society Orchestra
VOCALION 5496 (1940)
  I Can't Give You Anything but Love
  [reverse: without Turner]
VOCALION 5531 (1940)
  Low Down Dirty Shame
  [reverse: without Turner]

Benny Carter and His All-Star Orchestra
OKEH 6001 (1940)
  Joe Turner Blues
  Beale Street Blues

Big Joe Turner
DECCA 7824 (January 1941)
  Doggin' the Dog
  Rainy Day Blues
DECCA 7827 (February 1941)
  Careless Love
  Jumpin' Down Blues

Art Tatum and His Band
DECCA 8526 (February 1941)
  Wee Baby Blues
  [reverse: without Turner]

DECCA 8536   (March 1941)
  Last Goodbye Blues
  [reverse: without Turner]
DECCA 8563   (June 1941)
  Corrine, Corrina
  Lonesome Graveyard
DECCA 8577   (July 1941)
  Rock Me, Mama
  Lucille

Big Joe Turner
DECCA 7856   (September 1941)
  Ice Man
  Somebody's Got to Go
DECCA 7868   (October 1941)
  Nobody in Mind
  Chewed Up Grass

Big Joe Turner with the Freddie Slack Trio
DECCA 4093   (December 1941)
  Rocks in My Bed
  Goin' to Chicago

Big Joe Turner
DECCA 7885   (January 1942)
  Blues in the Night
  Cry Baby Blues

Big Joe Turner with the Freddie Slack Trio
DECCA 7889   (February 1942)
  Blues on Central Avenue
  Sun Risin' Blues

Joe Turner with Pete Johnson's All Stars
NATIONAL 9010   (February 1945)
  S.K. Blues, I
  S.K. Blues, II
NATIONAL 9011   (March 1945)
  Watch That Jive
  Johnson and Turner Blues

Big Joe Turner
DECCA 11001   (January 1946)
  Rebecca
  It's the Same Old Story

Joe Turner with Bill Moore's Lucky Seven Band
NATIONAL 4002   (May 1946)
  My Gal's a Jockey
  I Got Love for Sale
NATIONAL 4009   (August 1946)
  Sunday Morning Blues
  Mad Blues

Joe Turner
NATIONAL 4011   (December 1946)
  Miss Brown's Blues
  I'm Sharp When I Hit the Coast
NATIONAL 4016   (April 1947)
  Sally Zu-Zazz
  Rock o' Gibralter Blues
SAVOY 649   (April 1947)   [reissue of Varsity 8173]
  Shake It and Break It
  How Long, How Long Blues
DECCA 48042   (August 1947)
  I Got a Gal for Every Day in the Week
  Little Bitty Gal's Blues

Big Vernon
STAG 508   (c. 1947–48)
  Around the Clock Blues, I
  Around the Clock Blues, II

Joe Turner
NATIONAL 4017   (April 1948)
  That's What Really Hurts
  Whistle Stop Blues
MGM 10274   (September 1948)
  Mardi Gras Boogie
  My Heart Belongs to You
ALADDIN 3013   (October 1948)
  Low Down Dog
  Morning Glory
MGM 10321   (November 1948)
  Messin' Around
  So Many Women Blues

Joe Turner with the Flennoy Trio
EXCELSIOR 533   (January 1949)
  I Don't Dig It
  [reverse: Flennoy Trio without Turner]
EXCELSIOR 534   (January 1949)
  Oo-Ough Stomp
  [reverse: Flennoy Trio without Turner]

Joe Turner with Pete Johnson and His Orchestra
SWING TIME 151   (March 1949)   [also: Down Beat 151]
  Radar Blues
  Trouble Blues
SWING TIME 152   (March 1949)   [also: Down Beat 152]
  Wine-O-Baby Boogie
  B&O Blues
SWING TIME 153   (March 1949)   [also: Down Beat 153]
  Christmas Date Boogie
  Tell Me, Pretty Baby
SWING TIME 154   (March 1949)   [also: Down Beat 154]
  Old Piney Brown Is Gone
  Baby, Won't You Marry Me

Joe Turner
MGM 10397   (April 1949)
  I Don't Dig It
  Rainy Weather Blues
MGM 10492   (July 1949)
  Boogie Woogie Baby
  Married Woman Blues
MODERN 20-691   (August 1949)
  Don't Talk Me to Death
  High Tower Drive
CORAL 65004   (December 1949)   [reissue of Decca 7889]
  Blues on Central Avenue
  Sun Risin' Blues
NATIONAL 9099   (January 1950)
  It's a Low Down Dirty Shame
  Nobody in Mind
FREEDOM 1531   (January 1950)
  Adam Bit the Apple
  Still in the Dark
FREEDOM 1537   (May 1950)
  Just a Travelin' Man
  Life Is Like a Card Game
MGM 10719   (June 1950)
  Feelin' So Bad
  Moody Baby

Joe Turner with Dave Bartholomew's Orchestra
IMPERIAL 5085   (July 1950)
  Jumpin' Tonight
  Story to Tell
IMPERIAL 5093   (July 1950)
  Lucille
  Love My Baby

Joe Turner
FREEDOM 1540   (September 1950)
   You'll Be Sorry
   Feelin' Happy
NATIONAL 9100   (September 1950)
   Hollywood Bed
   New Oo-Wee Baby Blues
NATIONAL 9106   (October 1950)   [reissue of National 4002]
   My Gal's a Jockey
   Still in the Dark
FREEDOM 1545   (October 1950)
   I Want My Baby
   Midnight Is Here Again
FREEDOM 1546   (October 1950)
   Jumpin' at the Jubilee
   Lonely World
ALADDIN 3070   (November 1950)
   Back Breaking Blues
   Empty Pocket Blues
NATIONAL 9144   (March 1951)
   Rocks in My Bed
   Howlin' Winds
ATLANTIC 939   (April 1951)
   Chains of Love
   After My Laughter Came Tears
OKEH 6829   (September 1951)
   Cherry Red   [reissue of Vocalion 4997]
   Joe Turner Blues   [reissue of Okeh 6001]
RPM 331   (October 1951)
   Roll 'Em Boys
   Kansas City Blues
ATLANTIC 949   (October 1951)
   The Chill Is On
   Bump, Miss Susie
SWING TIME 261   (November 1951)   [reissue of Down Beat 153]
   Christmas Date Boogie
   How D'Ya Want Your Rollin' Done
FIDELITY 3000   (November 1951)
   Life Is Like a Card Game   [reissue of Freedom 1537]
   When the Rooster Crows   [reissue of Freedom 1545]
DOOTONE 305   (January 1952)
   I Love Ya, I Love Ya
   Born to Gamble
ATLANTIC 960   (February 1952)
   Sweet Sixteen
   I'll Never Stop Loving You
RPM 345   (March 1952)
   Riding Blues
   Playful Baby

FIDELITY 3007 (April 1952)
  After While You'll Be Sorry [reissue of Freedom 1540]
  Just a Travelin' Man [reissue of Freedom 1537]
BAYOU 015 (1952?)
  The Blues Jumped a Rabbit
  The Sun Is Shining
ATLANTIC 970 (May 1952)
  Don't You Cry
  Poor Lover's Blues
ATLANTIC 982 (December 1952)
  Still in Love
  Baby, I Still Want You

Joe Turner and Wynonie Harris
ALADDIN 3184 (July 1953)
  The Battle of the Blues, Part 1
  The Battle of the Blues, Part 2

Joe Turner
ATLANTIC 1001 (August 1953)
  Honey Hush
  Crawdad Hole
ATLANTIC 1016 (December 1953)
  TV Mama
  Oke-She-Moke-She-Pop
ATLANTIC 1026 (April 1954)
  Shake, Rattle and Roll
  You Know I Love You
DOOTONE 341 (June 1954)
  When I'm Gone
  No, There Ain't No News Today
ATLANTIC 1040 (September 1954)
  Well All Right
  Married Woman
ATLANTIC 1053 (February 1955)
  Flip, Flop and Fly
  Ti-Ri-Lee
ATLANTIC 1069 (July 1955)
  Hide and Seek
  Midnight Cannonball
ATLANTIC 1080 (November 1955)
  The Chicken and the Hawk
  Morning, Noon and Night
DECCA 29711 (November 1955)
  Piney Brown Blues [from Decca album 214]
  I Got a Gal for Every Day in the Week [reissue of Decca 48042]
ATLANTIC 1088 (March 1956)
  Corrine, Corrina
  Boogie Woogie Country Girl

DECCA 29924 (April 1956)
  Corrine, Corrina [reissue of Decca 8563]
  It's the Same Old Story [reissue of Decca 11001]
ATLANTIC 1100 (June 1956)
  Lipstick, Powder and Paint
  Rock a While
ATLANTIC 1122 (December 1956)
  Midnight Special Train
  Feeling Happy

ALBUMS

DECCA 214 (1941)
  Kansas City Jazz ("Piney Brown Blues")
COLUMBIA C-44 (1941)
  Boogie Woogie (one cut by Turner and Johnson)
DECCA DL-8044 (March 1953)
  Kansas City Jazz (LP reissue of Decca 214)
ATLANTIC 1234 (July 1956)
  Boss of the Blues
ATLANTIC 1235 (July 1956)
  Kansas City Jazz
ATLANTIC 8001 (1957)
  The Greatest Rock & Roll (two cuts by Turner)
ATLANTIC 8005 (1957)
  Joe Turner
ATLANTIC 8010 (1957)
  Rock & Roll Forever (three cuts by Turner)
SAVOY 14012 (1958)
  Joe Turner

Atlantic also issued four Turner EPs: *Joe Turner Sings* (No. 536), *Joe Turner* (Nos. 565 and 586), and *Rock with Joe Turner* (No. 606).

Index

Individual artists are listed separately from their bands. Italicized page numbers refer to photographs.

Grimes, Tiny, 6, 122
Griner, Flash, 78
Gunter, Hardrock, 83–87, *85*, 188–89
Gunter, Sid, 84

H

"Hadacol, That's All," 68
Haley, Bill, 7, 69, 73–77, *75*, 190–92
Hall, Roy, 78–82, *81*, 193
Halsey, Jim, 129
Hammond, John, 21
Hampton, Lionel, 41, 65, 71, 84
Handy, W. C., 32
Hank Ballard & the Midnighters, 114
"Hard Luck Blues," 58
Hardrock Gunter and the Pebbles, 85
Harlan Leonard and His Rockets, 14
Harris, Bill, *99*
Harris, Charles, 32
Harris, Wynonie, 2, 5, 6, 24, 37–43, *39*, 65, 66, 71, 72, 195–99
"Have Mercy Baby," 102
Hawkins, Coleman, 22
Hawkins, Hawkshaw, 79
Hawkins, Screamin' Jay, 120–27, *123*, 199–200
Hayes, Linda, 114, 137
"Heartbreak Hotel," 9
Heller, Eddie, 97
Henry, John "Shifty," 23
Hill, Don, 65, 66, 69
Hill, Raymond, 107, 108, 110
Hill, Smilin' Eddie, 5
Hines, Earl, 27
"Hi-Yo Silver," 68
Holland, Jack, 69
"Honeysuckle Rose," 28

Hotcha Trio, The, 61
"House of Blue Lights," 45–46, 89, 90
Hurte, Leroy, 4

I

Idol, Billy, 20
"I Got a Rocket in My Pocket," 118
"I Gotta Know," 129
Ike Turner and His Kings of Rhythm, 108, 110
Innis, Louie, 5
"Invitation to the Blues," 45
"I Put a Spell on You," 122–23, 125
Irwin, Frankie, 137
"I've Got You Under My Skin," 63
"I Wanna Be Mama'd, " 117
"I Wonder," 49, 50

J

Jackie Brenston and His Delta Cats, 74, 108
Jackson, Bull Moose, 5
Jackson, Joe, 20
Jackson, Little Son, 7
Jackson, Wanda, 128–32, *131*, 200–201
Jackson, Willis "Gator Tail," 7
Jackson Brothers, 7
Jacquet, Illinois, 28
James, Etta, 113
James, Harry, 3
Jennings, Waylon, 20
Jesse Stone and His Blue Serenaders, 12
Jimmie Lunceford Orchestra, 66, 227